THE ART
OF THE SPARK

12 HABITS TO INSPIRE
ROMANTIC ADVENTURES

MARY ZALMANEK

Many Pearls Press
Monument, Colorado

PUBLISHED BY
Many Pearls Press
P.O. Box 462
Monument, Colorado 80132
(719) 481-0270
Email: info@manypearlspress.com
Web: http:/www.manypearlspress.com

COVER ILLUSTRATION copyright © 2005 Collins Redman. All rights reserved.

References, information, concepts and quotes from *The Five Love Languages: How to Express Heartfelt Commitment to Your Mate* by Gary Chapman copyright © 1992. Used by permission from Northfield Publishing, Chicago, IL. All rights reserved.

Quote from *I Love You, Ronnie* by Nancy Reagan, copyright © 2000 Ronald Reagan Presidential Foundation. Used by permission of Random House, Inc.

"Let the fire of my passion..." poem used by permission of the author. Copyright © 1984 Steve Kowit.

EDITED BY Marylin Warner
COPY EDITED BY Ralph Verno
ILLUSTRATIONS BY Greg Barrington
AUTHOR PHOTO BY Suzanne D'Acquisto
DESIGN BY F + P Graphic Design, Inc.

ISBN: 0-9766879-0-9

Library of Congress Control Number 2005929883
First edition
Printed in the United States of America on acid-free paper.

Dedication

TO MY THREE JIMS,

To my husband,
JAMES EDWARD ZALMANEK,
who adds inspiration and passion
to our romantic adventures,

To my father,
JAMES WILLIAM ROSS (1930 – 2005),
who showed me the beauty and joy in loving one woman,
my mother, until death interrupted their happily ever after,

And to my father-in-law,
JAMES ALTON ZALMANEK (1925 – 2005),
who was the role model for his son
to be a loving and committed husband.

Testimonials

"Every moment of our wedding was absolutely, unbelievably perfect and we could NEVER have done it without Mary. I almost wish she had a boss so I could write and tell her what an incredible job Mary does and how much she cares about her clients!" **Sharon Thomas,** client

"I am in awe of Mary's creative spirit, her ability to orchestrate everything into a perfect package. I believe it meant as much to her as it did to me that every effort be made for this occasion to be a memorable experience." **Dick Hiegert,** client

"I highly recommend Mary's services to make special occasions even more special." **Bob Nordeman,** client

"This is a great experience for couples to really look at and think about their relationship in a different way." **LeNore Ralston,** Licensed Marriage and Family Therapist, workshop participant

"I not only endorse and recommend this class, but feel that Mary has put a creative and fun approach to a subject we sometimes take for granted in this fast paced world of ours." **Dr. John Daugherty,** workshop participant

"Mary has the passion to create a romantic adventure for anyone, anytime, doing anything." **Jim Young,** workshop participant

"Mary's course provides the inspiration, permission, and courage to live life as a romantic adventure." **Kat Jorstad,** workshop participant

"Mary guides you through the garden of romance letting you taste the possibilities to be with your loved one." **Deane Robertson,** workshop participant

"The course brought together all the things that have worked for us and were forgotten and many new ideas." **Tom Saponas,** workshop participant

"What I learned here was invaluable. I will use it every day of my life." **Colleen Allen,** workshop participant

"Here is an opportunity to come home to where your heart is." **Karen Burch,** workshop participant

"Mary embodies the romantic spirit in all of us…and she knows how to inspire us to exercise it." **Stephanie Stevenson,** workshop participant

"I found I am romantic, where I thought I would never be!" **Stephen Dellacroce,** workshop participant

"We spend so much time, effort and energy planning in our jobs and for our families. This course was a great reminder to spend time, effort and energy on the most important person in our life." **Kurt Ostrow,** workshop participant

Acknowledgements

I am awed when I think of the many people who helped me create this book. I'm most thankful for my husband, Jim. Without him to share my romantic adventures, this book would have had no spark, no reason for being. Not only is he my partner in romance and fun, he helped me plan adventures for clients, teach workshops, and edit this book.

To my clients, I thank you for the privilege of serving you in this most precious part of your life. To friends and acquaintances who shared your stories with me, I'm grateful for the opportunity you gave me to pass them on to others.

To Marylin Warner, thank you for being the best editor, mentor, writing coach, and cheerleader anyone could ever ask for. You helped me take a fresh look at what I'd written and make it better.

To the wonderful writers in my Wednesday morning critique group – Nancy Bentley, Annette Kohlmeister, Patricia McFarland, Louise Robinson, and Carol Stoffel – thank you for delivering your suggestions with kindness, laughter, and sincerity. Watching such a talented group of committed writers craft their stories has inspired me beyond words.

To Gina Olson, Jarla Ahlers, Ann Carlisle, Hillary Gale, Billi Lee, Ellen Powers, Peggy Ives, Denise Brown, Ruth Meinking, and the others who have come and gone in monthly writing groups, you've all made your mark on my book. Thank you, one and all.

To Kelly Young, thank you for coaching me, believing in me, and encouraging me every step of the way.

I send heartfelt thanks to Rebecca Finkel, who turned my manuscript into a book and patiently educated me in the process; to Greg Barrington, who understood exactly what I wanted to see in the Darlings and Dullards comics; to Collins Redman, who translated my vague wishes and childish line drawings into an eye-catching work of art for the cover; to Ric Helstrom, who captured the essence of Collins Redman's oil painting in a photograph; to Suzanne D'Acquisto, who made me look better on the book cover than I do in person; to Brenda Speer, who provided expert legal advice; and to Ralph Verno, whose careful last minute edits uncovered mistakes I'd been overlooking for months.

To my family – Doris Ross; Jim (my fourth Jim), Vicky, Sam and Zac Ross; Connie and Ross Barnhill; Rhonda and Sebastian Barnhill; Michael Elkins; Ryan Barnhill; Betty Zalmanek; Charlie and Roxanna Zalmanek; Linda, Tom, Justin, Colin and Caley Coulson; Mark Zalmanek; Karen, Marin, Byrnn and Josh Zalmanek – thanks for cheering me on during this l-o-o-o-n-g process.

Special thanks go to Debbie Robertson and Yella Werder, who read drafts of the book and offered suggestions. And to friends too numerous to mention, my life is so much richer with you in it.

Thank God It's Finished. Let's celebrate!

Contents

Foreword

So you're standing there, skimming through this book, asking yourself, "Does the world *really* need yet *another* self-help book on how to keep romantic love alive?" (The answer is "Yes.")

Some of you are saying to your self, "Hey, wait a minute! I already own a copy of *1001 Ways To Be Romantic* by the guy who wrote this foreword! What *more* could one need?" (The answer is "Plenty.")

You see, *my* book is all about the "what" of romance: *What* to do (tips, ideas, suggestions, creative expressions) to keep romance alive. Well, in addition to "what," people need to learn "how"—and that's what *this* marvelous book explores. The "how" of romance: *How* to apply romance into your life, and, perhaps more importantly, how to *think* about romance. In other words, *how to make romance a habit.*

Look, you've made it *this* far . . . (The title grabbed you; you skimmed the back cover and got intrigued; and now you're flipping through the book, trying to decide if you should buy it—or just grab a magazine and a cup of coffee in the bookstore café) . . . Like I said, you've made it *this* far, so let me encourage you to *go all the way* (double entendre intended) and purchase this wonderful book.

Why? *Why* should you buy this book? (No, not because I get a percentage of the royalties. I don't.) But because it *works*. Making romance a habit simply *works*. And, you should get it because you—or *someone you know* (wink-wink, nudge-nudge) needs a little help in the Romance Department. (Now, don't you feel better, admitting that to yourself? Confession is good for the soul, you know.)

Okay, *I'll* make a confession to *you*. (Turnabout is fair play.) I'm jealous of Mary. I'm jealous that I didn't think-up the concept of "Romantic Habits" *first*. Dang! And by the time I had the opportunity to read the manuscript of *The Art of the Spark* it was 99 percent complete. Meaning that Mary didn't need a co-author. Dang! Oh, and another thing. I'm jealous that I didn't think-up the concept of the "Romance Pyramid." Dang!

But I *do* have the honor of introducing Mary and *The Art of the Spark* to you. *And* I have the privilege of using what little influence I have, to encourage you to do yourself a favor and acquire this book. You—and your lover—will be glad you did.

—GREGORY J.P. GODEK, author of *1001 Ways To Be Romantic*

Introduction

It took me three long years to earn an MBA, but I've been working on an RA all my life. I'm a Romantic Adventurer.

I don't pretend to know it all, but I've learned a lot from being in love with love, and listening to other people. I'm always grateful when they trust me with their stories. My enthusiasm for romance translates into a gift for helping others plan their romantic adventures. Let me tell you about my journey.

In the early days of our relationship, Jim and I were in a romantic state of mind and excited just to be near each other. We were falling in love. Our passion was spontaneous. I can remember amorous moments when Jim was working on the car and covered in motor oil, and we still couldn't keep our hands off each other. As our relationship matured, however, we started to lose the excitement of those early days. Sweat and motor oil ceased to be an aphrodisiac for me.

To love is to receive
a glimpse of heaven.
KAREN SUNDE

Jim and I have been married since 1975. For the most part, we've enjoyed a very loving relationship. I'll admit we've had days when we wondered why we married each other, but our good days have far outnumbered the bad. Some days were so good that I wondered how much better heaven could be.

At the same time, I noticed what was happening to other couples I knew. Several were getting divorced; a few were having affairs. Some people may have felt there was something missing in their lives; others just assumed that's the way it goes after several years together. The couples who seemed to be adapting best to married life were having children, throwing themselves into their careers, or both. But romance had become a distant priority in most of their lives.

When some of my newly divorced friends started dating, I saw in them the excitement that comes with blossoming relationships. They were transforming right before my eyes. I remember Debbie's excitement about her first date after her divorce. We had spent the day together cross-country skiing. At the top of every rise in the trail we stopped to talk about her upcoming date that evening. We cut our ski day short to get her ready for her date.

Debbie showed me the pink denim mini-skirt she bought for the occasion. I helped with her makeup and hair while she did her nails. We looked through her music collection, discussing and rejecting a dozen titles until we found just the right music to be playing when he came to pick her up. We lit candles and turned on and off every light in the living room, dining room and kitchen until we found an appropriate level of lighting, not too intimate for a first date, but not so bright as to feel like a department store. Debbie chilled a bottle of white wine and put a bowl of cashews on the coffee table, a simple snack that would require no cleanup when they were ready to leave.

I felt like I was getting my little sister ready for her first date. As the big sister, I almost wished I could watch their interaction from the coat closet. Instead, I went home and left Debbie alone to experience her final thirty minutes of pre-date jitters.

Their date was fun, but it wasn't the start of a long-term relationship. Debbie and her date had a good time getting to know each other, and then decided they were better off as friends. The outcome didn't matter much to me; I still saw something that I wanted – the excitement typical of a new relationship.

I didn't want a new relationship, just the excitement that comes with one. After ten years of marriage, Jim and I were still compatible as mates, friends and lovers. We frequently reserved time for just the two of us – evenings at home and dates on the town. The time we spent together was good and comfortable, maybe too comfortable. I would pay more attention to my grooming when I was getting ready for work than I would for a Saturday night at home with my beloved. The conversations I had with a girl-friend over lunch were more intimate than most conversations I was having with Jim.

Without announcing my intentions to my husband, I decided to introduce some excitement into our marriage. Jim was away on business. When I picked him up at the airport, he complimented me on my pink mini-skirt. He noticed a cooler and gift-wrapped box in the back seat, but I offered no explanation. Instead, I tied a scarf around his eyes to blindfold him. I slipped a sexy saxophone instrumental into the tape player and told him to enjoy the ride. I drove to an unfamiliar part of town and checked us into a motel. Jim was a good sport about being led blindfolded into the unknown. He stood as still as a statue while I went to get the cooler and package. I gave him a big juicy kiss before I took off his blindfold.

As he looked around the room, the mirror on the ceiling above the bed gave him the first clue as to the type of establishment we were in. He opened the package, which contained some lingerie he had recently bought me for Valentine's Day and a few other items to enhance our afternoon delight. The cooler contained a bottle of chardonnay and shrimp cocktail. We enjoyed a few passionate hours before we checked out of the motel and went to a delicious dinner.

This interlude marked the start of the transition from the "passive romantic" to the "creative romantic" phase of our marriage. I initiated several adventures like this that we both enjoyed. I was always on the lookout for cre-ative new ways to say, "I love you," and our celebrations for birthdays, anniversaries, and Valentine's Days reached new heights. Years ago when it was Jim's turn to plan a celebration, his plans didn't exactly overflow with creativity. After all, as Jim says, he has a handicap when it comes to romance – he is an engineer. That didn't matter much to me; anything he did was appreciated and I enjoyed planning more elaborate celebrations.

Then it happened. Valentine's Day, 1992. Cupid pulled a creativity arrow from his quiver and scored a bull's eye on Jim's heart. Unbeknownst to me, he arranged with Don, my boss, for me to take an afternoon off work. Just before I left to meet Jim for lunch, Don reminded me that he had scheduled a meeting with me for that afternoon. He then handed me a sealed envelope addressed to one of Jim's co-workers, which I promptly gave to Jim when I saw him. Jim and I had a great lunch together, so good in fact, that he tried to talk me into taking the afternoon off. I told him I couldn't, that I had a meeting scheduled with Don. Jim took Don's envelope from his pocket and opened it, ignoring my protests about opening someone else's mail. The note, addressed to me, read,

> *Dear Mary,*
>
> *You may recall that we have a meeting booked for 2:00 this afternoon. The reason for this meeting was to block out time for your real mission. You are to go to space 2376 at the mall and ask for either Brenda or Indira.*
>
> *Don*

The designated space turned out to be a lingerie store. When I asked for Brenda or Indira, Brenda said, "Oh, you must be Mary. We thought you would never get here. We've been waiting for you."

Thus began an adventure that included shopping for a sexy outfit and picking up a dozen red roses (all prepaid on Jim's credit card). At each new step in the journey, I was given a card with further instructions. I loved the anticipation of wondering what was next, of wondering when I would see my man of mystery. Jim was waiting for me in a hotel suite, much swankier than the no-tell motel I had taken him to.

The next morning, two massage therapists showed up to give us two-on-one massages. I went first, then soaked in the oversized bathtub while Jim received his massage. Having two people massage me in unison was pure heaven. Their movements were synchronized to the point that there were times I couldn't tell if I had one leg or two.

From this point forward, Jim's creativity in planning romantic adventures surpassed my own. Whatever left-brained handicap he once claimed was gone forever.

I realized that we routinely had the excitement of a new relationship in a nearly twenty-year-old marriage. This did not go unnoticed in my circle of friends and acquaintances.

Two things happened to me in the mid nineties that eventually led me to Adventures of the Heart, the company I founded in 1997 to help people plan romantic and fun adventures.

First, I was attending a monthly women's group. We took turns selecting topics and conducting the meetings. When it was my turn, Rosie said, "Mary, you have more fun with your husband and your friends than anyone I know. Can you teach us your secrets?" For the next meeting I developed the "Fun Planner for Creative Celebrations," which contained eight questions to set parameters and a list of seventy ideas for romancing your beloved, celebrating events with friends and family, and building camaraderie in the workplace.

Next, I received a call from a man I'd never met. He said, "I heard through the grapevine that you're really good at celebrating special occasions. My anniversary is tomorrow. Would you give me some suggestions?"

I was delighted to help. I spent thirty minutes on the phone with him. I was even more delighted two days later when I received a huge bouquet of flowers and a note of thanks. He called later in the day and told me his wife said it was the best day of her life – even better than her wedding day.

About a year after I started my business, I was asked to speak to the Pikes Peak Romance Writers. As I was organizing my talk, I realized that many of the successful adventures had certain elements in common. It also

XVI The Art of the Spark

occurred to me that if I could identify some of the habits practiced by the most loving couples, I could teach people to plan their own adventures.

I developed two workshops to share these habits. A one-day class called *The Art of Romance and Fun* was open to singles or couples, and the *Couples' Romance Weekend* was designed as a romantic getaway. I used stories to explain the common elements and provided exercises for experiential learning. Each participant left with an adventure he or she had planned for a loved one. While my focus was frequently on romancing the beloved, people could apply these same principles to plan creative celebrations for anyone they cared about. Participants who were not in romantic relationships could use these same elements to plan a celebration for family or friends.

> *Habits are safer than rules; you don't have to watch them. And you don't have to keep them either. They keep you.*
> DR. FRANK CRANE

If the word "exercise" makes you think of hard work and sweat, you can relax. These exercises are fun. Invite your beloved to join you, settle into comfortable chairs, and pour yourselves something to drink. You'll start by narrowing in on each other's unique desires and personality traits. Once you've done that, you may want to work alone to surprise your loved one with a customized adventure. Your sweetheart will know that he or she is absolutely loved and adored by you, because you listened and learned.

While the bulk of my business has been planning romantic adventures for couples to celebrate anniversaries, birthdays and Valentine's Days, I've used these principles to plan numerous other adventures for adults and children:

♡ Marriage proposals,

♡ Weddings,

♡ Honeymoons,

♡ A divorce ceremony,

♡ A celebration of life on the anniversary of a loved one's death,

♡ Numerous team-building sessions for a large telecommunications company,

♡ Birthday parties for adults as well as for a nine-year-old boy and a thirteen-year-old girl, and

♡ Christmas party for a women's networking group.

The idea for this book originated in my workshops. In nearly every class participants asked if I had a book or was writing one. A book seemed like a good idea – good for the people who wanted more stories and examples to spark their creativity, good for the people who wanted the information without devoting a day or weekend to a workshop, and good for me to be able to reach a wider audience. This book focuses on romance for couples, although some of the habits can be used to spark adventures for other loved ones as well. Upcoming books in *The Celebrating Our Lives Series* focus on:

♡ Creative celebrations for special people and events in our lives,

♡ Activities to build happy and productive teams through camaraderie.

Stories in this book come from one of three sources. Many are adventures I've planned for clients, some are stories I've heard from others, and a few are my own adventures with Jim. Some happened exactly as I've written them. With the permission of the people involved, I've used real first names. Occasionally I've changed names, combined events, or added details to tell the tale. My goal was to illustrate points and provide creative inspiration, not to win a Pulitzer for accurate reporting.

General George S. Patton once said, "Never tell people how to do things. Tell them what to do and they will surprise you with their ingenuity." Practicing these habits can help you turn out your own adventures.

Surprise your beloved with your ingenuity. Add a dash of excitement and a pinch of passion to your own loving relationships.

If these habits spark your creativity such that you craft a unique, customized adventure for your beloved, then I have succeeded.

Build a Foundation for Adventure

You can pick them out anywhere. In shopping malls, restaurants, class-rooms, and conference rooms. At parties, soccer games, and parks.

Some couples just have that glow. There's a private buzz between them, as if they're holding onto a winning Powerball ticket just a few days longer, savor-ing their good fortune.

If you happen to meet some friends or even strangers who've recently experienced a romantic adventure, they will work it into the conversation with-in the first five minutes. The afterglow is so powerful they can't help but talk about it.

Once I sat at a banquet table with six strangers. I noticed a woman with a dreamy look and satisfied smile. An attentive and affectionate man was seated next to her. We introduced ourselves. With less than two minutes of chitchat under our belts, when I commented, "You seem very happy," she proceeded to tell me about the romantic weekend her husband of fifteen years had surprised her with only days earlier. Ordinarily, they led typical lives: two demanding careers, three school-aged children, and busy schedules for the entire family. The last truly romantic adventure they shared was their wedding day. He talked about how out of balance their lives had become, how his wife deserved this special time, and how much fun he had putting it together for her.

Then something magical happened at the table. Others started sharing stories of romantic adventures they had experienced or heard about from family or friends. The buzz expanded. A serious and reserved businessman was the last to enter the conversation with a tale about his niece's engagement.

> *We love because it's the*
> *only true adventure.*
> NIKKI GIOVANNI

The excitement of romance is contagious.

Even if the passage of time has dimmed the urgency of the feelings, once couples are reminded of an adventure, the emotions come rushing back. Let me tell you a story about Gina and Jon that happened over twenty years ago.

Still Glowing After All These Years
Gina and Jon's Romantic Adventure

Jon called his wife from work with some bad news.

"I'm sorry, Gina, but I just can't get away for lunch on our anniversary next week. Not only that, I'll probably have to work late that night. We've got a big deadline coming up."

"Oh, no!" Gina said, her voice heavy with disappointment. After a pause, she added, "I have an idea. I'll come to you. We can eat lunch in the cafeteria."

"That's a long drive for mediocre food."

"The drive wouldn't bother me as much as not being able to celebrate our anniversary, even if it's with mystery meat and bland veggies."

"I'm not even sure I can get you a visitor's badge. You know how security is around here."

"Jon, if I didn't know better I'd think you didn't want me around. I'm coming out there, and if I can't get in, we'll go on a picnic."

Gina pondered the situation after they hung up. She decided to get creative.

This was not a time to let business get in the way of pleasure.

In a burst of inspiration, she dialed Jon's manager. She explained her plan and boldly asked permission for her and a chef to gain access to the secured area. The manager's initial inclination was to deny the request. Then he changed his mind.

"You know, we've been putting in long hours. Maybe a little romance would help the morale around here," he said. "Sure, I'll reserve the conference room near Jon's office."

Later in the day when Jon checked into getting a badge for Gina, he was amazed at how easy it was. Just an inch or two of red tape, not the yards of it he'd expected.

Mid-morning on their anniversary, Jon sat in a meeting, unaware that a chef was setting up a bistro in a nearby conference room. He used a portable stove to prepare lunch, then set a romantic table for two with a tablecloth, flowers and fancy dishes.

When Gina arrived around noon, Jon met her at the entrance, expecting to eat lunch in the cafeteria.

"Can you show me your office before we eat?" Gina asked.

"It's not much to look at," Jon replied.

"That's okay. I just want to see where you spend so much time."

As they neared Jon's office, he sensed something was amiss. A mouth-watering aroma filled the air. Soft music down the hall drew his attention. Gina took him by the hand and led him past his office. His jaw dropped when he saw the sterile space had been transformed into a romantic café. Flickering candles replaced the harsh florescent lighting.

"Welcome to the Cozy Café. Please have a seat," the chef said as he pulled out a chair for Jon. "Today we have fresh tuna with a tarragon mustard sauce and toasted macadamia nuts. That is served with glazed carrots and a lemon rice pilaf. Shall I start you off with a Caesar salad, prepared table-side?"

Too stunned to speak, Jon nodded at the chef.

"How did you manage to do all this?" he asked Gina.

"Once I set my mind to it, things fell into place. Each roadblock made me more determined that this would be a special anniversary. I want you to know how much I love you."

"And I want you to know I've never felt more loved."

As they emerged from the conference room, Jon walked a little taller, feeling the adoration of his wife, the envy of his co-workers, and the satisfaction of being pampered.

That is what I call a romantic adventure. It's a story that shows the depth of their love. It was a defining event in their relationship.

> **adventure** – *1. an unusual and exciting experience*
> ILLUSTRATED OXFORD DICTIONARY

An adventure is an extraordinary demonstration of love and commitment. It's not defined by money, time or location, but by the feelings it arouses.

This book is about adventures.

Romance Pyramid

Sometimes when I tell a story about a romantic adventure, the listener will say, "If I did that for my wife, she would think I was apologizing for something I'd done wrong." What that tells me is they do not have the proper foundation for an adventure.

These romantic celebrations and the building blocks to them are defined in the three parts of the Romance Pyramid: loving gestures, dates, and adventures. Loving gestures are the little things lovers do to show how much they care. They may not even be consciously aware of what they are doing, yet their behaviors reflect their mutual respect and desire to care for and bring happiness to their partners.

A date is a social engagement with one's beloved. People who are considered to be romantic usually make a practice of loving gestures and dates.

A spark of creativity can turn dates into romantic adventures. Imagine a romantic celebration such that your beloved knows that he or she is absolutely loved and adored by you. That's an adventure. Loving gestures at the base of the Romance Pyramid provide a foundation for dates and adventures. Daily loving gestures create an atmosphere of love so those celebrations will be successful.

> *Chains do not hold a marriage together. It is threads, hundreds of tiny threads, which sew people together through the years. That is what makes a marriage last more than passion or even sex!*
> SIMONE SIGNORET

The time frames in the Pyramid are merely suggestions. There is nothing magical about monthly dates or yearly adventures. Loving gestures can be so easy and take such little time that you can do these several times a day, thousands a year. Do what works for you. Consider your current level of loving gestures, dates and adventures and crank them up a notch. Don't expect to make huge changes overnight.

Countless tips for romance have been written. Loving gestures are often included in the tips, and some have suggestions for more substantial dates. But how do you turn these suggestions into a customized adventure that is sure to hit home with your beloved?

That's what you'll discover as you read this book.

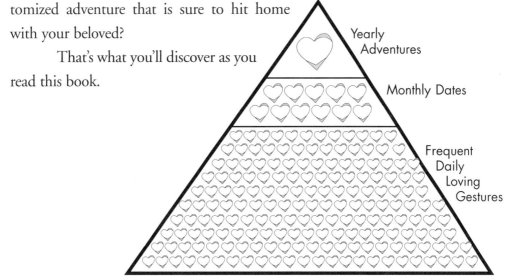

Yearly Adventures

Monthly Dates

Frequent Daily Loving Gestures

Romance Pyramid

Loving Gestures

Loving gestures can be defined in many different ways: a hug, a kiss, an "I love you," a card under the pillow, or a special look. When you give from the heart, you give an authentic, heartfelt gift of yourself. Create love in the moment with each connection. Let your expression of love be a sensual experience. Feel love when you touch your beloved, really feel it. Breathe in your sweetheart's unique scent. Gaze into your lover's eyes. Appreciate all the ways your senses of sight, hearing, taste, touch, and smell can enrich your connections.

In her book *Real Moments for Lovers,* Barbara DeAngelis defines "the loving gaze." She says, "When your partner looks at you with a loving gaze, you will feel more completely loved than if he gave you any gift, more perfectly beautiful than if he said any words, for the silence creates a sacred space in which you can receive his love in its purest form."

Making eye contact, either up close or across the room, while being present with your love is a simple yet powerful loving gesture. DeAngelis also says, "Looking *into* your lover's eyes, your intention is that the boundaries between you will temporarily dissolve, and for a moment, your souls will touch."

> *A kiss is a lovely trick designed by nature to stop speech when words become superfluous.*
> INGRID BERGMAN

A hug and kiss can be loving gestures, especially when they're genuinely given and received. My body reacts differently when I get a brief embrace from a friend than when my husband greets me with a lingering hug. We melt into each other and my nose nuzzles his neck. I take in his scent, which grounds me in our love.

Any act that demonstrates your love, and is recognized as such by your beloved, is a loving gesture. You can use words, either written or verbal, to express your love or appreciation. Use touch to connect with your beloved: hugs, kisses, caresses, massages, foreplay, and lovemaking. Thoughtful acts, such as making coffee, cooking dinner, or paying bills, when done with no strings attached, are loving gestures.

Laughing together also strengthens your love. Keeping a sense of humor, for better or worse, in sickness and in health, makes the good times better and the bad times easier to tolerate. When you see a couple laughing together in a restaurant, how often do you assume they are just getting to know each other? Next time imagine that

> *A good laugh is sunshine in a house.*
> WILLIAM M. THACKERAY

they've been together for five, twenty-five, or fifty-five years. Telling a funny joke or amusing story to your beloved says that not only do you love him, but you like him, too.

My parents had been married fifty-three years when my dad was diagnosed with stomach cancer that had metastasized to his liver and spine. During his treatment I spent many days and weeks with them at their home in New Mexico. As we settled into our routines, I watched love in action. My mom tended to his needs and my dad graciously accepted her new role as his caregiver. She would go to him as he rested in his recliner and caress him. One of them would make a comment that would make them both laugh. Their intimate laughter carried an assurance of eternal love sweeter than the truest love song.

Loving gestures are essential. They create an atmosphere of love. Frequent expressions of love are the foundation of successful adventures.

Sometimes people tell me they are too busy with work, children, church, or some other worthy cause to take time for romance. Nonsense! If a former President of the United States could find time for loving gestures, so can you. And I'm not talking about Bill and Monica; I'm talking about Ronnie and Nancy.

No matter what your politics, if you have a romantic bone in your body, you've got to be impressed by Ronald Reagan's heart. In the book, *I Love You, Ronnie: The Letters of Ronald Reagan to Nancy Reagan,* Nancy printed her collections of love letters Ronnie had written to her over the years. For nearly forty years, Ronnie wrote letters to his beloved. Whether he was making movies or serving as California's governor or President of the United States, he always found time to express his love to Nancy with written words. Some of these letters are the elegant, clever prose one would expect of the Great Communicator. Others are very simple. One of my favorites, a hand written note on White House stationery, reads:

I love you

I love you

I love you

I love you

I love you

I love you

I love you

I love you

And besides that –

I love you.

Now, seriously, how hard is that? This simple note, written by the President of the United States, a man who was almost certainly busier than any of us, is a constant reminder to Nancy of the love they shared. She had this note framed and still keeps it on her desk.

My husband is pretty good at writing love notes, but even better at leaving love voice mails. I remember times when I was too busy to answer my phone at work. I would be focused on the task at hand, maybe even cranky and irritable. When I had a chance to check my voice mail, there might be a message from Jim that would be something like this: "I was driving between meetings and saw a flower garden full of irises I knew you would like. I started thinking about how fortunate I am to have you in my life. I just wanted you to know how much I love you. I am really looking forward to tonight when we can sit in the hot tub and listen to the call of the poor-wills." That may have taken Jim a minute or two to dial the phone, get my voice mail, and leave the message. His loving words melted away the stress in my day. I saved those messages for as long as the voice mail system would allow and listened to them whenever I needed love.

Dates

The second tier in the Romance Pyramid is dates. The key is to date your beloved on a regular basis. Monthly dates are good; weekly is even better. Spend some quality time with the one you love. Allow time to focus on each other and have a real conversation. Go out to dinner and a movie, ride bikes, or dance the night away.

Dating your sweetheart at home can be fun, too. Get a babysitter if necessary, or reserve a night when the children have other plans. Light candles, use the good dishes, and dress for dinner. Unless one of you really loves to cook or it's something you enjoy doing together, this could be a good time to order take-out food. The main thing is to focus on each other, not cooking and cleaning. Top off the evening by giving each other a massage, or making love.

A couple of years into their relationship, Hillary and Joe are still celebrating the "month-iversary" of the day they met. Since they both have young children from previous marriages, they can't always have a date. Sometimes it's just remembered with a card or flowers. But when they do manage a "month-iversary" date, it's a special occasion. Once they told me about going to dinner at one restaurant, and moving to another one for a chocolate fondue dessert. When telling me the story, they both emphasized how romantic it was. They've created an atmosphere of love in which adventures can thrive.

Adventures

An adventure is a romantic celebration such that your beloved knows beyond a shadow of a doubt that he or she is absolutely loved and adored by you. The afterglow of an adventure can last for months, and the memory of an adventure never fails to bring a smile. Adventures are not every day occurrences. Once a year is a good rule of thumb. In a good year you may have more. Sometimes a year or two might fly by between adventures.

One common misconception is that adventures require travel and are expensive. You can travel if you want to, but it's not a requirement. Most of the adventures I have planned have taken place locally. People who travel frequently on business may prefer at-home adventures.

A $20 adventure can be every bit as memorable as a $2,000 adventure. Yes, really! A budget-minded wife surprised her husband with an elegant dinner complete with all the trimmings – a chauffeured limousine ride, an intimate corner table with a white tablecloth, fine china, and music softly playing in the background. Sound expensive? Not when the restaurant was Taco Bell, the limo was really a Jeep Cherokee driven by a friend, the tuxedoed waiter was another friend, and the music came from a CD player on the next table. You'll hear this full story in Habit Five.

Most memorable adventures start with a spark of inspiration. Many things can generate that initial spark: a book or movie, a problem or challenging situation, a memory or desire, a song, or just a few words, spoken or written. For Gina, the pressures of Jon's job and his remote location conspired to fire her imagination. I've had adventures inspired by events as simple as a walk in the woods or as unlikely as David Letterman's Top Ten Lists. Use the habits and stories in this book as kindling to spark your adventures.

> *Life is either a daring adventure or nothing.*
> HELEN KELLER

It's important to recognize where you are in your relationship and what is appropriate. If you are not living together and don't see each other on a daily basis, it could be difficult to do daily loving gestures. If you are living with your beloved, but loving gestures are rare, perhaps you could start with weekly loving gestures. If you have been married for twenty-five years and you have not had a date since your first child was born, monthly dates could be a bit much as a starting point. If you are starting at square one, take baby steps. If romance to you consists entirely of a card on Valentine's Day, don't try to develop an elaborate multi-day adventure on your own. It would be overwhelming. Wherever you are in the pyramid, think about what it would take to increase the frequency on each level.

For the hundreds of successful adventures I've planned for clients, I've had two failures. Those failures helped me rethink the plans. I'll share one of them with you now.

Once I set up an adventure for a couple that had not been getting along. The wife hired me to create an adventure to put some romance back in their marriage. Do you think it worked? No, they got into an argument before the adventure began and called the whole thing off. If your relationship is struggling, planning an adventure is a waste of time and money, and can actually be a threat to your progress. Start by building a foundation for adventures with loving gestures and dates.

If the situation warrants it, consider marriage counseling. Hosting an adventure is no substitute for professional guidance.

Your Own Romance Pyramid
An Exercise

Think about your own relationship in terms of the Romance Pyramid — not where you want it to be, or where it used to be, but where it is right now, today. Fill in the blanks with your beloved.

Dates and adventures are things you do *with* each other, which may also be true for loving gestures. For instance, you both say "I love you" and kiss each other good night.

However, loving gestures can be things you do *for* each other. For example, one of you makes the coffee and the other gives a card for no special reason.

Estimate the number of loving gestures you do in a day, then multiply by 365 to get a yearly total. Come up with a total as a couple, not as individuals. This is not a time to see who loves whom more, or to place blame if there's an imbalance. Not all loving gestures are created equal, nor do they need to be. Don't make two separate lists to see whose is longer. Make a combined list to form a solid foundation for adventure.

If you don't agree at first, find out why. Maybe what one of you thinks is a loving gesture is not perceived that way by the other.

If you are both satisfied with where your relationship is today, that's great. You can use this book to add more creativity to your loving gestures, dates, and adventures. If there's less than total satisfaction with the state of your union, this book can help you make some exciting changes.

Adventures _____ per year

Dates per year
_____

Loving gestures
_____ per day times 365 days per year=_____

Expressions of Love

Think about the ways you express love. In his popular book *The Five Love Languages: How to Express Heartfelt Commitment to Your Mate,* Gary Chapman suggests that people express and receive love in different ways. Dr. Chapman says the five love languages are:

♡ Words of affirmation   ♡ Acts of service
♡ Quality time   ♡ Physical touch
♡ Receiving gifts

Chapman believes we each have a primary love language. He says, "If you express love in a way your spouse doesn't understand, he or she won't realize you expressed your love at all. The problem is that you're speaking two different languages."

*It is not only necessary to love,
It is necessary to say so.*
FRENCH PROVERB

Even though I adored his book, it took me a long time to identify my own primary love language. Jim expresses his feelings for me in several love languages and I do the same for him. We each say "I love you" several times a day and frequently comment on qualities we admire in each other. We both enjoy giving and receiving gifts; some of my most treasured possessions have more sentimental than monetary value.

Over the years, we have each routinely performed acts of service for each other: Jim pays the bills and maintains our mountain bikes; I do most of the cooking and keep the house clean. All of the dates and adventures we arrange for each other are in pursuit of quality time. We often hug and kiss, sometimes as part of a routine, sometimes with more passion.

I finally realized that while we fully appreciate any expression of love, there is one expression of love we each crave more than any other. For me, it's physical touch. I appreciate it when Jim takes out the trash or tells me he loves me, but I feel his love to my core when he has his arms around me. It's what I miss most when we are mad at each other. His hugs and kisses when we make up are what let me feel that all is right in my world.

For Jim, his primary love language is quality time. He feels unloved when we don't make time to be together. Whether we are talking and laughing with each other or feeling connected in a quiet space together, quality time helps him feel grounded in our love and sustains him when we are apart.

Once you've identified your beloved's primary love language, don't feel you need to forsake all other languages. Other expressions of love can still communicate a powerful message.

One of my favorite examples

Too often we underestimate the power of a touch, a smile, a kind word, a listening ear, an honest compliment, or the smallest act of caring, all of which have the potential to turn a life around.
LEO BUSCAGLIA

involves my sister-in-law and her husband. Linda returned to nursing after raising three children. She was working the night shift at a nearby hospital. When her husband Tom woke up and saw several inches of snow had fallen during the night, he drove to the hospital just before the end of her shift. He scraped the snow and ice off her windows, warmed up her car, and added a few other finishing touches. After he settled in her car to wait for her, he noticed several cars in the sparsely populated parking lot with a full accumulation of snow. Assuming they must belong to other night shift nurses and hospital workers, he got busy cleaning off those windows, too.

The first thing Linda noticed as she walked toward her mini-van and opened the automatic side doors with the remote control was Mannheim Steamrollers music filling the air. It was then she realized someone had cleared the snow and ice from her windows. She expected to find Tom inside, but he was nowhere around. Instead she found a box of warm Krispy Kreme donuts on the dash and a cup of steaming coffee in the beverage holder. As she dialed his

Meet the Dullards

"I don't care if re-gifting has become popular. Re-carding is not acceptable."

Some might wonder why Bea and Moe Dullard ever got married in the first place. Sometimes they do, too. He's a tightwad, and her primary love language is receiving gifts. She's a workaholic, and his primary love language is acts of service. It's no wonder their 10-year marriage is a source of frustration for both of them.

number on her cell phone, she looked around the parking lot, noticing all the other scraped windows, and finally spotted Tom working on a car several rows away. She sat in the car to wait for him, feeling his love and being thankful for the man she married.

When they told me this story, I asked if her primary love language is acts of service. I knew they were fully versed in the subject since Linda was the first one to tell me about *The Five Love Languages* years ago. "No," she said, "It's receiving gifts, but Tom doesn't stop there."

By not stopping there, not only has he captured Linda's heart, but he's been elevated to a legendary status among Linda's envious co-workers.

The love language we appreciate most may change depending on the situation. Once Jim and I went backpacking for three days in a Utah canyon. I

Meet the Darlings

"I love you from the bottoms of my snow shoes."

Gracie married Frank 15 years ago. It was her first marriage, his second. They have one 11-year-old daughter, Angela. They've managed to have a very romantic relationship in spite of the demands of working and raising their daughter. Her primary love language is words of affirmation, and his is quality time.

found myself depending on him to do more for me on this trip because I had developed rheumatoid arthritis in my hands and knees since our last camping trip. He was especially attentive, making sure I was taken care of through his acts of service. He cut a walking stick for me so the hills would be easier on my knees. I felt very loved, and repeatedly expressed my appreciation with words of praise, thanks and love. After we climbed out of the canyon, we each resumed our primary love language.

When I read Chapman's book, a comment that a woman had made to me years earlier finally made sense. She had said, "My husband thought he could make me happy with a trip to Paris, but I'm still mad at him for not taking out the trash." I realized her primary love language is acts of service. She wants him to show his love on a daily basis by doing things like taking out the trash, helping with the dishes, or changing the oil in her car. Then she'll feel loved enough to enjoy that romantic trip to

> *You can give without loving,*
> *But you cannot love without giving.*
> ROBERT LOUIS STEVENSON
> ALSO ATTRIBUTED TO **AMY CARMICHAEL**

France with her beloved. Couples must share the responsibility of building a solid foundation. Just as she perceives acts of service as proof of her husband's love, he knows his love is reciprocated when she speaks to him in his primary love language.

Your own primary love language and that of your beloved may be obvious to you. However, even if you both agree on what your love languages are, I urge you to be multi-lingual and express your love in multiple ways, especially when you are on an adventure. An adventure is quality time that can be enhanced by loving words, gifts, physical touch, and acts of service.

Expressions of Love
An Exercise

The exercise on the following pages meshes the five love languages with the Romance Pyramid. Use this chart to communicate with your beloved about what is romantic to you. Customize it by adding or changing things as you desire. It may help you identify your primary love language, and which secondary love languages are worth speaking. It's just as important to know which ones, if any, don't appeal to you at all.

There is a page for each of the five expressions of love. The first column is titled "Don't even bother if –." Some people might think, "I already do a lot of this stuff, I must be romantic." But how is it received? Do you only praise your beloved when you want something in return? If so, it doesn't count. The next three columns are titled "It's a loving gesture, date or adventure when –."

For example, you can say, "I love you" in many ways. If your beloved has to ask, or if you say it when you don't mean it, then it isn't valid. Saying "I love you" may be a natural and welcome part of your routine. You can move it to the next level by writing a love letter and reading it to your sweetheart by candlelight.

It's an Adventure if...

- ♡ Your beloved knows beyond a shadow of a doubt that he or she is absolutely loved and adored by you.
- ♡ The afterglow lasts for months.
- ♡ Your experience was so powerful you can't help but talk about it.
- ♡ The memory of it never fails to bring a smile.
- ♡ You had outrageous fun with your beloved.
- ♡ It's an extraordinary demonstration of love and commitment.
- ♡ It's not defined by money, time or location, but by the feelings it arouses.
- ♡ You communicated in all five love languages, and your beloved got the message.
- ♡ It's quality time that can be enhanced by loving words, gifts, physical touch, and acts of service.

Many of us are at a loss for words when it comes to expressing our innermost feelings on paper. Michelle Lovric gives some useful advice in her book *How*

To Write Love Letters. She provides elegantly written samples for all kinds of situations: after a first date, for the newlywed, for separated lovers, to express thanks, and to apologize.

Love letters don't have to be memorable prose to strike a cord. There's no shame in simple yet honest words. Remember Ronnie's "I love you, and besides that, I love you" letter to Nancy? If that works for the Great Communicator, it can work for you, too.

> *To pay compliments to the woman we love is the first way of caressing her. A compliment is like kissing through a veil.*
> VICTOR HUGO

For an over-the-top expression, create a ten-day adventure around the "Top Ten Reasons" you love your sweetie. Brainstorm your list of reasons, then think of activities or gifts to celebrate ten of these items. For example, you could plan a romantic picnic in the woods if one of your reasons is your mutual enjoyment of the outdoors. If you appreciate that your beloved always has time for you, you could give a timepiece.

For each expression of love, there is a blank row at the bottom of the page. Use this row to note your own ideas for loving gestures, dates, and adventures.

Feel free to improve upon any of these suggestions. For example, on the Receiving Gifts page, the adventure for "Buy me a gift" suggests you design an adventure around the gift of a bicycle. This is only an example to make the point. If you're not a cyclist, plan your adventure around whatever your heart desires. If you'd rather have a guitar, create a musical adventure. In fact, all of these are suggestions only. Use them as communication points, not as the final word. There's more about planning an adventure around a gift in Habit Seven.

The "Rating" columns allow you and your beloved to rate the loving gestures, dates, and adventures with a plus (+) if you'd like to find yourself in a similar situation, or a minus (-) if you wouldn't. If you changed anything to make it more to your liking, do the rating based on your modifications. If you see something you especially like or dislike, give it extra pluses or minuses.

For situations that don't excite you one way or the other, assign it a zero or leave it blank, which will not affect the scoring. If the entire situation described doesn't apply to your relationship, skip that row. For example, if you don't have young children, the act of service on page 23 that says "Take the children so I have some time to myself" does not apply to you. Give everything in that row a zero or blank.

You may instinctively know the primary love languages for yourself and your beloved. Counting the number of pluses and minuses on each page may help you decide on your primary love languages. If you gave a particular situation two or three pluses or minuses, be sure to count each mark. The expression of love with the most pluses may be your primary love language. Consider it as a place to start your exploration. You may change your mind as you go through the book.

This exercise is not a carefully constructed scientific instrument, but it is useful as an idea generator. Use it as a checklist to facilitate your conversation. It doesn't matter if you score ten pluses or two on your primary love language. The important thing is to learn something about your beloved and yourself in the process.

EXPRESSIONS OF LOVE EXERCISE

Words of Affirmation

When you –	Don't even bother if –	It's a Loving Gesture when –	It's a Date when –	It's an Adventure when –
Say "I love you"	I have to ask or you don't mean it.	It's a natural and welcome part of our routine.	You write me a love letter and read it to me by candlelight.	You create an adventure around the "Top 10 Reason" you love me.
		Rating + or – HERS / HIS	Rating + or – HERS / HIS	Rating + or – HERS / HIS
Praise me	You want something in return.	You compliment the way I look or how I did something.	You sincerely praise me in the presence of others at a social or family gathering.	You serenade me with a love song in a fancy restaurant.
		Rating + or – HERS / HIS	Rating + or – HERS / HIS	Rating + or – HERS / HIS
Give me a card	It insults my age, weight, hair loss, etc.	It's my birthday, or Valentine's Day—it's expected although still appreciated.	It contains a personal note and an unexpected invitation.	You give me a card for each day we will be apart. Some cards contain small gifts.
		Rating + or – HERS / HIS	Rating + or – HERS / HIS	Rating + or – HERS / HIS
Express your thanks	It is delivered with sarcasm.	It is a sincere and heartfelt response.	You give me a thank-you card while dining out and you read your message aloud.	You express your thanks on a billboard or a handmade banner on our house.
		Rating + or – HERS / HIS	Rating + or – HERS / HIS	Rating + or – HERS / HIS
Fill in your own ideas				
		Rating + or – HERS / HIS	Rating + or – HERS / HIS	Rating + or – HERS / HIS
		HERS / HIS	HERS / HIS	HERS / HIS
Number of Pluses				
Number of Minuses				

EXPRESSIONS OF LOVE EXERCISE

Quality Time

When you –	Don't even bother if –	It's a Loving Gesture when –	It's a Date when –	It's an Adventure when –
Talk to me	It's a lecture.	You share about your day and ask about mine.	We laugh together, and the discussion lasts for hours.	We have a date that celebrates our past, present, and future (see page 264).
		Rating + or – HERS / HIS	**Rating + or –** HERS / HIS	**Rating + or –** HERS / HIS
Share common interests	You resent the time it will take.	You make time to work a crossword puzzle with me.	We spend a day or evening doing something we both enjoy.	We go on a mini-vacation to do what we both enjoy.
		Rating + or – HERS / HIS	**Rating + or –** HERS / HIS	**Rating + or –** HERS / HIS
Partake in one of my unique interests	You remind me that I owe you one.	You switch the radio to my favorite station when we are in the car together.	You take me to a "chick flick" when you prefer action movies.	You agree to a camping trip even though you really don't like roughing it.
		Rating + or – HERS / HIS	**Rating + or –** HERS / HIS	**Rating + or –** HERS / HIS
Spend time away from home focused on each other	You're on your cell phone with business issues.	We go for a walk in the neighborhood and talk to each other.	We go to dinner and talk to each other – really talk and listen.	You take me away for a romantic weekend.
		Rating + or – HERS / HIS	**Rating + or –** HERS / HIS	**Rating + or –** HERS / HIS
Fill in your own ideas				
		Rating + or – HERS / HIS	**Rating + or –** HERS / HIS	**Rating + or –** HERS / HIS
		HERS / HIS	HERS / HIS	HERS / HIS
Number of Pluses				
Number of Minuses				

EXPRESSIONS OF LOVE EXERCISE

Receiving Gifts

When you –	Don't even bother if –	It's a Loving Gesture when –	It's a Date when –	It's an Adventure when –
Buy me a gift	You will complain or brag about the cost.	You buy something inexpensive yet thoughtful – maybe a single rose or a book. **Rating + or –** HERS / HIS	You give me earrings or a tie as we are dressing for a dinner date. **Rating + or –** HERS / HIS	You plan an adventure around the gift. If you buy me a bicycle, plan a special ride. **Rating + or –** HERS / HIS
Make me a gift	You don't have the time or desire.	You make a special treat for my sack lunch. **Rating + or –** HERS / HIS	You put our vacation photos in an album and we take time to reminisce. **Rating + or –** HERS / HIS	You paint the bedroom while I'm away. We celebrate my return in our redecorated room. **Rating + or –** HERS / HIS
Send me flowers	Your assistant orders the flowers and signs the card.	You picked them up at the grocery store. **Rating + or –** HERS / HIS	You had a florist deliver them to our table at the restaurant. **Rating + or –** HERS / HIS	You sent a limo to take me to a florist where there were flowers waiting for me. **Rating + or –** HERS / HIS
Surprise me	I hate surprises or you cannot keep a secret.	You leave a card under my pillow for me to find when you're not home. **Rating + or –** HERS / HIS	You give me the new putter I wanted as I'm lining up a shot on the green. **Rating + or –** HERS / HIS	You propose with a diamond ring. **Rating + or –** HERS / HIS
Fill in your own ideas		**Rating + or –** HERS / HIS	**Rating + or –** HERS / HIS	**Rating + or –** HERS / HIS
		HERS / HIS	HERS / HIS	HERS / HIS
Number of Pluses				
Number of Minuses				

EXPRESSIONS OF LOVE EXERCISE

Acts of Service

When you –	Don't even bother if –	It's a Loving Gesture when –	It's a Date when –	It's an Adventure when –
Cook a meal	You make foods I do not like or should not eat.	You prepare a quick and easy meal and do the dishes.	You prepare a special dinner. We eat in the dining room on the good dishes.	You hire a chef to prepare and serve a feast for two. A harpist plays for us.
		Rating + or – HERS / HIS	**Rating + or –** HERS / HIS	**Rating + or –** HERS / HIS
Do a chore that is normally mine	You will remind me that I owe you one.	You make the bed by yourself, and I don't even have to ask.	You drop the car at Jiffy Lube so I don't have to change the oil.	You hire a gardener to plant flowers. We have a picnic in the garden when it's done.
		Rating + or – HERS / HIS	**Rating + or –** HERS / HIS	**Rating + or –** HERS / HIS
Listen to me	You don't care about what I'm saying.	You ask me how my day was and listen for the answer.	We go out for coffee You listen to me. You do not fix anything; you just listen.	You show me you've listened. Take me on a train trip to satisfy my fascination with trains.
		Rating + or – HERS / HIS	**Rating + or –** HERS / HIS	**Rating + or –** HERS / HIS
Take the children so I have time to myself	It won't be quality time for you or the children.	You adjust your schedule to care for the kids to give me some free time.	You take the kids to a you-paint-it pottery store. Use the dishes in a special family meal.	You watch the kids while I'm at the spa, then leave them with a sitter and meet me for dinner.
		Rating + or – HERS / HIS	**Rating + or –** HERS / HIS	**Rating + or –** HERS / HIS
Fill in your own ideas				
		Rating + or – HERS / HIS	**Rating + or –** HERS / HIS	**Rating + or –** HERS / HIS
		HERS / HIS	HERS / HIS	HERS / HIS
Number of Pluses				
Number of Minuses				

EXPRESSIONS OF LOVE EXERCISE
Physical Touch

When you –	Don't even bother if –	It's a Loving Gesture when –	It's a Date when –	It's an Adventure when –
Make love to me	Either one of us is too tired or I don't want to.	We have quick but satisfying sex before falling asleep at night.	We break out of our routine to make love. We enjoy foreplay, sex and conversation.	We hang the "Do Not Disturb" sign on the hotel door, opening it only for room service.
		Rating + or – HERS / HIS	**Rating + or –** HERS / HIS	**Rating + or –** HERS / HIS
Hug me	Your mind is elsewhere.	It's a natural and sincere part of our routine.	You hold me in your arms, talking and snuggling after we make love.	We take a bear-watching trip to Yellowstone to practice frequent bear hugs.
		Rating + or – HERS / HIS	**Rating + or –** HERS / HIS	**Rating + or –** HERS / HIS
Give me a massage	You hate giving massages.	You give me a 5-minute massage because you know my back hurts.	You give me a 30-minute massage in a candlelit room with gentle music playing.	You give me an hour-long massage under a palm tree on a sunny beach.
		Rating + or – HERS / HIS	**Rating + or –** HERS / HIS	**Rating + or –** HERS / HIS
Put lotion on my body	You don't have the time.	You see me putting lotion on my body and offer to do it for me.	You promise some pampering. You towel me off after a bath and rub me with lotion.	You set up a spa day at home. I don't need a salon-quality polish, just your touch.
		Rating + or – HERS / HIS	**Rating + or –** HERS / HIS	**Rating + or –** HERS / HIS
Fill in your own ideas				
		HERS / HIS	HERS / HIS	HERS / HIS
		HERS / HIS	HERS / HIS	HERS / HIS
Number of Pluses				
Number of Minuses				

Discuss the following questions with your beloved.

Which love language is most natural for you?

HER ANSWER	HIS ANSWER

Which is hardest for you to do?

HER ANSWER	HIS ANSWER

Which one means the most to you?

HER ANSWER	HIS ANSWER

Do you think the love language with the most pluses is your primary one? If not, how do you account for the difference?

HER ANSWER	HIS ANSWER

What was it you didn't like about the items you rated with a minus? Sharing your views about what didn't appeal to you is valuable information for your partner.

HER ANSWER	HIS ANSWER

Sparks that Ignite the Romantic Flame

♡ Build the foundation for successful adventures with daily loving gestures.

♡ Date your beloved on a regular basis.

♡ Celebrate your love with romantic adventures. It will let your beloved know beyond a shadow of a doubt that he or she is absolutely loved and adored by you.

♡ Give from the heart. It's an authentic, heartfelt gift of yourself.

♡ Make sure most of the daily loving gestures you do are in your beloved's primary love language.

♡ Express your love in multiple ways when you are on an adventure.

♡ Plan an adventure around the loving gestures that mean the most to your beloved.

Follow Your Own Romantic Bliss

*I*n the nineteenth century, Margaret Wolfe Hungerford, an Irish-born romance novelist, defined beauty for lovers. Over a century later, the truth in her words sparked the second habit to inspire romantic adventures. Just as beauty is in the eye of the beholder, romance is in the hearts of the beloveds.

> *Beauty is in the eye of the beholder.*
> MARGARET WOLFE HUNGERFORD

The truth in those words presents both the challenge and the reward of romance. There is no universal definition of what's romantic. The challenge is finding what romance means to each person. The reward comes with the unique love that honors and celebrates two people as individuals.

In the course of working with clients over the years, I've heard many romantic stories, some of which even brought tears to my eyes. Just because a story touches a place in my heart, however, does not necessarily mean I would want to find myself in the same situation. Romance is as individual as we are.

This is more than just romantic common sense. It also shakes up some traditional notions about romance. Advertisers lead us to believe red roses are one of the most romantic gifts, and for some people, that's absolutely true. But it's not a universal truth. Later in this chapter I'll share a story about a woman who received two gifts on the same day: roses, and a sporting goods item that very few would consider romantic. While the roses made her smile, it's the memory of the second gift that, years later, still makes her cry tears of gratitude.

Let your unique personalities and interests be reflected in your romantic adventures. Celebrate romance based on your own desires, not what society expects or advertisers sell.

But please, as you read the stories in this chapter, allow yourself to be touched by them without feeling the need to emulate them, unless they're a perfect fit for you. That's what this habit is about – giving you permission, encouragement, and inspiration to do your own thing. Don't worry about what others think of your ideas. If you know it's right for you and your beloved, go for it. Listen to your intuition when planning adventures. If some small inner voice tells you something's not quite right, it's not. Keep looking for new ideas.

> *When you follow your bliss... doors will open where you would not have thought there would be doors, and where there wouldn't be a door for anyone else.*
>
> JOSEPH CAMPBELL

On most of your romantic adventures, you'll celebrate the interests you have in common. But there may be times when you'll want to support and encourage each other by enjoying separate interests. In this chapter you'll see how people shared their partner's passion for golf or mountain biking without feeling pressured to take up a sport they personally did not care for.

The Longest Time
Ralph and Vicki's Romantic Adventure

This story was very romantic for Vicki and Ralph, but it wouldn't necessarily work for everyone.

Ralph asked me to help him plan a surprise for Vicki for their ninth anniversary. The inspiration for his surprise was a scene in *My Best Friend's Wedding* where the entire restaurant joined in singing Dionne Warwick's *I Say A Little Prayer for You*. With the help of some of Ralph's friends from the church choir, who just happened to be three members of a barbershop quartet, Ralph serenaded Vicki with a modified version of Billy Joel's *The Longest Time*.

Please understand this was not done at a restaurant where the wait staff gathers around the table to embarrass the birthday boy or girl with a rousing round of their own brand of a birthday song. On the contrary, this was done at an elegant restaurant. As diners enjoy the city lights, waiters clad in tuxedos prepare their tableside specialties.

I must admit that I let my desire to be a fly on the wall get the best of me. I had never before been present when any of the romantic adventures that I have planned for clients took place, but this one I had to see with my own eyes. Jim and I met some friends at the restaurant thirty minutes before Ralph and Vicky were to arrive. We requested a table on the opposite side of the dining room from where the action would take place.

Everything was ready. The three barbershop singers and their wives were seated near the entrance. Susan, a videographer, was waiting in the lounge to get this event on videotape. Right on time, Ralph and the unsuspecting Vicki entered the restaurant. Imagine their surprise when they passed the table of their friends and fellow choir members from church.

Ralph and Vicky were seated at their table. Lights! Camera! Action! Susan started

Always do right. This will gratify some people and astonish the rest.
MARK TWAIN

filming as Pat, Mike and Ross stood up and took off their jackets to reveal matching quartet vests. The trio walked over to Ralph and Vicky's table singing the chorus to *The Longest Time.* Ross handed Ralph a matching vest and the words to the song. He stood up, put the vest on, and began to sing.

Even though Ralph's nervousness was apparent in his voice for the first verse or two, the other diners in the restaurant were as enthralled as I was. Vicky's smile filled the room. I had goose bumps. My favorite line was the one Ralph modified about not caring what consequence it brings, but added "life with you just makes me want to sing." When the song ended, the applause was deafening.

After dinner, the couple drove to a mountain resort to spend the weekend in a condo. Ralph gave Vicky the words to the song printed in calligraphy on handmade paper, rolled in a scroll and tied with a ribbon. Vicky said her face hurt for days from smiling so much, and she'll always have a wonderful reminder of the love her husband feels for her.

When Ralph was setting up this adventure, he told a co-worker about it. She said, "If my husband did that to me, I would divorce him." Some of the comments directed to Ralph or me started to make me a little nervous. I asked him if he was sure this would be a hit with Vicky. He was confident this would be perfect for her. He frequently sings to her; music is very much a part of their life. Vicky is not a person who seeks the spotlight, but she would not be upset at being the center of attention. It was obvious that Ralph knew what would be romantic for his wife.

As much as I loved being witness to this, I personally would rather pull porcupine quills from a rabid dog than sing *a cappella* in front of a room full of strangers. But this adventure worked perfectly for Ralph and Vicky – proof that romance really is in the hearts of the beloveds.

Rate this adventure with a plus if you would like to find yourself in a similar situation, and with a minus if you wouldn't. Give extra pluses or minuses if you have strong feelings either way.

HER ANSWER	HIS ANSWER

Would you be thrilled or horrified if you were serenaded in a public place?

HER ANSWER	HIS ANSWER

If your beloved answered, "thrilled" to this same question, how would you feel about singing to him or her in public?

HER ANSWER	HIS ANSWER

Eloping with an Eight-Foot Train
Sharon and Paul's Romantic Adventure

On a Saturday morning in July, Paul called his girlfriend Sharon to tell her he was having a problem with his car. He called back several times describing the horrible noise coming from the engine and the progress the mechanic was supposedly making. He was so convincing that she called her brother, a service manager at a car dealership, to get some answers to his fictional car problem.

Mid-afternoon Paul asked her to come to his house. His story was that his car wasn't working well enough to make it to her house for their date that evening.

When he knew she was only a few minutes away, he began to light over fifty white candles in a dimly lit room. The candles were arranged in two circles; one circle large enough to surround Sharon and Paul and the other smaller circle surrounding an engagement ring box. The butterflies in Paul's stomach fluttered as he took a final look around the room.

Paul went outside to wait for Sharon. When she arrived, she asked him to start the car so she could hear the noise. Paul, clearly stressed over the situation, said he didn't think it was a good idea to try starting it again. She was preoccupied with thoughts of how much the repairs would cost and how he would get to work on Monday. Lacking any other useful advice, she asked to see the warranty book. He said it was in the house.

When he opened the door and she saw the candles and ring box, her tears began to flow. Never in her entire life had she been so lovingly surprised. He took her hand and led her to the center of the candle circle and helped her to get comfortable on the floor.

Paul picked up his guitar and sang a song he wrote for the occasion. He got to the heart of the matter in the fourth verse:

> *What it's about, my darling,*
>
> *Is you and me*

What I mean to say, my angel,

Is will you marry me?[1]

Sharon's answer, of course, was YES!

The perfect end to this romantic proposal would be a romantic wedding. Sharon knew she wanted to have a nice ceremony, but she did not want the stress of a big production. Several years earlier Sharon had broken an engagement to another man three weeks before the scheduled event. She was all too familiar with the pressure of planning a large wedding. Sharon and Paul wanted an intimate affair without the worry over napkin colors and bridesmaids' dresses, but unique wedding photographs were a must. They wanted a romantic, adventurous beginning to their life. They decided to elope.

The decision to get married in Colorado was made in a train museum in their home state of New Jersey. While following toy trains through miniature cities, canyons and mountains in the various rooms of the museum, the room with beautiful mountains enchanted Sharon. Paul said, "This is what Colorado looks like." Without hesitation Sharon asked, "Do you want to get married in Colorado?" From that point forward, they never even discussed another location. They had found exactly what they wanted without compromising their dreams of a romantic and adventurous wedding.

> *The more wild and incredible your desire, the more willing and prompt God is in fulfilling it, if you will have it so.*
> COVENTRY PATMORE

Eloping didn't mean giving up the private church ceremony, elegant wedding dress, or romantic photographs. It did, however, pose the problem of how to set this up two thousand miles away. Sharon began her search on the Internet for someone in Colorado to help with the logistics, eventually finding her way to my Adventures of the Heart web site.

When I got the call from Sharon, I knew this would be a special wedding. Sharon's request was unusual. She wanted a "romantic little wedding" complete with all the trimmings except one – no guests. In my limited experience,

[1] Written by Paul Chatham, Midland Park, New Jersey, 1999

people who eloped usually had a quick ceremony by a judge or in a wedding chapel on short notice. The bride would wear something nice from her closet – not a wedding gown with an 8-foot train.

I secretly wondered if one or both of their families were against this union. Even at the smallest weddings, the immediate family or a few close friends are usually present to share the joy – or so I thought. I found out later that both families where delighted to hear about the wedding, albeit sorry to have missed it.

Sharon and Paul taught me a lot about how to elope with style. They contacted me four months before their wedding. That's not exactly short notice.

I searched high and low for the right location. They wanted something intimate, yet elegant. Having lots of candles, reminiscent of Paul's proposal, was vitally important. I visited several possible locations and took pictures. They selected a small wedding chapel from the photographs I provided.

Keeping the upcoming wedding a secret from family and friends back in New Jersey while handling pre-wedding details presented a challenge in itself for Sharon and Paul. Sharon knew three years earlier that she'd picked the right bridal gown, just the wrong guy. The dress had been in storage at a dry cleaner. The owner was sworn to secrecy when Sharon shipped the dress to Colorado.

While most of the details on my side were coming together – the chapel, minister, photographers, videographer, hairdresser, dry cleaners to press Sharon's dress, flowers, tuxedo for Paul – there was still one item that left me in a quandary. Where would they have their first meal as husband and wife? Where could she wear her wedding dress with an eight-foot train and not feel conspicuous?

What they really wanted was a private dining room. I could not think of a single restaurant that would be appropriate. Finally I offered my home and sent pictures of the dining room and living room. Sharon and Paul were delighted with the invitation and graciously accepted. I hired Brooke, a chef, to prepare and serve dinner for them.

Sharon and Paul left New Jersey in early September on a 12-day vacation that would culminate with their wedding in Colorado. They were married in a very private ceremony on September 9, 1999. Just before the ceremony in the late afternoon sun, they posed for wedding photographs by the majestic red rocks in the Garden of the Gods. When they arrived at my home, delicious smells and enchanting music greeted them when Brooke welcomed them at the door. I retreated to my bedroom to give them the desired intimacy.

The day after the wedding they decided to face the music with their families. Sharon nervously called her parents. She chatted with her mom and dad about events at home. Her mom asked, "So what have you been doing for the last few days?" Sharon took a deep breath, looked at Paul for reassurance and said, "We got married."

After what seemed like an eternity, Sharon's dad said, "Congratulations. That's fantastic."

Then it was Paul's turn. After the initial shock, his family expressed their pleasure as well.

Eloping is not right for everyone, but it was perfect for Sharon and Paul. They embodied the second habit of planning romantic adventures: follow your own romantic bliss. It really didn't matter what anyone else thought; this day was theirs to celebrate how they wanted and with whom they wanted. By following their hearts, Sharon and Paul had the wedding that was perfect for them.

Rate this adventure with a plus if you would like to find yourself in a similar situation, and with a minus if you wouldn't. Give extra pluses or minuses if you have strong feelings either way.

HER ANSWER	HIS ANSWER

Have you made any plans based more on the expectations of others than your own desires? If so, when?

HER ANSWER	HIS ANSWER

If so, describe how the event would have looked if you had done exactly what you wanted.

HER ANSWER	HIS ANSWER

Bears in Yellowstone
Michael and Judy's Romantic Adventure

Judy has been a dear friend of mine for many years. When I asked her what the most romantic thing was her husband had ever done for her, she thought for a minute, searching the ceiling tiles for an answer. She suddenly looked straight at me, tears welling up in her eyes.

Wow, I thought, *this is going to be good.*

Her voice broke as she whispered her answer. "Bear repellent."

As she relived her experience, I waited patiently for any possible explanation that could transform bear repellent into an aphrodisiac.

Judy loves to go to Yellowstone National Park in Wyoming. She has been going once or twice a year for many years. Sometimes she goes alone and sometimes her husband, Michael, goes with her. She enjoys the solitude, relaxation, sunshine and wildlife. Watching grizzly bears is one of her favorite pastimes. One year she found a guide who took Michael and her into the backcountry to view bears.

> *We can only learn to love by loving.*
> IRIS MURDOCH

She went back the following year by herself, and Michael planned to join her several days later. He knew she would spend a lot of time bear watching. Additionally, part of her daily routine was an early morning run in the backcountry. Naturally, he was concerned about her safety.

When she arrived at her hotel room, a large bouquet of red roses and a hastily wrapped gift greeted her. Tears came to her eyes when she opened the package to find a can of bear repellent. Judy was touched to know that Michael cared enough to call around and find someone willing to buy and gift-wrap bear repellent. It wasn't a professional wrapping job, if you know what I mean. In Judy's mind, she could see a local man going to the sporting goods store to buy bear repellent, stopping at a grocery store for wrapping paper, and rummaging through his junk drawer at home for tape and scissors. He may have cursed a few times trying to wrap the odd-shaped package, then shook his head thinking this was the strangest request he'd ever had from a tourist. The image still makes her laugh.

As she was telling me this story, the memory of it choked her up. I'd never heard anyone get so emotional over a can of bear repellent. This was further evidence that romance is in the hearts of the beloveds.

Rate this adventure with a plus if you would like to find yourself in a similar situation, and with a minus if you wouldn't. Give extra pluses or minuses if you have strong feelings either way.

HER ANSWER	HIS ANSWER

Have you given or received an unusual gift that was especially meaningful to you? If so, what was it?

HER ANSWER	HIS ANSWER

What made it so meaningful?

HER ANSWER	HIS ANSWER

Pennies in a Fountain
Pete and Joanne's Romantic Adventure

Paulette, the concierge at a local luxury hotel, called to ask if I could help one of their guests plan a wedding proposal. "In a heartbeat," I responded. "This is the stuff I live for."

Paulette explained that Pete wanted to let his girlfriend find the question – "Will you marry me?" – in an unusual location. Paulette had initially contacted a hiking tour company they frequently recommended for their guests. Their suggestion was to take Pete and Joanne on a hike and let Joanne find the question spelled out with small stones on the trail. Pete was okay with this idea except for two things. First, a snowstorm was predicted for the weekend. Second, Pete walks with a cane and wasn't sure if he could handle the trail. Pete was looking for Plan B.

I called Pete to find out more about what he wanted. The weather dictated the proposal would need to happen indoors. My first suggestion was that he order roses for their room and have the question spelled out with rose petals in front of the bouquet. He liked that initially, and then called back a little while later when he realized why it wouldn't work. Joanne is a good Catholic woman, and it wouldn't be proper for him to be in her room. Pete, a perfect gentleman, wanted something Joanne could tell her family and friends about.

My challenge was to come up with an indoor location, not in her room, where passersby would not disturb the message before Pete and Joanne arrived. The hotel had several beautiful indoor fountains. One of them was in a quiet lobby. I asked Pete if he would like the message to be presented in pennies in the fountain. This plan was perfect for him. He would get Joanne to the lobby by telling her he had to meet a client there.

> I truly feel that there are as many ways of loving as there are people in the world and as there are days in the life of those people.
>
> MARY S. CALDERONE

On the day of the proposal, I had a previous commitment so my husband agreed to help me out. Jim went to the hotel, arranged the pennies in the fountain, and put a long-stem red rose on the fountain by the message to draw Joanne's attention. He sat in the lobby to be sure no one took the rose or disturbed the message before they arrived. Out of the corner of his eye, he saw a man with a cane and a woman get off the elevator. As soon as Joanne noticed the fountain and the rose, Jim left the hotel lobby.

When I saw Jim, I wanted to know all the details. "Did she say yes?" I asked.

"I don't know. I didn't want to watch and invade their privacy," Jim said.

"You mean you didn't even watch her body language from a distance?"

"No, that didn't seem right."

Jim must have a more highly evolved sense of decency than I do. I would have been tempted to glance in their direction. How would I know her answer?

Fortunately, I didn't have to wait long. Pete called to thank us for our help and he reported that she did, in fact, say yes. Joanne had been telling and retelling the story to family and strangers alike.

For Pete, following his own romantic bliss meant knowing when to pay attention to his inner voice. He listened to several options that could have worked just fine for other people, but realized they weren't quite right for him and Joanne. He kept looking for other ideas until he hit one that resonated a big yes.

Rate this adventure with a plus if you would like to find yourself in a similar situation, and with a minus if you wouldn't. Give extra pluses or minuses if you have strong feelings either way.

HER ANSWER	HIS ANSWER

While Pete didn't know exactly what he wanted in the beginning, he set some parameters around the event, which made it easy to work toward a solution. Do you or your beloved have any reason to limit certain activities?

HER ANSWER	HIS ANSWER

Do you or your beloved have religious or moral beliefs that would restrict the timing or location of your adventures?

HER ANSWER	HIS ANSWER

Telling Romantic Stories
An Exercise

We can learn from hearing and telling romantic stories. Whether the story is about ourselves or someone else, if we can identify why we liked a certain story, we learn about our own romantic preferences.

One of my favorite stories is how Princess Diana fell in love with Dodi Fayed. They were on Dodi's yacht shortly after they met. Food was being served. Dodi dropped a piece of fruit. Diana picked up the fruit and threw it at him. A full-scale food fight broke out. There was mayhem on the yacht. When the food fight ended, they looked deeply into each other's eyes. From that moment on, everything between them changed. It was their playfulness that touched me, which for me is essential for romance.

Tell your partner a romantic story you have experienced or heard. Some topics to consider are:

♡ Favorite times with your beloved

♡ A story about your friends or family

♡ A story from the news

♡ A scene from a movie or novel

♡ Your parents' first date

♡ A story from your own imagination

Summarize your stories.

HER ANSWER	HIS ANSWER

What did you like best about your story?

HER ANSWER	HIS ANSWER

What did you like best in your beloved's story?

HER ANSWER	HIS ANSWER

Were there elements in either story that did not appeal to you? If so, why?

HER ANSWER	HIS ANSWER

Take an inventory of your own best romantic memories. List several and tell your beloved what you liked best about them.

HER ANSWER	HIS ANSWER

Celebrating Shared and Separate Interests

Ideally, you and your beloved have a balance of shared and separate interests. There's a good chance you enjoy many of the same activities. That may be what drew you together in the first place.

> *If we all pulled in one direction, the world would keel over.*
> YIDDISH PROVERB

It's easy for lovers to celebrate the interests they share, but celebrating interests they don't share requires more creativity. There's no reason to expect your beloved to enjoy all of the same leisure activities you do. Having your own pastimes makes you a more fascinating individual.

Celebrating a separate interest doesn't necessarily mean you should make it a shared interest. When I brought this issue up in a workshop, a woman mentioned that her husband played golf and she didn't. Some other people in class tried to convince her to take it up. "It's fun," they promised, "and you'll enjoy the view." No, that's not the point. First of all, if her husband is a competitive golfer, neither of them would find much satisfaction in a mismatched game. More importantly, they each should do what they enjoy. Life's too short to be lived according to someone else's desires.

Celebrating separate interests means giving support and encouragement to each other. Mark was an avid mountain biker. His girlfriend Jeannine wasn't. On a camping trip Jeannine encouraged Mark to take a challenging daylong bike ride with his friends. She drove them to the trailhead, and then returned to the campsite to relax with a good novel. When Mark and the other bikers returned to camp, they found a 10-by-3-foot sign marking the finish line. Shouts of "Congratulations!" filled the air. Mark was covered with streamers and Silly String. Jeannine never took up mountain biking, but she encouraged Mark to pursue his passion.

David wanted to show his favorite golf course to his wife, Gail. She wasn't a golfer, but she loved to garden. He knew she would enjoy the beautifully landscaped twelfth hole. Having never been on a golf course before, she was fascinated by the short grass on the green. As they sipped champagne and watched several groups of golfers go by, Gail got a sense of the game and the friendly people who play it. While strolling along the cart path, Gail shared her knowledge about some of the plants growing on the course. It was a magical evening. Gail better understood why David loved golf, and he gained an appreciation of his wife's gardening talents.

Here are some ideas for celebrating separate interests:

> *It is not a lack of love, but a lack of friendship that makes unhappy marriages.*
> FRIEDRICH NIETZSCHE

♡ He likes shooting, she doesn't. She gift-wraps a box of clay pigeons, and puts his shotgun and a picnic lunch in the trunk. They enjoy a picnic in the park. She gives him the box, and he drives to a nearby skeet shooting range. She reads a novel while waiting for him to return.

♡ She loves *The Oprah Winfrey Show,* he doesn't. He keeps an eye on Oprah's web site to see when his beloved can be in the audience, and gets tickets for her and her sister. He spends the day pursuing his own interests in Chicago, while the sisters enjoy the show and a nice brunch. The next day he takes his wife for their special exploration of the city.

♡ He restores vintage automobiles, she doesn't. She finds out about an automobile show in their area and gets tickets for him. She joins him for the classic car rally prior to the show, then meets him that evening for a nice candlelit dinner.

♡ She knits, he doesn't. He arranges for a limo to take her and her knitting friends to a yarn store for some shopping and a private group lesson. After enjoying champagne and hors d'oeuvres during the ride home with her friends, she joins her beloved for a romantic dinner.

Par Three on the Stairs
Carol and Richard's Romantic Adventure

When Richard's fortieth birthday was coming up, Carol hired me to help her plan a celebration for him. Richard loved golf, but Carol didn't play. She wanted this to be a memorable day for him, centered on golf.

She started out with big dreams. Richard had always wanted to see Tiger Woods play. I searched the web for tournaments Tiger would be in for the next six months. Tiger's tournaments were either sold out or too costly to consider. We moved down on her wish list.

Carol eventually arranged for Richard and a friend to play eighteen holes with a golf pro at a nearby country club. The pro gave them both tips to improve their games. When they finished, they enjoyed a leisurely lunch.

While this was going on, Carol was getting ready for the surprise party for Richard in their home. She set up a miniature golf course in the house. The first hole used a tic-tac-toe golf game; the second lay on the other side of a bridge fashioned out of cardboard boxes, and another was a dog dish at the bottom of a flight of stairs. The last hole, an indoor putting green, led to the last big surprise in their bedroom.

When Richard left the house that morning, Carol went into action. A neighbor watched their two children while Carol hurriedly painted the alcove behind their bed in their master bedroom. She chose a soft yellow that complemented the oil painting Richard had recently seen and liked. Carol bought it for his birthday, and hung it on the newly painted wall.

As their friends arrived for the party, they played a round of golf, which also gave them a tour of the new house. Everyone knew about the painting.

When Richard arrived, he was surprised to see so many friendly faces. After the initial excitement subsided, one of his friends challenged him to a game of miniature golf. The crowd moved with him through the house. Carol and the kids waited for him in the master bedroom.

Just outside the bedroom door, he lined up his shot. He did a double take when he realized the wall had been painted, and then he noticed the artwork he had recently admired. He looked from the painting to Carol.

"Happy birthday," Carol said. The kids jumped up and down with excitement.

Gift giving had always made Carol uncomfortable, but Richard's reaction told her the gift and the golf celebration were a success.

Rate this adventure with a plus if you would like to find yourself in a similar situation, and with a minus if you wouldn't. Give extra pluses or minuses if you have strong feelings either way.

HER ANSWER	HIS ANSWER

Carol wanted to honor Richard with a golf-centered celebration, even though she didn't play. What interests does your beloved have that you don't share. How can you honor these interests?

HER ANSWER	HIS ANSWER

Lifestyle Profile
An Exercise

Rate each of these interests or hobbies with a plus (+) if you love it, a minus (-) if you have no interest in it, and a question mark (?) if you'd be willing to give it a try.

Number	Interests or Hobbies	Her Answer	His Answer	Comments
1	Acting			
2	Aerobics			
3	Animals			
4	Antiques			
5	Archery			
6	Aromatherapy			
7	Art shows			
8	Automobile racing			
9	Automobile restoring			
10	Backpacking			
11	Baking			
12	Beer making			
13	Biking, mountain			
14	Biking, road			
15	Body work, massage or other (specify type)			
16	Bowling			
17	Camping			
18	Canoeing			
19	Caving			
20	Children's activities (specify type)			
21	Church activities (specify type)			
22	Collecting (specify type)			
23	Concerts (specify type)			
24	Cooking			

Number	Interests or Hobbies	Her Answer	His Answer	Comments
25	Craft shows			
26	Crossword puzzles			
27	Dance performances			
28	Dancing (specify type)			
29	Dining out			
30	Directing plays or movies			
31	Drawing			
32	Exercise (specify type)			
33	Family activities			
34	Film festivals			
35	Fishing (specify type)			
36	Flying as passenger			
37	Flying as pilot			
38	Foreign language studies (specify language)			
39	Gambling			
40	Games, board			
41	Games, cards			
42	Gardening			
43	Glider planes			
44	Golf			
45	Gymnastics			
46	Hang gliding			
47	Health spas			
48	Hiking			
49	History			
50	Home decorating			
51	Home improvements			
52	Horseback riding			
53	Hot air balloons			
54	House boating			
55	Hunting (specify type)			

Number	Interests or Hobbies	Her Answer	His Answer	Comments
56	Kayaking, sea			
57	Kayaking, white water			
58	Kite flying			
59	Knitting or crocheting			
60	Martial arts			
61	Melodramas			
62	Motorcycles			
63	Movies (specify favorites)			
64	Music, listening (specify type)			
65	Music, playing (specify)			
66	Music, singing			
67	Mysteries			
68	Opera			
69	Painting			
70	Parties			
71	Personal growth			
72	Photography			
73	Poetry			
74	Politics			
75	Pottery			
76	Quilting			
77	Racing (specify type)			
78	Reading (specify type)			
79	Recreational vehicles			
80	Relaxing (specify how)			
81	Religious studies			
82	Rock climbing			
83	Running			
84	Sailing			
85	Scuba diving			
86	Sculpture			
87	Sewing			

Number	Interests or Hobbies	Her Answer	His Answer	Comments
88	Shooting guns			
89	Shopping			
90	Skating (specify type)			
91	Skiing, cross country			
92	Skiing, downhill			
93	Sky diving			
94	Snorkeling			
95	Snowboarding			
96	Snowshoeing			
97	Soaking in hot springs			
98	Soaking in hot tubs			
99	Soaking in mud baths			
100	Spiritual growth			
101	Sports, attending events (specify)			
102	Sports, coaching			
103	Sports, playing (specify)			
104	Sunbathing			
105	Surfing			
106	Tennis			
107	Theater			
108	Trains			
109	Travel			
110	TV (specify favorites)			
111	Vineyards			
112	Water skiing			
113	Watsu (hot water massage)			
114	Weaving			
115	Wind surfing			
116	Wine making			
117	Wood working			
118	Writing (specify type)			
119	Yoga			
120	Other (specify)			

Celebrating Separate Interests
An Exercise

Each of you pick out your five favorites and record them below. Indicate whether they are shared (two pluses) or separate interests (one plus, with one minus or question mark). If you don't have at least one separate interest for each of you, look over the Lifestyle Profile again and pick one out or identify one together.

Number	Interests or Hobbies	Her Answer	His Answer	Shared or Separate?

Up until now, sharing your answers with your beloved has been a way of learning more about each other's romantic preferences. As you move forward in this workbook, you may prefer to keep some of your answers to yourself as you collect ideas for an adventure for your beloved. Separate his and hers answer spaces are provided; however, if you want to keep your answers secret to surprise your beloved at a later date, record them in a private notebook.

How can you celebrate your beloved's separate interest?

HER ANSWER	HIS ANSWER

or record your answers in your private notebook.

Sparks that Ignite the Romantic Flame

♡ Remember, just as beauty is in the heart of the beholder, romance is in the hearts of the beloveds. Romance is as individual as you are.

♡ Let your unique personalities and interests be reflected in your romantic adventures.

♡ Allow yourself to be touched by another's love story without feeling the need to emulate it, unless it is a perfect fit for you.

♡ Celebrate romance based on your desires, not society's expectations.

♡ Don't worry about what others think of your ideas. If you know it's right for your beloved and you, go for it.

♡ Listen to your intuition when planning adventures for your beloved. If some small inner voice tells you something's not quite right, it's not. Keep looking.

♡ Support and encourage each other by celebrating separate interests.

Do Something Outrageous

How many times have you been told to "think outside the box"? That's what this habit is suggesting you do. Many people have put a box around their definitions of romance – flowers, champagne, chocolates and heart-trimmed cards. There's nothing wrong with those things, but they're limiting. Be creative. Try doing something outrageous for your beloved, but be outrageous in a loving way. Don't do anything that would cause your beloved to be frightened or embarrassed. Expand your definition of romance. Depart from your routine.

> *Love is the only thing that keeps me sane.*
> SUE TOWNSEND

Some of my favorite romantic stories have outrageous, unreasonable and unexpected components to them. Hollywood movies are full of unpredictable characters and extreme behaviors. Is the story line in *Sleepless in Seattle* reasonable? Can you imagine an engaged woman traveling across the US to meet a man simply because she hears on a radio talk show a young son wishing for a wife for his widowed father? No, of course not. And in fact, almost all of Meg Ryan's romantic comedies push the limits of credibility, which is the first reason her films are so captivating. The second reason is that the unreasonable plots always end up so successfully for the lovers.

It's not just movies that capture our imaginations and our hearts with unbelievable storylines. In *The Man Who Ate the 747*, novelist Ben Sherwood tells the story of a quiet, heartsick farmer, Wally Chubb, who eats an entire 747 – "the airplane with a hump on top" – to help him win the heart of Willa Wyatt, who writes for the local newspaper. Every day Wally grinds up pieces of the 747 and eats some, "no matter how bad it tastes." In this unreasonable love story, an airplane gets eaten and Wally and Willa find true love, although nothing turns out quite like you'd expect.

> *Nothing is impossible to a willing heart.*
> JOHN HEYWOOD

Reality TV and daytime talk shows know how to do something outrageous — and some of them do it in a nice way. *Extreme Makeover: Home Edition* surprises deserving families by remodeling their homes. The best part is when the show's producers talk to family members about their individual needs and wants. They really listen, and it shows in the results.

The Oprah Winfrey Show does segments on making your wildest dreams come true. Oprah asked *Desperate Housewives* star Felicity Huffman about her wildest dream. Felicity admitted she'd once wanted to be a backup singer for a rock star. On the next program, Oprah made it happen. Tina Turner was on the show promoting a new CD, and Felicity was behind her, singing and dancing like a pro. Watching Felicity after her performance, radiant and overcome with emotion, was almost as much fun for the viewing audience as watching her during her performance.

This habit does not suggest that you fly around the world on a whim searching for a potential lover or even eat a smaller vehicle, like a Ford Focus. However, it does show how making an unnecessary flight to meet your lover or using the shell of a broken-down Volkswagen can be incredibly romantic.

Listen to your beloved's needs, wants, wildest dreams, and even fanciful musings. You'll see how one man used his creativity — without the budget and celebrity connections that Oprah has — to satisfy his wife's wildest Irish dreams.

Love in a 1964 Volkswagen Bus
Maggie and Frank's Romantic Adventure

Whether or not you remember the Summer of Love – 1967 in San Francisco – you'll enjoy this story about Frank and Maggie. They met that summer. Frank drove a 1964 VW panel bus, wore tie-dyed t-shirts, and listened to the Grateful Dead. Maggie wore flowers in her hair and lived in a Haight Ashbury apartment with three other people. He spotted her dancing at a Jefferson Airplane concert and was mesmerized by her movements and her smile. He worked his way through the crowd to be near her. They fell in love during the Summer of Love.

Thirty-some years later Frank and Maggie still have fond memories of that summer, but their lives could not be more different today. He owns a successful construction business and she is a social worker. Together they've raised three children, doing their best to steer their kids away from the lifestyle they experienced during the sixties. Nowadays, they dote on their grandchildren and tend their garden.

While Frank and Maggie never wanted to go back in time to the sixties, they both longed for the spirited passion they felt that summer. When a co-worker mentioned to Maggie that he had an old 1964 VW bus that he needed to tow to the junkyard, she had an idea.

A few weeks later, Frank offered to help their son build a deck on his home. Since the son lived several hours away, Frank planned to spend the night on Saturday and return home on Sunday afternoon. This gave Maggie the opportunity she needed to execute her plan.

Just after he left, she had the old VW towed to their back yard. They lived in a rural area with five acres of land, so it was easy to keep the VW out of sight from the street. The backseats had been taken out of the bus long ago. The paint on the body was faded or eaten away by rust. The windows were dusty and cracked. Just the sight of this dilapidated old vehicle made Maggie laugh.

Maggie tackled the mess, eager to clear out the junk left in the bus, wondering what she'd find under the tattered carpet. She hoped the bus would be as enchanting as the original, the original that drove them to concerts, broke down on the second date, and provided a love pad away from their roommates.

From one of Frank's construction sites Maggie had picked up a carpet remnant. In the attic she found a couple of beanbag chairs. At a discount store she bought some pillows, curtains and twelve cans of spray paint in rainbow colors. By Saturday evening, she had transformed the beat-up VW into an inviting love pad.

When Frank returned home late Sunday afternoon, Maggie met him at the front door wearing a colorful sundress and Birkenstock sandals. She covered his eyes with a blindfold. Frank was excited when she unbuttoned his shirt and removed it, but confused when she pulled another shirt over his head. He could tell he was being led to the back yard. He heard Jefferson Airplane music and smelled sandalwood incense.

Maggie took off his blindfold. Frank was speechless at the sight before him – a 1964 VW panel bus just like the one he had when he met Maggie. She had begun the paint job on the bus with a few slogans like "Flower Power" and "Summer of Love" and one big daisy around a rust spot. A dozen cans of spray paint sat on a tray just waiting for Frank and Maggie to finish the paint job. Frank walked around the bus, running his hands along the body as if to make sure it wasn't a dream. He laughed when he noticed he now wore a tie-dyed t-shirt and she had a daisy in her hair.

She led him inside the van and closed the door behind them. The floor of the cozy love nest was sprinkled with flower petals. Posters of the Grateful Dead, the Beatles, Bob Dylan and Jefferson Airplane covered the walls and ceiling. Tie-dyed curtains covered the windows; the only light inside the van came from a lava lamp.

> *Think big thoughts but relish small pleasures.*
> H. JACKSON BROWN, JR.

On a blanket inside, Maggie had laid out a dinner reminiscent of their favorite foods that summer: garden salad with Italian dressing, vegetarian lasagna, and San Francisco sour dough bread. A bottle of Lambrusco, their wine of choice in 1967 but far too sweet for their current sophisticated palates, was chilling in a wine bucket.

While nibbling on lasagna and sipping wine, Maggie told Frank the story of how she acquired the VW bus. Frank couldn't take his eyes off Maggie. In that moment, their love for each other seemed to take on a surreal quality. It was as if their love had a tangible element that colored the walls and sweetened the music. When she confessed that her motive was to rekindle the passion of that summer, he reached over to kiss her, slowly at first, then building with some urgency. After just a few bites, the dinner went untouched. They made love with the passion of a couple of twenty-two year olds, but with the depth and tenderness and understanding that comes from being lovers for over thirty years.

A little while later, Frank said, "I would say your mission was accomplished."

"It was even better than I expected," Maggie replied.

Having finally worked up an appetite, Frank tasted the lasagna. "Hey, this really is like our Summer of Love. I remember several times when our food got cold before we ever got around to eating it."

"Eat up because you'll need some energy to paint this bus," Maggie advised.

Under the light of a full moon, Frank and Maggie had a grand time painting their love nest. All twelve cans of spray paint were nearly empty when they finished. When the sun came up the next morning, they were able to admire their handy work. What a fine job they had done!

The bus still sits in their back yard, offering a pleasurable retreat from the pressures of everyday life. About once a month, Frank and Maggie spend the evening in the "Love Bus."

Who would have thought that a useless old VW bus could inspire such passion?

Rate this adventure with a plus if you would like to find yourself in a similar situation, and with a minus if you wouldn't. Give extra pluses or minuses if you have strong feelings either way.

HER ANSWER	HIS ANSWER

What do you remember about your initial attraction to each other?

HER ANSWER	HIS ANSWER

What kind of car did you drive? What romantic memories do you have of that car?

HER ANSWER	HIS ANSWER

How did you dress? Ask your beloved to describe your sexiest outfit. Would you be willing to dress like that again some time?

HER ANSWER	HIS ANSWER

Are there certain smells or tastes that remind you of an especially romantic date?

HER ANSWER	HIS ANSWER

What were your favorite activities? What is your favorite erotic memory from that time? Is there a way to recapture or recreate it?

HER ANSWER	HIS ANSWER

Wild Irish Dream
Randy and Loretta's Romantic Adventure

Before Randy and Loretta were married, they took a trip to Ireland. Loretta fell in love with the castle at Powerscourt. One of the most beautiful locations in Ireland, Powerscourt House and Gardens sits on a thousand-acre estate. As she admired the landscaped gardens and grounds, she told Randy that she wished they could be married there. Thinking of their guest list of several hundred, Randy knew this was not possible, but he didn't forget Loretta's wish. They took rolls of pictures, not wanting to forget anything about this magical experience.

Randy and Loretta were married the following year in a garden wedding in one of Colorado Springs' most romantic wedding sites. The finely grained pink sandstone Tudor Manor was reminiscent of an English Country House – perhaps a miniature version of Powerscourt. It was a storybook wedding.

The photographer captured the spirit of the day, recording the anticipation, nervousness, humor, and, of course, the romance. Looking at the wedding pictures afterward, I nearly developed a case of sympathetic jitters remembering Randy waiting at the altar. I laughed out loud at the image of Loretta hurling a dinner roll at a rowdy table during dinner at the reception. (Okay, I admit it was my table, but I wasn't the instigator.) One of the most romantic pictures was a perfect you-may-kiss-the-bride shot from a distance of about 15 feet. The details on Loretta's dress looked like an advertisement in a bridal magazine. The wedding party watched and smiled in the background.

When their first anniversary neared, Randy thought long and hard about a unique approach to the traditional first year anniversary gift of paper. Randy remembered Loretta's wish to be married at Powerscourt. He looked though their pictures from Ireland and found the perfect location for a wedding – the very spot where they were standing when Loretta expressed her desire. The picture showed a corner of the castle on the left, a lush flower garden in the distant right, and a manicured lawn in the center. There wasn't a soul in the picture, but that was about to change.

Randy took the pictures of Powerscourt and the wedding kiss to a photographer who did custom darkroom work. After deciding where he and Loretta would stand in the picture, Randy left the rest to the photographer.

On their first anniversary, Randy took Loretta to dinner. He said, "Loretta, I know you wanted to get married in Ireland, and I'm sorry that we couldn't. I hope this present will make up for that."

Loretta protested. "Oh Randy, I knew we couldn't do that. I was just wishing out loud. And besides, I thought our wedding was perfect."

When you love someone all your saved-up wishes start coming out.
ELIZABETH BOWEN

When she opened the package, it took her a minute to figure out what she was looking at in the framed photograph. It was their wedding – but it wasn't. It was their wedding at Powerscourt.

Randy had given her a fantasy, the memory of two special events commemorated in one photograph. Loretta still feels like a princess with her Prince Charming when she looks at the picture of their fairy tale wedding.

Rate this adventure with a plus if you would like to find yourself in a similar situation, and with a minus if you wouldn't. Give extra pluses or minuses if you have strong feelings either way.

HER ANSWER	HIS ANSWER

Do you have some pictures of a favorite place? Or maybe some postcards of a place you would like to visit someday? You could have some fun putting yourself and your beloved into an exotic location without ever leaving home. This could be a unique way to build anticipation around an upcoming vacation.

HER ANSWER	HIS ANSWER

or record your answers in your private notebook.

What are your wildest dreams? Notice when your beloved expresses a desire, no matter how fanciful. You don't have to have Oraph's resources or connections to make it come true in some fashion.

HER ANSWER	HIS ANSWER

or record your answers in your private notebook.

The Great Birthday Give-Away
Our Romantic Adventure

For the fourth time in as many years, Jim and I were planning a trip to Lake Powell for Labor Day with the same group of friends. And for the fourth time, I would be celebrating my birthday there. Thinking about the last three celebrations, I started feeling just a bit undeserving to be the guest of honor at yet another Lake Powell birthday party. I knew better than to suggest they not celebrate my birthday. Since there was no entertainment on the lake, any excuse for a party was a good one.

"Too bad we're not going in May so we could celebrate Jim's birthday. He always draws the short straw when it comes to birthday parties." I pondered this thought

> *Most of us can remember a time when a birthday — especially if it was one's own — brightened the world as if a second sun had risen.*
> ROBERT LYND

for a few minutes when I had an epiphany – I could give Jim my birthday!

I approached my friends with this idea. No one understood it at first – who ever heard of giving a birthday to someone else? "It won't make you any younger," they teased.

"That's not the purpose," I promised. "Jim doesn't get to celebrate his birthday with friends very often, especially in a beautiful place like this. He would never suspect that a celebration on my birthday would honor him. Let's roast him."

This was an idea our friends could stand behind – any lighthearted excuse to poke fun at Jim was good enough for them. He was known for his good sense of humor.

It was only logical to let him think the group was planning a party for me. Someone suggested to Jim that he should take me for a nice, romantic walk after dinner. We were both happy to have an excuse to get away for a while, since a houseboat with ten of our closest friends was not conducive to intimacy. Staying away long enough for the party preparations to take place gave us some intimate time while we enjoyed the magnificent red rocks at sunset.

When we came back to the houseboat after our walk, the group greeted us by singing "Happy Birthday" while standing around a flaming UN-birthday cake. Jim sang along and I acted like the guest of honor until the rest of the group turned their attention to him as they sang the line "Happy UN-Birthday Dear JIM, Happy UN-Birthday to you."

He had not really gotten the message by the time the singing stopped. I pointed to the message on the cake and said, "This celebration is for you. I've been celebrated enough down here. Tonight we are roasting you." I placed a tacky crown on his head and the party began.

No one had ever been more surprised at a birthday party than Jim was that night. Each gag gift brought rounds of laughter: fake hair for his chest, a t-shirt proclaiming him "Lake Powell Houseboat Captain," and a "Lake Powell Weather System" to predict the weather (a rock on a string: if the rock is wet, it's raining; if the rock if swaying, the seas are high). The best memento of the event was a photo album with twenty-five pictures of Jim with various newspaper and magazine headlines and hilarious captions written by the group.

Of all the birthdays I celebrated at Lake Powell, this is the one I remember best.

Rate this adventure with a plus if you would like to find yourself in a similar situation, and with a minus if you wouldn't. Give extra pluses or minuses if you have strong feelings either way.

HER ANSWER	HIS ANSWER

Does your beloved, or anyone else you normally celebrate, have a birthday around the holidays or any other time of year that is very busy? Maybe their celebration was preempted due to unexpected events. Have you ever noticed how kids will report their ages to be, say, four and a half or seven and a half? Why not celebrate the half birthdays of adults? When birthdays slip by without a little fanfare for whatever reason, consider picking another date to celebrate. It's one way to ensure surprise.

HER ANSWER	HIS ANSWER

or record your answers in your private notebook.

Tips on Marriage Proposals

Sir Winston Churchill, Great Britain's World War II prime minister, once said, "My most brilliant achievement was my ability to be able to persuade my wife to marry me." Considering his many accomplishments, that's quite a statement.

Are you working on your own most brilliant Churchill-like achievement? If you're thinking about proposing to your beloved, think about these three points.

> *How bold one gets when one is sure of being loved!*
> SIGMUND FREUD

First, who (other than your beloved, of course) would you like to be present when you propose? If you decide you want to have others present – family, friends or strangers — be sure you know that the answer will be yes before you ask it. For some, proposing marriage is an intensely private affair. For others, it's a cause for public celebration. Often, a public wedding proposal will be as memorable for the witnesses as it is for the happy couple.

If you choose to propose in public, be certain your beloved will be comfortable with it, too. When I see marriage proposals on national television I'm always relieved when the answer is "Yes" rather than "Honey, we need to talk."

Second, do you want to ask the question yourself, or do you want the question to present itself? Just saying the words sounds easy enough – unless you're nervous. Having the message present itself, whether in Christmas lights, a fortune cookie, or rose petals, is a grand and memorable gesture.

If you have musical talents, this could be the perfect opportunity to use them. Write a song and sing it to your beloved.

Third, where do you want to propose? What common interests do you share that could provide a unique opportunity? The location and the activities surrounding the proposal can be as varied and interesting as each couple.

I heard a story about a couple who loved movies. He filled a theater with their family and friends, and then brought his beloved into the darkened room after the previews had started. I can only imagine the emotions filling the room when his video asking for her hand in marriage began. If that weren't enough of a shock for her, when the video ended the house lights came on and the audience cheered in celebration. If you love movies, you don't need to be a movie star to find yourself in a starring role *at* the movies.

While in reality it's usually the man who pops the question in our society, proposals can provide equal opportunities for both sexes. These tips work regardless of who's doing the asking.

John had asked Nancy to marry him three times, and three times she said no. When she finally decided she was ready, it was up to her to break the news. She asked, and he said yes. When she told her friends what she had done, they asked her if she got down on one knee. "No," she said with a twinkle in her eyes, "I got up on one elbow."

I'll end with a word of caution about marriage proposals. It is a special moment in your life, so it would be nice if it were treated that way, but a proposal doesn't need to be grand or extravagant for the marriage to work. I speak from experience here: Jim and I had an argument and as part of making up, he asked me to marry him. It was probably the least romantic proposal I know of, but the marriage has worked. Our romantic adventures in subsequent years, many of them on his initiative, have more than made up for that rocky start.

Make romance a life long commitment, not just a one-time event.

Flying United Makes Time Fly
Dennis and Brenda's Romantic Adventure

I ran a promotion called the Great Romantic Payback on a local radio station, asking listeners to fax in romantic stories for which they are grateful. The person with the best story would win a weekend for two in Breckenridge, which would include lodging, dinner at a fine restaurant, lift tickets, and massages, among other prizes. Of all the entries I received, I selected Brenda's story as the winner because of the outrageous and unexpected way Dennis showed his love for her.

Brenda met her husband-to-be when she came to Colorado from Manchester, England to visit her brother. During her brief visit, a romance with Dennis developed. For the next year, they nurtured a long distance relationship with letters, phone calls, and a few vacations. As she began making plans for her next trip, she admitted to Dennis that as much as she was looking forward to seeing him, she was dreading making the long flight again.

Brenda's journey was to take her from Manchester to Chicago to Dallas, and finally to Colorado Springs where Dennis would be waiting for her. After arriving at Chicago's O'Hare Airport, she waited for her next connecting flight at the departure gate. She had just settled down with a paperback to pass the next fifty minutes when someone stood before her and snapped a picture. She tried to ignore the photographer but the flash was so close she couldn't help but look up. The moment she looked up another flash went off and it was clear that the unwelcome photographer was taking pictures of her. She was about to protest when a familiar voice said, "Hello, Beautiful."

"Oh my God! What are you doing here?" Brenda exclaimed.

"I knew you weren't looking forward to that long flight alone, so I decided to keep you company," Dennis answered.

Brenda was stunned. "You flew all the way to Chicago just so I wouldn't have to be alone for a few hours?"

Who travels for love finds a thousand miles not longer than one.
JAPANESE PROVERB

Brenda couldn't imagine anyone doing something so impulsive and impractical. The very idea that someone would spend the money and take the time to do something like this rendered her speechless.

Dennis helped her gather her belongings and they found a quiet lounge. "Actually, there is more to this trip than just keeping you company," Dennis confessed. "I have a question for you that just couldn't wait any longer. I figured if you knew how anxious I was to see you, you couldn't possibly say no."

"What's the question?" Brenda asked, holding her breath.

Dennis reached into a bag that he was carrying. He pulled out a single long-stem red rose. Upon closer inspection, Brenda realized she was looking at a ring box shaped like a rose. Dennis flipped open the top and presented a lovely diamond engagement ring.

"I love you. Will you marry me?" Dennis asked.

"I want you to know I would have said yes no matter when or where you asked. But the fact that you went to such great lengths makes me love you even more."

Dennis slipped the ring on her finger – a perfect fit.

Brenda was swept away by Dennis's surprising and creative way of showing his love for her.

Rate this adventure with a plus if you would like to find yourself in a similar situation, and with a minus if you wouldn't. Give extra pluses or minuses if you have strong feelings either way.

HER ANSWER	HIS ANSWER

Think back on your life with your beloved. Is there something he or she really dreads doing? Is there a way you could have turned that chore or journey into an adventure you enjoyed together?

HER ANSWER	HIS ANSWER

The Magic of Christmas Lights
Todd and Jenny's Romantic Adventure

Todd's hands trembled as he dialed his girlfriend's number. "Hi, Jenny. Guess what? I won a contest on the radio."

"Todd, that's fantastic. What did you win?" Jenny asked.

"I won dinner for two at a fancy restaurant and a limousine for the evening. We get to drive around town and judge which houses have the best Christmas decorations. The DJ on the morning show is a judge, too."

The fact that Jenny had not heard of this contest didn't surprise her. They listened to different radio stations. She listened to National Public Radio; he listened to the stations with chatty DJs. He had won several contests in the past, but this was by far the best.

On a Saturday night in December, Todd dressed up in his best suit for the night on the town. The sight of Jenny as she opened the door to her apartment nearly took his breath away. She looked beautiful – and very sexy – in a sequined red dress. When Jenny invited Todd inside, he found himself standing under a sprig of mistletoe. After a passionate Christmas kiss, he showed her the letter from the radio station with the night's itinerary. They were ready and eager when the limo arrived.

Josh, the videographer who went along to record their every move, made them both feel like celebrities. When they arrived at the restaurant, the hostess led them to a corner table by the window. A white candle burned in the center of an arrangement of red roses, holly and ivy. The attached card from the florist congratulated Todd on winning the contest.

Jenny and Todd enjoyed their four-course meal and a bottle of wine. With Josh coming by occasionally to video each course and the special attention they received from the staff, it was clear to the other diners that Jenny and Todd were VIPs.

As they finished their dessert, Mark, a DJ from the radio station, showed up. He joined Jenny, Todd, and Josh in the limo. They sipped champagne as they drove through several neighborhoods to admire the decorations and to pick their favorites.

The limo driver drove to an area where the houses were far apart. He slowed down as they passed a house with thousands of lights and numerous displays. As they approached the far side of the house, Jenny noticed a display with lights spelling out a message. It was obviously not "Merry Christmas," so she started to spell out the words.

"W-i-l-l y-o-u — will you marry me? Isn't that romantic? It's a proposal."

It didn't occur to Jenny that this message might be for her until she felt Todd take her hand. As she turned to face him, the look on his face told her this was the real thing. He pulled a ring from his pocket and offered it to her in silence. After she recovered from the shock, she said, "Yes!" He slipped the ring on her finger.

The celebration in the limo exploded with cheers.

Realizing she had been set up, Jenny asked if he really won a contest. "No," Todd confessed. "When I got the idea, I called Mark and asked him if he would help me pull this off. Initially I only asked for a sheet of the station's letterhead, and then I asked him if he would like to ride along with us in the limo."

"It sounded like fun to me," Mark said, "and when Todd told me there would be free champagne and single women, I couldn't resist."

"Mark, you're too easy. I don't see any single women, do you?" Jenny asked.

"We're just getting to that part," Todd said. The limo pulled into the driveway of the house with the proposal. "Let's go inside and break the good news."

"Who lives here?" Jenny asked.

"My mom's friends. They helped me put up the sign and offered to host a small celebration, assuming you said yes."

"You were pretty sure of yourself, weren't you?"

"I was a little nervous, but when your friend Carla heard about what I had planned, she said if you said no, she would marry me."

Jenny's parents, Todd's mother, several siblings and numerous friends greeted them as the party moved inside. After hugging everyone and showing off her ring, Jenny made her way to Carla.

They had a good laugh about Carla's offer to marry Todd. Jenny said, "He's officially taken now, so you'll have to keep looking. Let me introduce you to Mark."

Mark and Carla were still getting acquainted when Jenny and Todd were ready to leave in the limo. Carla offered Mark a ride home. Last I heard Mark and Carla were still dating.

Todd wanted the question to present itself, and found a clever way to record her reaction. He also wanted family and friends to share in his happiness.

Rate this adventure with a plus if you would like to find yourself in a similar situation, and with a minus if you wouldn't. Give extra pluses or minuses if you have strong feelings either way.

HER ANSWER	HIS ANSWER

Drum Roll

Seth and Dennette's Romantic Adventure

Seth, a musician, was ready to propose to Dennette, a fourth grade teacher. He had previously studied drumming in Africa and was happy to oblige when Dennette asked him to show her class what he had learned. Afterward, the fourth graders wrote thank you notes. Seth was charmed by what the students asked in their thank you letters: if he could visit their classroom again, if he'd bring cookies next time, and if he was going to marry Miss Dennette.

That last question sparked his plan for his return visit, his big day, his marriage proposal. Seth returned to answer their questions with a smile on his face, a box of cookies in his hands, and a diamond ring in his pocket. To his delight, the questions rolled forward from the lips of the captivated fourth graders: Did you see any wild animals? Did you get any African tattoos? Are you going to marry Miss Dennette?

> *Three grand essentials to happiness in this life are something to do, something to love and something to hope for.*
>
> JOSEPH ADDISON

To that he replied, "Well, in Africa it's customary to ask the woman's community for permission to marry. Is it okay with you if I marry her?"

"Yes!" thirty young voices squealed in unison.

Seth turned to Dennette, dropped to his knees, and struggled with his emotions. He felt the tension build as the question crept forward on his tongue; Dennette felt the tension intensify as silence filled the air; a student in the back row broke the tension with two words: Drum roll!

As if on cue, thirty sets of little hands started beating rapidly on their desks. When Seth found his voice, he raised his hand for silence. He asked Dennette to comply with the wishes of their community, to share his life, to be his wife.

While her heart screamed YES, only a tiny whisper managed to squeeze by the lump in her throat, but it was enough to put the class in a frenzy. The girls rushed forward to surround their beloved teacher; the boys high-fived each other.

With all the commotion in the classroom, word spread quickly throughout the school. Shortly the band teacher appeared and insisted that the newly engaged couple come to the band room. In just a few minutes the band had learned to play a barely recognizable version of *Here Comes the Bride.*

There's a class of fourth graders who will remember their teacher and her fiancé for years to come. They learned much more than what was on the lesson plan that day. They learned the thrill of romance.

Rate this adventure with a plus if you would like to find yourself in a similar situation, and with a minus if you wouldn't. Give extra pluses or minuses if you have strong feelings either way.

HER ANSWER	HIS ANSWER

Money is No Object
An Exercise

This is a brainstorming session. Do this with your beloved or with a small group. Working with several others is encouraged to get ideas from multiple sources; however, it's not mandatory.

Pick six random numbers between 1 and 120 and write them in the "Number" column in the space provided below.

Number	Interests or Hobbies	Celebration

Refer to the numbered activities in the Lifestyle Profile in Habit Two. List the interests or hobbies that correspond to the numbers listed above. Circle three or four of them that appeal to you. Come up with a way to celebrate these interests with an unlimited budget. It doesn't matter if you don't know much about these activities; in fact, it could be a benefit not to have preconceived notions about how to celebrate them. Money is no object.

> The best way to have a good idea is to have lots of ideas.
> LINUS PAULING

Remember the name of this chapter: Do Something Outrageous. It's okay to let your thinking run wild.

The purpose of this exercise is to free your thinking so that you are not limited by financial constraints. This isn't to assume that everyone doing this exercise has thousands or even hundreds to burn on romance. In the next chapter, we return to financial reality and work with limited budgets.

Sparks that Ignite the Romantic Flame

- ♡ Think outside the box.
- ♡ Make romance outrageous, unreasonable, and unexpected.
- ♡ Surprise your beloved by showing up in unexpected places.
- ♡ Use unpredictable ideas to bring back romantic memories.
- ♡ Find unconventional ways to deliver your message of love.
- ♡ Let your favorite daydreams and fantasies inspire your adventures.
- ♡ Celebrate your beloved when it's least expected. Observe half birthdays or give your birthday to your beloved.

Accommodate Your Beloved's Surprise Tolerance

Some people love surprises; others hate them. Before you go out and plan an outrageous surprise for your beloved, consider his or her Surprise Tolerance.

Surprise Tolerance Types

Your beloved's Surprise Tolerance Type is	1	2	3
If your beloved...	...is uncomfortable with surprises	...likes to know some of what will happen	...loves surprises
Prepare for adventures this way:	Plan together	Build anticipation with hints	Keep it a secret until the big day

What is your Surprise Tolerance Type? This is just your first impression. You'll be building on this answer as we go along.

HER ANSWER	HIS ANSWER

If Your Beloved Is a Type 1
Plan Adventures Together

People who say they hate surprises have a variety of reasons for feeling that way. Some possibilities are:

♡ They dislike being the center of attention. Surprise parties for people like this will be a source of anxiety and discomfort.

♡ They prefer having control over their own time and celebrations.

♡ They have specific tastes and are more likely to be satisfied with the outcome if they are involved with the planning.

♡ Most surprises they've received in the past have been embarrassing, poorly planned or executed, or awkward.

♡ They've never been surprised in a good way.

♡ Their hearts won't take it.

If you or your beloved has a Type 1 surprise tolerance, have a conversation to further explore the subject. If being the center of attention is the only problem, throwing a surprise party or serenading your beloved in a restaurant would be a bad idea, but a surprise weekend getaway could be a winner.

> *Surprises are foolish things. The pleasure is not enhanced, and the inconvenience is often considerable.*
>
> JANE AUSTEN

Having a Type 1 surprise tolerance isn't a bad thing. It's just the way some people are. Some very romantic people have low opinions of surprises. I would guess Jane Austen was one of them.

If your beloved absolutely hates to be surprised, plan your adventures together. This is foreign to me since I love surprises, but I remember the second habit: "Follow your own romantic bliss." If he or she has an unpleasant history of surprises for whatever reason, you will have a more comfortable and memorable adventure if you plan it together.

Just because you agree on the major event and plan it together, that doesn't mean you can't throw in a few minor surprises, like a well-timed card or love note.

Some people may find themselves distanced from their beloveds during the planning of a surprise. A certain amount of secret keeping is necessary during that process. If you are used to sharing almost everything with your beloved, it will take a conscious and perhaps uncomfortable effort to keep things to yourself.

When Rhenee was planning Russ's fiftieth birthday celebration, she found herself avoiding even mundane conversations with him so that she wouldn't let slip some important piece of information. For several days leading up to the big event, she really missed her time with him.

I've felt that, too, at times. I censure my discussions and make mental notes of all the things I want to tell Jim about once the adventure is underway or after it's over. For me, it's worth the tradeoff because the outcome is so satisfying.

A Moment with the Dullards

"I hope this means you ordered the big fight on Pay-Per-View. You know how I hate surprise parties with your boring friends."

This is something to consider not only in determining your beloved's tolerance for surprises, but also in determining your tolerance for planning surprises for your beloved.

The Gentlest Surprise
Ann and Matt's Romantic Adventure

Matt's birthday was approaching, and Ann knew better than to plan a surprise party. Being the center of attention made Matt uncomfortable. At his insistence, Ann let most of his birthdays come and go with a minimum of fuss. Ann wanted to do something different this year, while still honoring that basic part of who he is.

Ann asked Matt if she could take him out to dinner for his birthday, and he was happy to comply. When they got to the restaurant, they waited for their table in the bar, where Matt was surprised to see their dear friends, Gina and Jon. They chatted for a few minutes, avoiding the fact that it was Matt's birthday. Matt asked them if they would join Ann and him for dinner. Of course they said yes.

Shortly after they were seated at their table, Gina gave Matt a birthday card. He realized he'd been set up, but he didn't mind one bit. He thoroughly enjoyed spending time with Gina and Jon. It was a gentle, comfortable surprise. He wasn't blindsided by people jumping out of hiding places yelling "Surprise!", nor did he have to endure the restaurant's own birthday song. Ann listened to the feelings behind the "No surprises" request. She let Matt be the one to extend the invitation. It's one of Matt's fondest birthday memories.

Rate this adventure with a plus if you would like to find yourself in a similar situation, and with a minus if you wouldn't. Give extra pluses or minuses if you have strong feelings either way.

HER ANSWER	HIS ANSWER

Do you have any negative memories or feelings associated with surprises? If so, what are they?

HER ANSWER	HIS ANSWER

If you are a Type 1, let your beloved know why. Do any of the reasons listed on page 80 apply to you? Are there other factors as well?

HER ANSWER	HIS ANSWER

If you are a Type 1, can you identify some circumstance in which a gentle surprise would be okay?

HER ANSWER	HIS ANSWER

If Your Beloved Is a Type 2
Build Anticipation with Hints

When an out-of-the-blue surprise is out of the question, use anticipation to build up to a secret adventure. Drop plenty of hints, but don't make them too obvious if the destination or adventure is to remain a surprise. Giving a few obscure hints can pique curiosity, and maybe even serve as red herrings to make things interesting.

> *The days on which one has been most inquisitive are among the days on which one has been happiest.*
> ROBERT LYND

Once my husband Jim told me we were going away for my birthday. Prior to our departure, he gave me three gifts with Kokopelli images on them: a pair of earrings, a metal sculpture for the garden, and a book about the dancing Anasazi flutist. I was tickled pink as I assumed we were going mountain biking on the Kokopelli Trail between Grand Junction, Colorado and Moab, Utah. I was astounded when we left town heading the opposite direction. Jim had found a remarkable cave carved into the side of a cliff in Farmington, New Mexico that had been converted into a bed and breakfast called Kokopelli's Cave. I've never enjoyed being misled as much as I did that day.

You may want to let the time and date be known, but keep everything else a mystery. No matter what a person's surprise tolerance, sometimes this is the only way to hold time open in a busy person's calendar. Giving a heads up that you've got something planned allows your beloved to manage his or her time around the adventure and avoid any scheduling conflicts.

A Christmas Gift of Time
Bob and Becky's Romantic Adventure

Bob and Becky were busy professionals. They had everything they wanted except more time together. As well as being partners in marriage, they were partners in a successful consulting business that required frequent travel.

Scheduling a long weekend meant they would have to reserve the time at least six months in advance.

Christmas was approaching and Bob was stymied as to what to give Becky. She had everything she needed and wanted. I suggested the gift of time, with a unique and promising presentation.

Looking ahead in their calendars, Bob found three weekends throughout the year that they could get away. Over the next week, he collaborated with their assistant and their kids to schedule bogus events on Becky's calendar to keep those times free.

Bob selected an invitation format and found a lovely, handcrafted box to hold the invitations. He decided where he wanted to go for those weekends and we thought of hints to put in the invitations. His invitation for a long weekend trip to Mexico is shown on the right.

Robert N.
Requests the Honor
of your Presence
From Friday, August 23
To Monday, August 26.

Warm water and
The warmth of your love –
A winning combination.

I printed the invitations for Bob and he wrapped them up inside the box. On Christmas morning their family gathered together to open gifts. With all the scheming that had gone on to create this gift, all eyes were on Becky as she opened the box. The box itself was handsome enough to warrant several oohs and aahs.

When Becky looked inside and saw the cards, she was intrigued. As she opened each card, she became even more excited until she remembered her busy schedule. She said, "I'll have to check my calendar to see if these dates will work for me."

Bob pulled her calendar from behind a pillow on the sofa. "Here, you can check it now."

Becky opened to the first date and said with some disappointment, "Jeanie has me in Seattle for a conference, returning mid-afternoon on Saturday."

Bob smiled and said, "I had Jeanie put that on your calendar just to save the date. That conference ends on Thursday."

"Perfect timing. We'll need a break after that." Becky said, flipping to the next date. "Oh, this one won't work. Nicole has a concert that weekend."

Nicole said, "I wasn't entirely honest about the date. It's really Wednesday of the following week. You'll be back by then."

Becky was starting to sense a conspiracy as she checked the last dates. "Do we really have a fund raiser to attend that weekend?"

"I'll skip it if you will," Bob said.

Becky nodded in agreement.

"So, it looks like you're available after all," he said. "What do you say?"

She realized the entire family was in on his scheme to help get her away. With tears in her eyes, she said, "This is the best gift anyone has ever given me. I'd love to go away with you, Bob."

Rate this adventure with a plus if you would like to find yourself in a similar situation, and with a minus if you wouldn't. Give extra pluses or minuses if you have strong feelings either way.

HER ANSWER	HIS ANSWER

If your beloved has a busy calendar, think of people you can ask to help "fill it," people who could willingly and believably put a "placeholder" on your beloved's calendar. These people could be family, friends, or co-workers.

HER ANSWER	HIS ANSWER

or record your answers in your private notebook.

Clues for San Francisco Trip
Randy's Staff's Playful Adventure

This story isn't necessarily romantic, but it is so clever it could easily be adapted to a romantic adventure for two. I've gone to the same dentist for at least fifteen years. Randy is a good friend as well as a good dentist. He is also creative and generous, as shown in this story about how he rewarded his employees.

One morning Rhonda, one of the hygienists, walked into the break room at the office and found a box of Rice-A-Roni on the table. She thought nothing of it until it sat there untouched for several days. No one in the office admitted to knowing where the Rice-A-Roni came from.

Several days later some Ghirardelli chocolate appeared. As with the Rice-A-Roni, no one admitted to having any knowledge about it, but unlike the rice, the chocolate quickly disappeared.

When the Napa Valley wine showed up, it caused quite a stir. "I don't know who brought this, but we'd better get it out of here before Randy sees it," worried Linda, the other hygienist. "This is a dental office. We can't be drinking here."

That night when the women in the office arrived home, they received a mysterious card in the mail. Each card contained a piece of a puzzle. One card said, "Be at the airport at 11:30 a.m. on April 4." Another said, "You will be away from home for 3 nights." A third card said, "Pack for average temperatures in the high 50s and low 60s in the day and in the 40s at night." The two most mysterious clues, and read alone not altogether comforting, said, "The office will be closed on Friday and Monday" and "You will leave your husband and kids at home for 3 days."

Randy thought he was being clever by writing with his non-dominant hand, but he did use the green ink pen he uses for everything in the office. Seeing the familiar ink in the non-familiar and obviously left-handed writing was the clue that tied everything together.

Amy called Rhonda and said, "I got a card that tells me when to be at the airport. Do you know what this means?"

Rhonda said, "My card tells me what to pack. It sounds like Randy is up to something."

Within an hour, all five women in the office were swapping phone calls about the clues. Debbie was pleased to find out her husband had already agreed to take care of the kids for the weekend while she was off on her trip. With the San Francisco foodstuff showing up in the office, they were fairly certain where they were going.

The next morning as the women arrived at the office filled with excitement, Randy pretended ignorance. "I have no idea what you are talking about. I'm not taking you to San Francisco. I have a business to run."

Over the course of the day, they wore him down until he finally admitted to being the mastermind of this plan and the benefactor of their trip. Since there would be six of them on the trip and they would be gone three nights, two people were responsible for planning activities for each night.

The anticipation of the trip and the planning that went into it was almost as much fun as the trip itself.

Rate this adventure with a plus if you would like to find yourself in a similar situation, and with a minus if you wouldn't. Give extra pluses or minuses if you have strong feelings either way.

HER ANSWER	HIS ANSWER

Use this story to spark an idea for a romantic adventure of your own. Even for a night out in your hometown, you could send cards to arrive several days apart to extend the invitation and build anticipation. Do you have an upcoming event that you could announce this way?

HER ANSWER	HIS ANSWER

or record your answers in your private notebook.

Consider giving small gifts as hints for the big event. If you are going away, what are the hints you could give about the destination? If you are planning dinner at a special restaurant, give cards or small gifts that will pique curiosity. For this exercise, name a destination that you may or may not be planning to visit. Brainstorm a list of items that could be used as clues.

HER ANSWER	HIS ANSWER

or record your answers in your private notebook.

Costa Rican Breakfast
Nuria and Mainor's Anniversary Adventure

While innsitting for two months in Costa Rica, Jim and I had the pleasure of getting to know the employees at the Villa Decary. Mainor and Nuria were a married couple who worked at the inn. Mainor spoke some English, but in the entire time we were there I only heard Nuria speak one word in English.

I asked Nuria how long she and Mainor had been married. She pointed to a date on the calendar just a few days away and said, "un año" (one year). Well now, there's a reason to celebrate.

Later in the day, Jim and I talked about how we could honor their anniversary. We decided to ask them to be our guests for breakfast on Monday morning.

Naturally, my initial inclination when they arrived for work was to surprise them as if they had won the Publishers Clearing House sweepstakes, lead them to a beautifully set table and serve them a gourmet breakfast. Fortunately, Jim remembered what we teach: "accommodate your beloved's (or guests of honor's) surprise tolerance." Not only could a surprise be uncomfortable for them, but the anticipation of the event could add to their pleasure. It was wise to let them know not to eat breakfast before they came to work. Jim and I asked them in broken Spanish if we could help them celebrate their anniversary by serving them breakfast. Their looks of surprise and wide grins left me anticipating the event as much as they were.

I picked birds of paradise for a bouquet for the dining table and several varieties of ginger for a large bouquet for a side table in the entry way. We served a fruit plate with papaya, pineapple, watermelon, tangerines and star fruit, and honey-pecan baked French toast. After breakfast, we gave Nuria and Mainor a hand-painted butter dish from a local art gallery. They seemed to feel a little awkward being served at first, but by the end of the meal I detected an unmistakable twinkle in Mainor's eyes whenever Jim would jump up to get him more coffee or juice.

Rate this adventure with a plus if you would like to find yourself in a similar situation, and with a minus if you wouldn't. Give extra pluses or minuses if you have strong feelings either way.

HER ANSWER	HIS ANSWER

If Your Beloved Is a Type 3
Keep It a Secret Until the Big Day

Nothing makes me feel more like a queen for a day than to unexpectedly find that I am the star of some unfolding adventure. If your beloved responds the same way, go ahead and plan a surprise, making sure a block of time is reserved. One possible approach is to ask your beloved's manager, co-worker or friend to schedule a meeting or celebration under false pretenses.

> *Nearly all the best things that came to me in life have been unexpected, unplanned by me.*
> CARL SANDBURG

Annette was invited to a baby shower, but when she arrived the gathering turned out to be a birthday party for her instead.

Another possibility is to tell your beloved that you are planning something for the occasion, but just leave it at that – no hints. You can really get creative with this approach.

For my birthday one year, Jim took me out to dinner. We watched the sunset on the mountains as we enjoyed drinks and appetizers. I had just suggested we order our entrees, when suddenly a horrified look came over Jim's face. "We've got to leave right now," he whispered. "I have diarrhea."

I tried to be sensitive to his predicament – I really did. I paid the bill and went to get the car. But I was unable to stifle my giggles as I watched him waddle with tight cheeks to the restroom. When he met me at the car, I drove straight home. We rushed into our house to find several friends had gathered for a surprise dinner party.

Jim admitted we were having such a good time he didn't know how he was going to convince me to leave the restaurant. His line was so unusual that I never questioned his motive, never suspected a conspiracy.

If you need to pack for your beloved for a surprise overnight trip, observe what he or she uses when dressing in the morning. This is usually harder for men than women, particularly when it comes to cosmetics, but I've seen resourceful men accomplish this in clever ways. In the following stories, Tom took Jill's entire makeup tray to cover all the bases, and Jim devised an ingenious scheme to get me to pack my own cosmetics.

Limousine-Driven Treasure Hunt
Tom and Jill's Romantic Adventure

Limousine-driven treasure hunts have been very popular with my clients. These adventures have ranged from a couple of hours on a limited budget to an all-day affair with a high dollar price tag. Tom and Jill's anniversary celebration was the most extravagant.

Tom was a successful executive in the large company I worked for when I was just starting Adventures of the Heart. He was a driven, type A manager. I had the pleasure of seeing the softer side of Tom when he hired me to help him plan an anniversary celebration for his wife.

"I'd like to take Jill out for a really special weekend," Tom said. "We need to have some fun – without the kids." Tom explained his idea of fun: fancy dinner, formal attire, and a musical. He was one of the few men I knew who owned his own tuxedo. The only thing I knew about Jill was that she was an attractive woman who was always impeccably dressed.

Since Tom had a good idea of what he wanted, all I needed to do was most of the legwork. One of my challenges was to find a restaurant in Denver that could assure me Tom would not look like a member of the wait staff wearing a tux. Weeks of planning went into this adventure. Whenever Tom talked about Jill, his manner changed. His voice was softer. His eyes sparkled. I loved seeing this serious, driven businessman morph into a loving husband right before my very eyes.

Early on the Saturday morning of the adventure, Tom made an excuse to leave the house and take their children with him. He worried that Jill might see through his flimsy excuse, but she seemed pleased to have a little time alone with her coffee and newspaper. As soon as he was out of the driveway, he called Jill to say he'd forgotten to give her an anniversary card. Even though she didn't understand the urgency, when he told her where it was, she promised to get it right away.

> *Surprise is the greatest gift which life can grant us.*
> BORIS PASTERNAK

The card instructed Jill to be ready to leave the house in thirty minutes for a very special day, and to dress casually. The mystery intrigued her, and she eagerly followed his directions.

Thirty minutes later a limo arrived. The driver rolled out a red carpet, and said, "Your husband has a great day planned for you. I'll take you to all of your destinations." Upon entering the limo, Jill found a light breakfast with mimosas. Tom wanted her to be comfortable and well fed during the one-hour drive from Colorado Springs to Denver. She was delighted Tom was acting like the romantic man she married.

Jill's first stop was an upscale mall in southern Denver. When Ruth, a personal shopper from Jill's favorite store, met her at the limo, she began to feel like a celebrity. She noticed a couple of middle-aged women studying her as if trying to figure out which magazine recently featured her on their cover.

Ruth escorted Jill to the women's department and gave her a card from Tom instructing her to buy whatever she needed to go with a sequined top she recently purchased. Tom had secretly brought her new top to the store the previous day. Jill was amazed that Tom had taken the time away from work to drive two hours roundtrip to drop off an outfit with Ruth – Tom NEVER took time off work. Since he'd hired me to help him, I was equally impressed with the effort he personally put into this adventure. Jill enjoyed a few uninterrupted hours shopping and found the perfect shoes and skirt to go with her new top.

Next on Jill's unfolding itinerary was a spa in downtown Denver. The owner greeted her at the door. Jill received a three-hour treatment, including a massage, steam bath, body masque, foot reflexology, and aromatherapy. Being pampered was something Jill had always enjoyed and didn't get enough of with two small children underfoot.

> *What is least expected is the more highly esteemed.*
> BALTASAR GRACIAN

Jill felt like she floated out of the spa and into the limo when it returned for her. The driver took her to one of Denver's finest hotels. He said, "I'll be leaving you here. As much as I've enjoyed driving you today, I don't think I'll tell my wife about it. Your husband gave you the royal treatment. I don't want to put ideas into her head." Jill agreed that she felt like royalty.

Before Jill's arrival, Tom had prepared their suite with flowers, candles, music and personal belongings. The bellman greeted Jill and took her directly to her suite, bypassing the registration desk. He lit the candles and started the CD player. Jill read a card from Tom that instructed her to dress for the evening in her new clothes and meet him in the lounge downstairs.

Now that the minutes until their reunion were ticking down, Jill was as excited to see Tom as she had been on their first date. When it was nearly time for her to leave to meet her sweetheart, the bellman returned and gave her another card from Tom that said simply, "Look under your pillow." There she found jewelry to complete her outfit. While Jill was at the spa, Tom visited Ruth at the mall to choose earrings to compliment her clothes. Jill felt absolutely loved and adored.

Tom was waiting for her in his tuxedo with a bottle of champagne on ice. His wait seemed like an eternity. When Jill entered the lounge, all eyes were on her. She hesitated at the door to look for that familiar face. A hush came over the room. When their eyes met, their smiles lit up the room. He crossed the room to hug her.

Tom led her to their table. "Happy anniversary," he said, raising his champagne glass to hers.

"What a wonderful day I've had!" Jill gushed, unable to contain her excitement.

"There's more to come," Tom promised.

They shared the adventures of their day as they enjoyed dinner. After dinner they attended a performance of the traveling Broadway hit musical *Chicago*. This was a perfect day for Jill, and Tom enjoyed setting it up for her.

Back at the office, Tom seemed different, more relaxed, for days. I overheard several people comment on his good mood, and one puzzled woman asked if he'd gotten a haircut.

With the initial success of limousine-driven treasure hunts, I thought I'd found a magic elixir, a one-size-fits-all formula for romantic adventure.

I found out the hard way how wrong I was. It took a failed adventure to show me the error of my ways.

John Doe asked me to help plan an anniversary adventure for his wife, Jane (names changed to protect the disappointed). Even though I'd never met Jane, I suggested a surprise limo ride, lingerie shopping, several hours at a luxury spa, and dinner at a fine restaurant. I'd love an adventure like this, and so had many satisfied clients. My enthusiasm convinced John that Jane would, too.

I blissfully handled the details, oblivious to any potential problems. When Jane's mother showed up unexpectedly to watch the children on their anniversary, Jane managed to get her mother to admit what was going on. Jane called John and explained that while she appreciated his efforts, it wasn't what she wanted. She didn't like surprises and she was uncomfortable with the extravagance.

They canceled the activities and went out for a quiet dinner and a movie. John said they had a great time, and he learned a lot about his wife's preferences.

I appreciated this turn of events for the valuable lessons it taught me. Successful adventures must accommodate the beloved's surprise tolerance and allow participants to follow their own romantic bliss.

Rate Tom and Jill's successful adventure with a plus if you would like to find yourself in a similar situation, and with a minus if you wouldn't. Give extra pluses or minuses if you have strong feelings either way.

HER ANSWER	HIS ANSWER

Discuss John and Jane's attempt at adventure. How do you feel about his efforts and her response? Can you think of a time you did something that didn't work out? What did you learn?

HER ANSWER	HIS ANSWER

If you'd like a limousine-driven treasure hunt, what stops along the way would you like to make?

HER ANSWER	HIS ANSWER

Are you comfortable getting massages and other body work at spas? If not, what would you prefer instead?

HER ANSWER	HIS ANSWER

Called on the Red Carpet
Our Romantic Adventure

When Jim told me he wanted to plan Valentine's Day, I was delighted to let him.

A few days later I got a call from my friend Judy who asked me to go for a walk with her before work on Friday prior to the long Presidents' Day weekend. That sounded like fun to me. I got up early that morning, dressed in walking clothes, packed my cosmetics and work clothes in the car, and left to meet Judy.

I went to work invigorated from the walk and happy that I'd spent time with my friend. That afternoon Lauren, a friend and co-worker, stopped by my desk and told me to pack up my things.

"I can't right now. I have to finish this report," I argued.

"It can wait," Lauren said without smiling. "You have to leave now." She tried to make it sound like I was in trouble for something, but just between you and me, she's not that good of an actress, or maybe the script wasn't that believable. She kept insisting, so I acquiesced.

I turned off my computer and she escorted me to the door. A red carpet was rolled out in front of long white limousine. I wondered who the limo was for.

I looked around for Jim, but he was nowhere in sight. Lauren walked me to the limo and told me to get in.

"This is for me? Why? Where am I going?" I asked plenty of questions and got no answers.

Lauren took my picture as I poked my head out of the limo sunroof and waved like a beauty queen in a parade. The driver poured me some champagne and handed me a card from Jim. It said, "You'll want to go by your car and pick up your bag with your cosmetics in it."

I am so gullible. Jim had found a very clever way to get me to pack my own cosmetics for a trip. Judy is a good actress; I never suspected a thing. I was off to somewhere but I had no idea where. With each turn, I would eliminate or add possible destinations. It finally became apparent I was going to the airport.

Jim was waiting on the curb. He had already checked my bags. We went through airport security and walked to a gate with a flight to Salt Lake City. Skiing – that sounded good to me.

In Salt Lake I found we were only changing planes there. Our final destination was San Diego. I was thrilled to be going to a place I'd never been. In San Diego there was another limo waiting to take us to a beachside hotel.

I was curious to see what Jim had packed for me. Most things fit, and a few things matched. I was a good sport in that I didn't whine; Jim was a good sport in that he took me shopping for the missed essentials.

That trip kept a smile on my face for months to come.

♡　♡　♡　♡　♡

Rate this adventure with a plus if you would like to find yourself in a similar situation, and with a minus if you wouldn't. Give extra pluses or minuses if you have strong feelings either way.

HER ANSWER	HIS ANSWER

If You and Your Beloved are Both Type 3s
Let a Third Party Do the Planning

For the truly courageous, one or both of you can hire a third party or ask a friend to plan a surprise adventure. It is important that this is someone you can trust. After you set some parameters around cost and time, discuss your likes, dislikes and goals for the adventure.

This Guy Loves Surprises
Carey and Kim's Romantic Adventure

My most courageous and trusting client was Carey Parker. He let me create a surprise for him and his wife. Here's his story in his own words:

> My wife, Kim, and I were married on Nov 29, 1996. For our second anniversary, I decided that I wanted to do something special and different. Thanks to pure serendipity, I found Mary and ended up with more than I could have wished for.
>
> A couple months ago, my mother ran across an article in the Fort Wayne, Indiana newspaper about this woman in Colorado named Mary who plans romantic events and vacations for people. She read a little of the article to me and I decided it was worth a shot. She gave me Mary's number and promised to send the article.

I contacted Mary shortly after that and we began to correspond via email. After just a couple emails, I decided this was a great idea. Now, I've actually planned many such things for my wife in the past, but Kim and I were in the middle of a countrywide job search and my free time was already limited. Plus, Mary and I agreed that this trip would also be a surprise for me, which clinched the deal.

Over the course of the first few weeks, I sent her a ton of info on Kim and me: our interests, hobbies, background, history, likes, dislikes, and previous adventures. Mary also sent me some surveys and questionnaires. We established a budget and timeframe, and Mary took over from there.

She planned the adventure around our Thanksgiving trip to Atlanta. She ran the itinerary by my best friend and Kim's best friend via email to make sure it would be good for us and just told me the final cost estimate. Here's how it unfolded:

At Thanksgiving dinner, our hostess in Atlanta, Kim's aunt, brought in two boxes. At this point, Kim still believed that I planned all this and only she was in the dark. So I told her that I didn't know what was going on either, and quickly explained. The first box contained a one-pound fortune cookie. The fortune read, "Take I-85 north to exit 48. Turn left into the hotel." The second box contained seven numbered envelopes, each with a note telling us when to open them. We opened Card Number One, which had literature about the chateau, a very posh resort with four golf courses, seven restaurants, a large hotel, a vineyard, and a European health spa.

We arrived Thursday night and checked in. We stayed in the spa, which only has fourteen rooms, each with a particular theme. We were in the Vintage Room, which was decorated like a Victorian home, complete with antique furniture and accessories, including a huge porcelain bathtub, big enough for two.

Card Number Two was to be opened Friday morning at 8:30 a.m. We woke up and eagerly opened it. It told us we had full body massage appointments at 10:00. After breakfast and our massages, we spent the rest of the day wandering around the chateau. They were having an annual festival highlighted by the moment when they flip on all the Christmas lights around the property. We took a helicopter ride to get an overview of the grounds, visited the craft booths, sampled some wine, and basically relaxed and enjoyed our surroundings.

On Friday afternoon we opened Card Number Three, which was attached to a box. The wooden box itself was a puzzle. I'd indicated on the Romance

> *Love withers with predictability; its very essence is surprise and amazement. To make love a prisoner of the mundane is to take away its passion and lose it forever.*
> LEO BUSCAGLIA

Profile that Kim and I both liked puzzles. We managed to open the puzzle after trying for a couple minutes. The box contained a small jigsaw puzzle. We put the pieces together, which revealed our next surprise. It told us that we had an appointment Saturday morning at 6:30 a.m. for a hot-air balloon ride.

Saturday morning we got up for our balloon ride, which was wonderful, if a bit chilly at first. It was so peaceful.

When we got back, we opened Card Number Four. Inside was Mary's Gift Giving Exercise *(described in Habit Seven)*. The plan was for us to go shopping and buy each other some anniversary gifts, since I'd previously told Mary I wouldn't have time to shop for a gift before the trip. We filled out the lists, and then exchanged them with each other. We set an overall cost limit, and drove to a local mall. We were to buy three things for each other and get them wrapped. We spent several very enjoyable hours shopping.

Back at the chateau, we opened Card Number Five, a little too late. It began "Over lunch..." and it was about 4:00. Oh, well. This was a deck of fifty-two cards, and each card had a paragraph about a neat place to visit or thing to do in Atlanta. It was too late to go back to do much of anything in Atlanta, which was about thirty-five minutes away. We relaxed, got some dinner, and did a bit of a pub-crawl through various bars on the property, including an authentic Irish pub. The bar in the pub was actually flown over from Ireland and almost all the staff were from Ireland. We joined the Irish piano player for some sing-alongs.

Sunday morning we opened Card Number Six. It told us to order room service and exchange our gifts over breakfast. Here's what we got each other, based on what we marked on the Gift Giving checklist:

Kim to me:

♡ Shiny and playful from a department store: a Christmas ornament of Santa hanging from a hot-air balloon

♡ Contains text and is humorous from a book store: *Dirty Minds* board game

♡ Mystical and unexpected from a department store: a geode that you put oils in for aromatherapy

Me to Kim:

♡ Sensuous, fuzzy, and playful from a specialty store: emerald green velvet lingerie from Victoria Secret

♡ Irregular shape and frivolous from a specialty store: various candies and gum from a bulk candy store. (You'd have to see them; they weren't just simple things.)

♡ Natural and adventurous from an art store - 1999 Sierra Club wolf calendar

I got another massage that afternoon and Kim got a facial. After an intimate dinner, we returned to the room, lit candles, and turned on some music. We played the board game *An Enchanting Evening,* which a friend bought for us a long time ago and Mary had instructed me to bring along.

Card Number Seven was a summary of the trip and thank you note from Mary.

We returned to Memphis Monday afternoon after our wonderful, relaxing, romantic get-away vacation. We told and retold the story for the weeks, and we'll certainly cherish it for many years to come.

Rate this adventure with a plus if you would like to find yourself in a similar situation, and with a minus if you wouldn't. Give extra pluses or minuses if you have strong feelings either way.

HER ANSWER	HIS ANSWER

If you and your beloved both love surprises, do you know a creative person you could trust to create a surprise adventure for both of you? Be sure it's someone you can trust with your credit card number and someone who's good with details.

HER ANSWER	HIS ANSWER
or record your answers in your private notebook.	

After hearing several stories containing various elements of surprise, has your opinion changed about where you fall in the Surprise Tolerance Type? If so, where are you now?

HER ANSWER	HIS ANSWER

Determine Your Surprise Tolerance Type

An Exercise

Select the sentence that best describes your comfort level for each item:

1. Center of attention:

   a. I'd rather avoid any situation where I'm the center of attention.

   b. I'm comfortable being the center of attention, but it's not something I seek out.

   c. I feel honored when I'm the center of attention.

HER ANSWER	HIS ANSWER

2. Time management:

   a. I like to make my own plans.

   b. I don't mind if other people make plans for me as long as I know when and for how long I'll be gone.

   c. I know you respect my time enough that I can be flexible. Take me; I'm yours.

HER ANSWER	HIS ANSWER

3. Tastes:

   a. I want to choose my own activities and make my own purchases, since my tastes are very specific.

   b. I enjoy being surprised with activities or gifts, if someone knows my tastes well.

   c. I crave new adventures.

HER ANSWER	HIS ANSWER

4. Attitude about surprises:

a. There's no such thing as a good surprise.

b. I don't mind a few surprises now and then, as long as I'm not embarrassed.

c. I never met a well-intentioned surprise I didn't like.

HER ANSWER	HIS ANSWER

5. Flexibility:

a. If my beloved planned an adventure I didn't enjoy, I would be very uncomfortable.

b. Even if my beloved planned something I wouldn't have chosen, I'd make the best of it.

c. If my beloved created a new experience, I would love it.

HER ANSWER	HIS ANSWER

Add up the total number of a, b and c answers for each of you. Record them below and plan your adventures accordingly.

	Number of a's	Number of b's	Number of c's
Her Answers			
His Answers			
Surprise Tolerance Type	1	2	3

Sparks that Ignite the Romantic Flame

♡ If your beloved absolutely hates to be surprised, plan your adventures together.

♡ If you or your beloved is uncomfortable with surprises, figure out the reason and honor it.

♡ Even if your beloved doesn't like surprises, that doesn't mean you can't throw in a few unexpected surprises, like a well-timed card or love note.

♡ When an out-of-the-blue surprise is out of the question, use anticipation to build up to a secret adventure.

♡ If you decide to surprise your beloved, make sure the block of time is reserved on the calendar.

♡ If you both love surprises, hire a third party or ask a trusted friend to plan an adventure to surprise both of you.

♡ If you find yourself censuring your discussions with your beloved before a surprise for fear of letting something slip, make a note of all the things you wanted to say but couldn't. You'll both enjoy reminiscing.

Transform the Ordinary into the Extraordinary

The nineteenth century French painter Jean Francois Millet said, "It is the treating of the commonplace with the feeling of the sublime that gives to art its true power." The same can be said for the art of romance. By paying special attention to the details, you can turn a commonplace event into a sublime romantic adventure.

As my friend Susan used to say, "It all about the presentation." Years ago we used to vacation together at Lake Powell on a houseboat. There were usually eight to twelve of us, and we always took turn preparing meals. Susan never liked to cook, so she volunteered for cocktail hour every day. For her it was more about presentation than the actual beverages or food. She'd bring cute tablecloths and napkins and paper umbrellas for the drinks. She spent more time arranging the food than preparing it, and we all looked forward to cocktail hour. It was when the party started. We would dress for dinner, which could be something like a sarong for the women, and a swimsuit and a bowtie held on with elastic for the men. It simply wouldn't have been the same to pop a beer and open a bag of chips, although most of the time the menu wasn't much more complicated than that.

Susan's preparations made us all feel special. I've learned to apply that lesson to romantic adventures.

You don't have to go away to create a romantic setting. Spending an evening at home can be a passionate adventure. It's something you may do frequently, and practicing this habit can make it memorable. If you are going away for a romantic interlude, these same suggestions can help you turn an impersonal hotel room into a sensual retreat.

Going somewhere? Remember that the journey can be as much fun as the destination. Choosing unique transportation can make getting there as much fun as being there.

It's important to remember that the adventures don't need to be expensive. You'll read a story about an adventure that cost around twenty dollars that is every bit as memorable as an adventure that would set you back a couple thousand dollars.

Using Your Senses for a Sensual Adventure

Once or twice a year, set aside some time for a "Sensual Day," a day that you devote to being together, touching, loving. Bathe together, exchange massages, make love, and then feed each other. It can be a full day or just several hours in an afternoon or evening. Schedule it, write it on the calendar in ink, anticipate it, make it a priority. Get away or do it at home. Just do it.

> *Love and sex are things that give life some value, some zest.*
> ISAAC BASHEVIS SINGER

Where can you possibly feel more comfortable than at home? Feeling comfortable can be good or bad. Comfortable isn't necessarily special, but you can make it special with some attention to the details. Make this a sensual experience. Engage as many of the senses as you can. With a little planning, you can do many of theses things when you go away for a romantic weekend. Here are a few ideas.

Touch

♡ Wear clothes that feel good on your skin and invite touch. If you're doing the planning, suggest something for your beloved to wear or pick out clothing for the adventure.

♡ Prepare a space to give a massage. Heat some massage oils. Make sure the room is a comfortable temperature.

♡ Have an ostrich feather available to caress your beloved's skin.

♡ Share a hot tub, sauna or steam shower with your beloved.

♡ Put fresh linens on the bed and spray the sheets with scented linen water.

♡ Heat towels in the dryer or on a heated towel rack while your beloved's taking a shower or bath.

Taste

♡ Provide various foods considered to be aphrodisiacs. If you have your beloved sample the foods while wearing a blindfold, the taste will be enhanced. When deprived of sight, the remaining senses will be focused on determining what the food is. Martha Hopkins and Randall Lockridge wrote the cookbook entitled *InterCourses: An Aphrodisiac Cookbook.* They provided delicious recipes, sensuous photographs and romantic stories for foods they considered to be aphrodisiacs: chocolate,

> *A tale without love is like beef without mustard: insipid.*
> ANATOLE FRANCE

asparagus, chilies, coffee, basil, grapes, strawberries, honey, artichokes, black beans, oysters, rosemary, edible flowers, pine nuts, avocados, libations, and figs. Try some.

♡ Indulge in some edible massage oils or dusting powders. Taste them on your beloved.

♡ Feed each other.

Smell

♡ Smell foods, essential oils and other pleasant substances while blindfolded.

♡ Burn candles or incense.

♡ Flowers are great because they are pleasing to the nose and the eyes. When making your choices, close your eyes and smell the flowers to get ones that are especially fragrant.

> *Nothing awakens a reminiscence like a scent.*
> VICTOR HUGO

♡ Light a fire in the fireplace on a cool evening.

♡ Wear perfume or aftershave that's pleasing to your beloved.

♡ Consider having a scent that you wear only for lovemaking – not to a party, or to work, or to church – only in bed. If you happen to pass someone wearing it while you're out, your mind will drift back to the sweet memories of your beloved.

♡ Use any scent that evokes a special memory. If you enjoy reminiscing about erotic times in a certain room that had a unique smell, bring it back. Whether it's lilacs or pumpkin pie, sauerkraut or motor oil, if it triggers a fond memory, use it again.

Hearing

♡ Play music on a CD player.

♡ Consider having a song recorded especially for your beloved.

♡ Make sure other sounds in the environment will be conducive for what ever you have planned. If you want to have a romantic environment, make every reasonable effort to ensure you won't be interrupted by cars honking, telephones ringing, children playing or dogs barking.

♡ Relax to the sounds of running water in a fountain.

Sight

♡ Decorate and clean the space according to the adventure. A cluttered, messy room is often a distraction to romance. Arrange the space so that it will be pleasing to your beloved's eye.

> *A dress makes no sense unless it inspires men to want to take it off you.*
> FRANCOISE SAGAN

♡ Dress up if it enhances the situation.

♡ Take pictures. You'll enjoy reliving the adventure in years to come.

♡ Use your best dishes and silverware. Bring out anything you are saving for a special occasion. This is it.

The time spent in preparation to create the mood will not go unnoticed. Set the stage. Consider writing a note and tucking it some place your beloved will find it hours before the adventure begins. Here is a sample, but feel free – and creative – to make yours unique and personal:

"I have a special afternoon planned. To get in the proper mood, listen to our favorite CD – you know which one I mean. Think about the memories it brings back. Dab some of our favorite perfume behind your ears and knees. Do you remember the last time you wore it? I do."

An Elegant Evening at Taco Bell
Donna and Pat's Romantic Adventure

This is a story about a couple who, in spite of a tight budget, celebrated a memorable anniversary. Donna did all the planning. She told Pat to get dressed up because she was taking him out for a fancy dinner. Pat protested, saying they couldn't afford an expensive dinner.

The normally frugal Donna said, "Trust me, honey, I've got this one covered. Wear your new suit and put on your dancing shoes."

Just after Donna finished putting the final touches on her makeup, the doorbell rang. Pat answered the door and was surprised to see their friend Joe dressed in a coat and tie. Joe told him he would be their chauffeur for the evening. Joe led Pat and Donna across the red carpet to their "limousine," a 15-year-old Jeep. Joe opened the door for them and they slid into the back seat. After he closed the door, he rolled up the red bath mat and tossed it in the back of the Jeep.

Pat had no idea what Donna had in mind, but Joe's arrival assured him it would be fun. He was surprised when Joe stopped the car near the door at Taco Bell, his favorite fast food restaurant. Joe opened the door for them, and then drove off to park the car. Another friend playing hostess, formally attired in a long blue dress, greeted them at the door. Vicki asked them if they had a reservation. Donna replied that they did indeed.

> *Creativity requires the courage to let go of certainties.*
> ERICH FROMM

Vicki looked over her list and said, "Of course, ma'am, your table is ready for you."

Pat laughed when he saw their table. "Wow, this really is a fancy dinner," he said.

"Nothing but the best for my dear husband," she said with a smile.

Donna, a regular customer at Taco Bell, had arranged with management to cordon off a section of the restaurant. The table was set with a tablecloth, real silverware and glasses, and flowers. A CD player on a nearby table played soft dinner music.

Ralph appeared as their waiter and asked with stiff formality if they would like to have something to drink before dinner. They ordered iced tea with lemon. Ralph returned with a napkin over his arm, proudly displayed the large purple Taco Bell cup, and asked them if it was the proper vintage. He offered the plastic lid to Donna to smell. She nodded her approval. The waiter proceeded to pour their tea into elegant wineglasses. Pat got into the spirit of the adventure and swirled the tea in his wine glass to check out the "legs" of this fine "wine."

Ralph then asked to take their order. Donna ordered "the usual" for both of them. The waiter disappeared around the corner, stood in line, placed the order and paid for the food. The burritos and tacos were presented with an exaggerated flair.

After they finished eating, dance music replaced dinner music. To the delight of their friends, the staff and fellow diners, Pat and Donna took a few turns around the dance floor to a slow Neil Diamond song. Applause erupted when they finished the dance with a twirl and a dip. The Eagles livened things up a bit, and their friends and a couple of innocent bystanders joined them for the final dance.

The entire dinner costs less than $20. Attention to details transformed the ordinary into the extraordinary. When Pat realized the "fancy dinner" Donna had promised him was from Taco Bell, his worries about money vanished. With their sense of humor and sense of adventure intact, they laughed all the way through the evening.

Rate this adventure with a plus if you would like to find yourself in a similar situation, and with a minus if you wouldn't. Give extra pluses or minuses if you have strong feelings either way.

HER ANSWER	HIS ANSWER

Would you feel self-conscious if your beloved arranged a dinner like this in a fast food restaurant?

HER ANSWER	HIS ANSWER

A Valentine Retreat

Janet and Ken's Romantic Adventure

When Janet's eight-year-old daughter Chelsea asked if she could go to her friend's Valentine's slumber party, an idea flashed in Janet's mind. That meant she and Ken would have a rare Friday evening together. And for the first time in eight years, they would be without their child on Valentine's Day.

While asking all the necessary motherly questions about the party before giving her permission, a voice inside her head was yelling, "Yes, yes, YES! Tell her yes and get on with your own plans."

Janet worked shifts at the hospital and her day off just happened to fall on Valentine's Day. Janet asked Ken to take the day off to make the most of this exceptional opportunity. They began to plan their day of romance.

Before Chelsea was born, they used to go all out for Valentine's Day, birthdays and anniversaries. Now with a daughter and a limited budget, they couldn't afford the time or the money for extravagant romantic interludes. Even with their daughter away for the evening, they needed to be frugal with their Valentine's Day plans. They agreed to spend the day at home, and they both had some ideas on how to make the day special.

On the Wednesday and Thursday evenings prior to the big event, Janet put Chelsea and Ken to work cleaning the house. Chelsea put up a typical eight-year-old's protest of having to clean her bedroom and dust the living room before the regularly scheduled cleaning day on Saturday. Janet insisted this was part of the deal for Chelsea to be able to go to the slumber party.

> *Say "I love you" to those you love. The eternal silence is long enough to be silent in, and that awaits us all.*
>
> GEORGE ELIOT

Janet took Chelsea to school on Friday morning with an overnight bag for the slumber party. After kissing her daughter goodbye, she hurried home with the eagerness of a teenager who had just escaped the bonds of her parents and was heading for an illicit rendezvous with her boyfriend. When Janet opened the door, she found a card wishing her a memorable Valentine's Day. Upstairs she found Ken relaxing in a bubble bath. Several candles lit the darkened room, and slow, sexy music filled the air. A bouquet of roses sat on the countertop. Ken held his hand out to her as an invitation to join him. In a flash, she was naked and sinking into the bubbly warm water with her lover.

When the bath water had cooled, they realized they had worked up an appetite. Ken made a smoked salmon omelet for breakfast. While he was cooking, Janet put the finishing touches on a basket she had prepared for him. In her closet, she stored a large assortment of massage oils, personal lubricants, and lotions, some of which had never even been opened. She arranged these in the basket, along with a few items she had purchased just for this occasion, including a CD of Ella Fitzgerald's love songs, *The Piano* with Holly Hunter and Harvey Keitel on DVD, and a jar of

A Moment with the Darlings

"Here's to the only woman I know who can turn a new bar of soap into a cause for celebration. I love you, Gracie."

chocolate body paints. Janet also added a book from her bookshelf to the basket, *The Gryphon*, by Nick Bantock. Janet topped off the basket with a large pink ostrich feather.

When they finished eating a leisurely breakfast and reading the paper, a real luxury for them, Janet left the kitchen and returned with the basket. She explained that the basket contained enough activities to keep them busy all day long and then some. Ken could pick out his favorite items and Janet would happily partake in the festivities. Ken's first pick was the massage oil and the ostrich feather.

Janet closed the living room blinds, unplugged the phone, and arranged the pillows from the sofa into a massage table. She lit a fire in the fireplace to warm the room for a massage. Janet covered the pillows with sheets, and invited Ken to slip between them. Ken and Janet had taken a couple's massage class years earlier, but had only used their sensual skills a few times on each other. As soon as Janet started kneading Ken's muscles, the moves came back to her. She started on his back, arms and hands, and then moved to his buttocks, legs and feet. When Ken turned over, she worked on his chest and legs and improvised with a few moves they hadn't taught in class. She followed this with a face and scalp massage. For a finishing touch, Janet traced the ostrich feather all over his body.

While Ken fully intended to give Janet a massage in return, she suggested that they do something else first to give Ken's body a chance to relax. Her beloved was grateful to have some time to transition from receiver to giver.

Janet poured champagne and took *The Gryphon* from the basket. Nick Bantock wrote a series of books composed of beautifully illustrated postcards and letters between the fictional characters Griffin and Sabine. Janet and Ken enjoyed reading these books aloud to each other, with Janet reading the correspondence from Sabine and Ken reading Griffin's parts. They snuggled in blankets on the pillow-less sofa and read *The Gryphon*, the latest in the series, to each other. Ken regained his strength and gave Janet her massage, which she fully enjoyed.

They were amazed that the day had passed so quickly. It was time to fix dinner. Ken marinated and grilled some lamb chops. Janet made a salad and steamed the asparagus. To give the dinner the special atmosphere it deserved, they set the table in the dining room with the good china and silverware. Ella's love songs played on the CD player. The dinner was better than anything they could have had in a crowded restaurant on this commercialized, busy night for lovers.

After dinner, Ken loaded *The Piano* in the DVD player. They arranged the sofa pillows on the floor for comfortable viewing. They enjoyed watching the movie until just after that steamy love scene between Holly and Harvey. At that point things in their own space seemed far more compelling than watching the rest of a movie they had already seen once.

Janet and Ken slept in on Saturday morning. When they woke up, they stayed in bed, talking about how much they had enjoyed their day together. Janet had just applied the chocolate body paint to Ken's chest when they heard a car pull into the driveway. It was almost 10:00 – two hours before they expected Chelsea – when they heard the front door open and Chelsea yelled, "I'm home!"

At that moment Janet remembered the intimate mess they had left downstairs. She grabbed a robe and headed downstairs. Janet saw Chelsea looking over the sofa pillows on the floor with sheets twisted on top of them, empty massage oil and champagne bottles nearby and dirty dishes in the sink. For the second time in just over twenty-four hours, Janet felt like the mother-daughter roles had been reversed.

"Just look at this mess," Chelsea cried. "What did you do? I just cleaned this house."

"I know. Your dad and I had a good time together. You don't have to help me clean this time," Janet said, fighting the feeling that she had been caught doing something wrong. Janet heard the shower running and could imagine all that delicious chocolate going down the drain.

Chelsea studied the pillows and sheets in the middle of the living room floor. "You know, Mom, we did the same thing last night at the slumber party."

"Really? What did you do?"

"We made a fort out of pillows. Ours was bigger though," Chelsea replied with pride. "Can I rebuild it before you put the pillows up?"

"Of course," Janet said, feeling once again like the adult in their relationship.

Rate this adventure with a plus if you would like to find yourself in a similar situation, and with a minus if you wouldn't. Give extra pluses or minuses if you have strong feelings either way.

HER ANSWER	HIS ANSWER

Do you have a closet full of massage oils, dusting powders, romantic games and lingerie that have only been used once or not at all? Plan an adventure to have some fun with these items.

HER ANSWER	HIS ANSWER
or record your answers in your private notebook.	

The Ultimate Bubble Bath

Justin and His Wife's Romantic Adventure

In an earlier chapter, I mentioned a promotion called the Great Romantic Payback that ran on a local radio station. People faxed in romantic stories. This was Justin's entry in his own words:

The blustery January wind caught the screen door as I opened it, slamming it against the house. "Good, no harm done," I said to myself as I checked the house and the door for damage. "I wish I could say the same for the day I've had."

Fumbling my way through the door, trying not to drop the load I was carrying, I rushed to the dining room table and emptied my arms without noticing the stage that was set all around me. "Why is it so dark? I know I'm late again, but is she already in bed?"

At that moment I came to my senses and picked up the heart-shaped card perched against a glowing cinnamon-scented candle. "Follow your heart," the card prompted. A trail of red rose petals led around the corner. Smiling inside and out, I was beginning to understand.

As I followed the fragrant smell of roses, my obsessive-compulsive nature couldn't help but gather the petals from the floor. Each and every petal had been carefully trimmed into a heart. "Why in the world would anyone take so much time?" Another note, also with a flickering, cinnamon-scented candle, answered my question. "Just because," the card explained. She knows me so well.

> *For it was not into my ear you whispered, but into my heart. It was not my lips you kissed, but my soul.*
>
> JUDY GARLAND

Continuing to pick up the petals, I journeyed up the stairs following the soft glow of candlelight. Just before I reached the top of the stairs, Peter Cetera began quietly singing, "I Wanna Take Forever Tonight" — one of my favorites. What I saw next I would never forget.

My beautiful wife, with her long, red hair falling down over one of Victoria's lacy best, stood in the candlelight holding a basket out to me. Without a word, I put the rose petals in the basket. She then emptied the basket of roses into the bathtub, which was still filling and nearly overflowing with inviting bubbles. My evening was looking much better than my day.

Romantic interludes such as this are not rare occurrences. They're not always so elaborate, but for my wife, romance is a lifestyle. Breakfast in bed, surprise picnics in the park, fireside foot-rubs — the list could go on. She's so good at making our life together special.

As a pragmatic, "by-the-book" male, I've finally come to realize that, well, I need a new book. The same tired, cliché Valentine's gifts won't cut it this time. I need to take my wife on an adventure of the heart . . . PLEASE help me show her that her gamble on me wasn't a losing wager.

Justin's wife knew how to turn a bath into a sensual adventure. Justin is a lucky guy.

Rate this adventure with a plus if you would like to find yourself in a similar situation, and with a minus if you wouldn't. Give extra pluses or minuses if you have strong feelings either way.

HER ANSWER	HIS ANSWER

Put yourself in the position of being Justin's romance coach. How would you recommend Justin show his wife that her gamble on him wasn't a losing wager? Would this work for you?

HER ANSWER	HIS ANSWER

or record your answers in your private notebook.

Just a Card and a Cake, Please
A Birthday Adventure from the Comics

One of my favorite comic strips is *For Better or Worse*. John is a dentist who was having a fiftieth birthday. He told his wife, Lynn, he absolutely did not want a big party. All he wanted was a card and a cake, and he repeated this several times.

Of course, as the day approached he was convinced that a surprise party had been planned for him. Lynn asked him to take their young daughter, April, around the neighborhood to sell something for a school fundraiser. John was afraid this was to allow time for his family and friends to sneak inside the house for a surprise party. He dreaded going home and braced himself for the onslaught of well-wishers.

Things inside the house were perplexingly normal. There were no shouts of "Surprise!" There were no "Happy Birthday" banners. In fact, everyone seemed a bit preoccupied with normal activities. After he had been in the house for a few minutes, Lynn came to greet him and led him into the dining room. On the dining room table stood a large handmade card that was probably 3 feet high by 5 feet wide containing birthday greetings from family, friends, co-workers, patients, and former professors. There were pictures, stories, poems and plenty of sentiment.

This was perfect for John. He loved reading all the notes. Immediately connected by memories to all these people so important to him in his past and present, he didn't have to suffer though being the center of attention.

After he finished reading, he said jokingly, "Thanks for the card. Now where is my cake? I wanted a cake too."

Lynn said with a smile, "Yes, you will get your favorite cake. In fact your favorite cake maker flew all the way from Toronto to make your cake."

At that moment, his mother entered the room carrying a cake with candles blazing. Knowing he had been heard and understood, he said, "Thank you for giving me exactly what I wanted."

It's important to honor the wishes of the guest of honor. John was not a man who enjoyed the limelight. Lynn listened to his request. The presentation of the card and cake transformed the ordinary to the extraordinary.

Rate this adventure with a plus if you would like to find yourself in a similar situation, and with a minus if you wouldn't. Give extra pluses or minuses if you have strong feelings either way.

HER ANSWER	HIS ANSWER

Are you comfortable being the guest of honor at a party or the center of attention? Is your beloved? If not, take that into consideration when you plan something. Think of ways to make simple requests more special.

HER ANSWER	HIS ANSWER

Romantic and Erotic Movies

Romantic movies may leave viewers with tears dripping off their chins. Erotic scenes in movies may cause them to slip out of the theater to satisfy their own passions.

Here's a list of movies that might be considered romantic or have erotic scenes in them.

- 10 (1979)
- 50 First Dates (2004)
- 9½ Weeks (1986)
- A Place in the Sun (1951)
- A Woman of Affairs (1928)
- African Queen (1951)
- Amelie (2001)
- American Gigolo (1980)
- An Affair to Remember (1957)
- An Officer and a Gentleman (1982)
- Annie Hall (1977)
- Arthur (1981)
- As Good As It Gets (1997)
- Basic Instinct (1992)
- Before Sunset (2004)
- Benny & Joon (1993)
- Blossoms in The Dust (1941)
- Body Heat (1981)
- Brief Encounter (1945)
- Broadcast News (1987)
- Bull Durham (1988)
- Camelot (1967)
- Carefree (1938)
- Casablanca (1942)
- Chocolat (2000)
- City Lights (1931)
- Cold Mountain (2003)
- Crouching Tiger, Hidden Dragon (2000)
- Dangerous Liaisons (1988)
- Dirty Dancing (1987)
- Don Juan Demarco (1995)
- Double Wedding (1937)
- Emmanuelle (1974)
- Eternal Sunshine of the Spotless Mind (2004)
- Eyes Wide Shut (1999)
- Flashdance (1983)
- Frankie and Johnny (1991)
- From Here to Eternity (1953)
- From the Terrace (1960)
- Funny Girl (1968)
- Ghost (1990)
- Gone with the Wind (1939)
- Henry & June (1990)
- Hold Your Man (1933)
- In America (2002)
- It's a Wonderful Life (1946)
- Jerry Maguire (1996)
- Key Largo (1948)
- LA Story (1991)
- Lady Chatterly's Lover (1981)
- Last Tango in Paris (1972)
- Legends of the Fall (1994)

♡ Life is Beautiful (1997)

♡ Like Water for Chocolate (1992)

♡ Lolita (1962)

♡ Lonesome Dove (1989)

♡ Love Affair (1994)

♡ Love in Paris (1997)

♡ Love is a Many-Splendored Thing (1955)

♡ Manhattan (1979)

♡ Message in a Bottle (1999)

♡ Moonstruck (1987)

♡ Moulin Rouge (2001)

♡ Much Ado about Nothing (1993)

♡ On Golden Pond (1981)

♡ On the Waterfront (1954)

♡ Out of Africa (1985)

♡ Picnic (1955)

♡ Play Misty for Me (1971)

♡ Prelude to a Kiss (1992)

♡ Pretty Baby (1978)

♡ Pretty Woman (1990)

♡ Quills (2000)

♡ Raintree Country (1957)

♡ Red Shoe Diaries (1992)

♡ Return to Me (2000)

♡ Romancing the Stone (1984)

♡ Romeo & Juliet (1992)

♡ Sabrina (1954)

♡ Saratoga (1937)

♡ Scent of a Woman (1992)

♡ Sense & Sensibility (1995)

♡ Sex, Lies & Videotapes (1989)

♡ Shadowlands (1993)

♡ Shakespeare in Love (1998)

♡ Shrek (2001)

♡ Singin' in the Rain (1952)

♡ Sirens (1991)

♡ Six Days, Seven Nights (1998)

♡ Sleepless in Seattle (1993)

♡ Snow Falling on Cedars (1999)

♡ Some Like It Hot (1959)

♡ Something's Gotta Give (2003)

♡ Splendor in the Grass (1961)

♡ Stealing Beauty (1996)

♡ Stealing Heaven (1988)

♡ Strike up the Band (1940)

♡ Suddenly Last Summer (1959)

♡ Summer of 42 (1971)

♡ Sunrise: A Song of Two Humans (1927)

♡ Talk to Her (2002)

♡ The American President (1995)

♡ The Big Easy (1987)

♡ The Big Sleep (1946)

♡ The Bodyguard (1992)

♡ The Bridges of Madison County (1995)

♡ The Enchanted Cottage (1945)

♡ The English Patient (1996)

♡ The Fabulous Baker Boys (1989)

♡ The General (1927)

♡ The Ghost and Mrs. Muir (1947)

♡ The Graduate (1967)

♡ The Man from Snowy River (1982)

♡ The Marrying Man (1991)

♡ The Notebook (2004)

♡ The Piano (1993)

♡ The Princess Bride (1987)

♡ The Red Violin (1998)

♡ The Sailor Who Fell From Grace with the Sea (1976)

♡ The Unbearable Lightness of
   Being (1988)
♡ The Way We Were (1973)
♡ The Wedding Singer (1998)
♡ The Woman in Red (1984)
♡ Titanic (1997)
♡ Top Gun (1986)
♡ Top Hat (1935)
♡ True Lies (1994)
♡ Truly Madly Deeply (1991)

♡ Two Moon Junction (1988)
♡ Unfaithful (2002)
♡ Untamed Heart (1993)
♡ Vertigo (1958)
♡ When Harry Met Sally (1989)
♡ Wide Sargasso Sea (1993)
♡ Wild Orchid (1990)
♡ Women in Love (1969)
♡ Y Tu Mama Tambien (2001)
♡ You've Got Mail (1998)

What are your favorite romantic or erotic scenes? Pick your five favorites from this list or add your own. Even if you didn't like the whole movie, but there was a scene you liked, mention it.

HER ANSWER	HIS ANSWER

What movies did you dislike? Why? It's just as important to let your beloved know what you don't like. The more specific you can be about your likes and dislikes, the more valuable this exercise can be for you. Maybe the food scene in *9 ½ Weeks* looked like great fun to you, if you could just get someone else to clean up the mess. Maybe you thought it was degrading to women. In either case, this is important information for your beloved.

HER ANSWER	HIS ANSWER

Is there a scene in a movie that makes you want to learn something new or travel to an exotic destination? Maybe you want to dance the tango like Jamie Lee Curtis and Arnold Schwartzenegger in *True Lies* or go on an African safari like Meryl Streep and Robert Redford in *Out of Africa*. What do your favorite movies make you long for?

HER ANSWER	HIS ANSWER

Think about a romantic scene in a book or movie that is too outrageous to be believable, or so sweet that it made you cry. What was it about that scene that got your attention? Is there an element of it that you can recreate?

HER ANSWER	HIS ANSWER

or record your answers in your private notebook.

Enjoy the Journey

Remember to enjoy the journey, as well as the destination. How will you get there? The transportation can be a celebration all by itself. Even going by car can be fun, but consider some less common alternatives.

♡ Limousine

Limos are fun, albeit expensive. For a less expensive alternative, ask a friend to act as your limo driver.

♡ Horse and carriage

One of the most dramatic entrances I ever saw a bride make was in a horse-drawn carriage. Her groom and his best man arrived on horseback.

♡ Sleigh

Many winter resorts offer dinner sleigh rides. It can be very cozy to snuggle under the blankets.

♡ Glider

If your frequent flier has become bored with air travel, a side trip on a glider can make the air fun again.

♡ Hot air balloon

Floating in a hot air balloon is an awe-inspiring way to see your own town or new scenery.

♡ Train

Trains conjure up images of the old west with all its excitement, unless that's how you commute to work. Train trips that are almost a guaranteed good time have some of that mystique built in: the wine train in the Napa Valley, the cog railroad to the top of Pikes Peak, the ski train from Denver to the Winter Park ski area.

♡ Boat

Whether you are going by kayak, canoe, yacht, sail boat, cruise ship, or Venetian gondola, going by boat promises a sense of adventure.

♡ Helicopter

Seeing the Grand Canyon or Hawaiian Islands from helicopter provides a unique view of the sights.

♡ Skis or snowshoes

Like to mix outdoor recreation with romance? Some remote restaurants in ski resorts require that patrons cross-country ski or snowshoe to their location. The gourmet meals are well deserved after burning off a bunch of calories to get there.

♡ Bicycle

If different fitness or skill levels prevent togetherness when bicycling, consider renting a tandem bike.

♡ Motorcycle

Rent a Harley and hit the open road. Physical closeness and a sense of freedom can make this a memorable journey.

♡ All Terrain Vehicles (ATVs) and Snowmobiles

These agile vehicles can get you into beautiful, secluded and romantic locales faster than anything else.

♡ Recreational Vehicles

If you don't have an RV or camper, rent one. The close quarters almost guarantee more physical contact.

A Train Ride to Remember
Wayne and Angela's Romantic Adventure

In July of 1981, Wayne had two long-time dreams come true. First, he married his college sweetheart, Angela, in his mother's prized rose garden under a brilliant blue Colorado sky. Second, they started their honeymoon with a train trip to Portland.

More than twenty years later, memories of their picture-perfect wedding still make Angela smile. The train trip, however, is another matter altogether. She always blushes when she talks about her most embarrassing moment. Far from being embarrassed, Wayne stands tall and proud when she tells this story.

Wayne had been fascinated with trains ever since he earned a Boy Scout merit badge for railroading as a youngster. He had built several model railroads, and two of his favorites along with several hundred cars were stored in his parents' basement. Wayne's contribution to the wedding planning was to resurrect one of the model railroads and reconstruct it as the cake table. Wayne and the baker put their creative talents to work planning the table to have the train run under four cake "bridges" placed strategically near the corners. The guests seemed to enjoy watching the train's journey around the cake table as much as they enjoyed the dinner and dancing.

The day after their wedding, Wayne and Angela arrived at Union Station in Denver early in the morning to board the train to Salt Lake City. The terminal, made from volcanic stone and pink sandstone in 1881, awakened Wayne's longing for the romance and adventure of train travel of bygone days. Even Angela noticed the difference in the excitement of their fellow train passengers compared to the complacency of seasoned travelers in airports. They selected their seats in the observation car and settled in for the journey through the majestic Rocky Mountains. Everyone seemed eager to get underway and trade the view of the terminal through the domed windows for the view of the canyons and valleys through which they would travel. A shudder, originating in the train's powerful engines and rippling through the passenger cars, only served to intensify Wayne's excitement. The shudders and shakes grew into a constant rocking motion as the train picked up speed and left downtown Denver for the mountains.

The first leg of their journey would take them to Winter Park, a Colorado ski resort. There are thirty-one tunnels between Denver and Winter Park. The shortest is seventy-eight feet and the longest — the Moffat Tunnel — measures an amazing 6.2 miles.

When they traveled through the tunnels, they made a game of kissing and caressing under the cover of darkness, and behaving like interested sightseers in the light of day. Emerging from the West Portal of the Moffat Tunnel after six miles of foreplay, they were both in an aroused state. After all, they were newlyweds.

During their brief stop in Winter Park, they decided to check out the rest of the train. They passed through several passenger cars, a dining car and a lounge car. Each passenger car had separate men and women's restrooms. The lounge car had one unisex bathroom. This gave Wayne an idea.

Late in the afternoon, most of the other passengers were taking naps or reading. The excitement of traveling though the magnificent mountains had subsided as they traveled across a stretch of flat land. Wayne took Angela's hand and led her to the lounge car. They ordered Bloody Marys, chatted briefly with the bartender and a couple at the bar, and then slipped away as nonchalantly as possible. As they passed the unisex bathroom, Wayne opened the door and pulled Angela in with him. He locked the door behind them.

They were soon doing what newlyweds often do and what they had wanted to do ever since the Moffat Tunnel. When someone grabbed the doorknob, Angela said, "It's occupied." Knowing there were plenty of other restrooms on the train, they made no effort to hurry. Sounds of passion were muffled by the sounds of the train, or so they thought. After they were both satisfied and the Bloody Mary glasses were empty, they readied themselves to leave the restroom. Angela was not prepared for what awaited her on the other side of the door.

A line of people waiting for the bathroom had formed. Angela immediately lowered her eyes and took in four pairs of shoes of various shapes and sizes belonging to four people who undoubtedly knew what they were doing and probably heard them doing it. She rushed by without looking at their faces. She was mortified. Newlywed or not, she felt like she had just been caught doing something she shouldn't have been doing. Her face glowed neon red. She tried to keep her face hidden behind her long hair as she walked quickly by them. In contrast, Wayne nodded to them and gave them a big smile.

Once out of the lounge car, they burst into laughter. Wanting to avoid anyone who saw them leave the bathroom, Angela asked Wayne what the people looked like. When they went to dinner, they were paired with a mother and her young son at a table for four. Did they know? Angela looked at their shoes, but she couldn't be sure. She watched the other diners, looking for signs of recognition.

> *Man is the only animal that blushes. Or needs to.*
> MARK TWAIN

When Wayne and Angela arrived in Salt Lake City, they left most of their fellow travelers behind as they boarded the train for Portland. Angela felt more at ease, no longer wondering if every person she passed heard them making love in the bathroom. They spent the night in their sleeper car, enjoying their privacy.

The next afternoon around lunchtime, they left their sleeper to get a bite to eat. Just ahead of them in line were the two people they had talked to while they ordered their drinks on the Denver-Salt Lake City train. The four of them made small talk while waiting to order at the snack bar. The man ordered a sandwich, and then commented to his wife, "I'd order a Bloody Mary, but I'm afraid I'd lock myself in the bathroom and miss the view."

His wife gave him a playful poke in the ribs and made an apologetic comment to Angela. Angela looked at his shoes for confirmation. Not only did they know what the newlyweds had done, but there was a good chance they'd heard them in the act. She was embarrassed and emboldened at the same time. "There's more to enjoy on this journey than the scenery," Angela replied.

Rate this adventure with a plus if you would like to find yourself in a similar situation, and with a minus if you wouldn't. Give extra pluses or minuses if you have strong feelings either way.

HER ANSWER	HIS ANSWER

For your next vacation, think about alternative means of transportation – anything other than a car or commercial airplane – for at least a segment of the trip.

HER ANSWER	HIS ANSWER

or record your answers in your private notebook.

Adventures on a Limited Budget
An Exercise

Larry told me he had looked at my web site for some ideas for Susan's fortieth birthday. He decided if he had a billion dollars, he would take his homesick wife back to their hometown in Texas, fly in all of her old friends, and visit her favorite places. Since he wasn't a billionaire, he modified his plan a bit. He did take her to their hometown. He hired a limousine to take her, her par-

> *It is better to have enough ideas for some of them to be wrong, than to be always right by having no ideas at all.*
>
> EDWARD DE BONO

ents and siblings by all of the homes they lived in when they were growing up. At each house, they piled out of the limo and took pictures of themselves in front of the house. Rather than flying in her old friends, he asked each of them write letters to her. When Susan, Larry and her family returned to her parent's current home, she found a ribbon leading her from one card or letter to the next. It was an excellent birthday adventure, inspired by wishes free of financial constraints.

This brainstorming exercise is the follow up to the Money is No Object Exercise on page 77. Using the same six numbers and activities, come up with a way to celebrate these interests with a limited budget.

Number	Interests or Hobbies	Celebration

Sparks that Ignite the Romantic Flame

♡ Pay attention to the details. You can turn a commonplace event into a sublime romantic adventure.

♡ Make the journey as much fun as the destination by using unique transportation.

♡ Engage the senses for a sensual experience.

♡ Notice the small touches at fancy restaurants and hotels. Use their ideas to make your own adventures more elegant.

♡ Spend an entire day focused on each other in the privacy of your own home.

♡ Recreate scenes from your favorite romantic movies.

♡ Listen to your beloved's simple requests. Go the extra mile when you fulfill them.

♡ Start brainstorming ideas for your next adventure with a money-is-no-object attitude. Then apply your budget, figuring out how to capture the spirit without the expense.

HABIT SIX

Invite People To Help

In Paulo Coelho's novel, *The Alchemist,* the old king says, "When you want something, all the universe conspires in helping you to achieve it."

This belief seems to be especially true for romance. Friends and strangers alike may enjoy helping you carry out parts of your adventure. It's like being part of a conspiracy for fun and romance. Who can resist that? When others participate in your adventure, they get to share in the "WOW." If you have a hard time asking for help, just imagine how honored you would be to help someone else if the situation were reversed.

Including other people in the planning invariably adds to the creativity of the event. Listen to their ideas and consider using the ones that enhance your adventure, but remember to follow your own romantic bliss. Do what works for you.

You can practice this habit whether you're the planner or the guest of honor. Inviting people to help as you're setting up an adventure lets them share in the anticipation. If you find yourself the star of some unfolding adventure, asking a friend or stranger to participate multiplies the excitement.

Don't take it personally if someone, especially a stranger, is unable to help. Just because you ask doesn't necessarily mean that person has the time,

> *To ask is no sin and to be refused is no calamity.*
> RUSSIAN PROVERB

skills, or opportunity to help. Some of these stories happened before the events of September 11, 2001, which caused heightened security in public places, particularly airports, so they would

require additional consideration today. Take that into account before you make your plans and ask for help.

Mixing Technology and Romance
Our Romantic Adventure

For one of our anniversaries, I gave Jim a global positioning system. A GPS is a handheld device that can pinpoint your location anywhere on the planet by using input from satellites. Rather than just hand him a package, I decided to have him use the GPS gift to find me in a bed and breakfast.

Our anniversary was on a Saturday. Early in the week I started setting up the adventure, using hints to build his anticipation. I wrote him a letter setting up a fantasy. He would be a spy, and his enemies would capture me on Friday at noon. It would be his job to find me. As a spy he was told to notice anything out of the ordinary during the week that could be a clue to my location on Friday afternoon.

We would be staying at a bed and breakfast on Broken Arrow Lane in Lake George. I left a broken arrow in his car. The owner of the archery shop had a hard time understanding why I wanted to buy a cheap wooden arrow that I could break, but he took the time to find one for me.

I also left *A Spy in the House of Love* by Anais Nin in Jim's car. There was no direct clue here, but it added to the anticipation.

Jim and I enjoy crossword puzzles. I bought software that helped me create my own crosswords. I designed one that had the names of many places in Colorado where we had visited over the years. His destination for the weekend was hidden in the puzzle. It wasn't obvious since "Lake" and "George" were parts of two different answers.

When the Garmin GPS that I ordered came in the mail, I gave it to my friend Scott. His job was to figure out how to use it and put in the waypoints leading to the inn. Being a computer whiz, he was thrilled to have a new toy to play with.

On Friday Jim arranged to duck out early of an all-day meeting. I left the GPS with Jim's boss who would give it to him at noon. Jim endured some good-natured teasing as several of his co-workers gathered around as he was presented with the gift-wrapped GPS. A card instructed Jim to find a bench in the center of a downtown park and figure out how to use it.

Two of my co-workers Jim had never met agreed to deliver lunch to him. To help them recognize Jim, I blew up a picture of him and pasted it over Denzel Washington's face on the cover of *People Magazine's* Sexiest Man Alive issue. When they found Jim, they got his attention with a squirt gun and negotiated for a joke and his autograph on the magazine cover in exchange for his lunch.

A friend and I watched the entire interaction from a sandwich shop across the street. We laughed at the surprised look on Jim's face when a stream of water from the squirt gun hit his shirt. We watched the look of disbelief when he saw himself on the cover of *People*. We noticed how his expression softened when he told a joke. After a while, a small crowd had gathered around us to watch this entertaining trio.

Jim settled on a park bench with a sandwich in one hand and an instruction manual in the other. He hadn't made it much past page three when Lori came along.

"Hi, Lori," Jim said, surprised to see her.

"Hi, Jim. What are you doing here?"

"I'm figuring out how to use the new toy Mary gave me."

"Do you know how to use it yet?" she asked.

"No."

"Gee, that's too bad because your time is up. Now you have to buy me a drink."

Lori and Jim walked across the street to a Mexican restaurant. Waiting for them were Lauren and Scott. Knowing full well that Jim may not have time to figure out the intricacies of the GPS in the allotted time, I had asked Scott to show him how to use it. They ordered drinks and chatted about the GPS. After reviewing the basic functions, Jim paid the bill and they left the restaurant.

The group followed the waypoints from the restaurant back to the park, and then to one of my favorite clothing stores. Regina, the store owner, gave Jim a box I had left for him. In the box were ten greeting cards and a one-pound chocolate fortune cookie, dipped in white chocolate and rolled in walnuts. The fortune in the cookie told him the name of the route in the GPS he was to follow to find me, and the ten cards corresponded to each of the waypoints in the route. Cheers of best wishes from sales clerks and customers followed him out the door as he set out on his mission.

> *Happiness is not in the mere possession of money; it lies in the joy of achievement, in the thrill of creative effort.*
> FRANKLIN D. ROOSEVELT

His instructions were to pull over and read a card when he arrived at each waypoint. I didn't want him fiddling with this new toy in traffic. At a few of the waypoints, I asked him to get out of the car to buy something. At the supermarket in Woodland Park, he bought a picnic lunch to put in a cooler I had left in his car. At the general store in Lake George, he asked what flies the trout in the river were biting and bought a few.

In the meantime, Judy drove me to Lake George. Since we did not have a GPS and did a lousy job of following Scott's clear directions, we got lost and barely beat Jim to the B&B. I had just a few minutes after Judy dropped me off to get settled before Jim arrived.

Our reunion was filled with the excitement of busy friends getting together for the first time in years, even though we had parted just hours before. I wanted to know all the details, and Jim was amazed with the number of people who had helped with this adventure. Mission accomplished!

Some people went above and beyond the call of duty to help make this adventure successful. When I was thinking about it, the only part I dreaded was figuring out how the GPS worked. That's just not my thing. When I mentioned to Scott I was buying a GPS, he asked if he could play with it for a while, as if I were doing him a favor. That alone would've been a blessing, but then he drove all the way to Lake George to put the waypoints in. I didn't realize when I planned this adventure how essential that would be.

Judy took an afternoon off work to drive me to Lake George. I didn't even have to ask her; she offered when I told her what I had planned.

The people who helped so enthusiastically confirmed the value of this habit. Most people enjoy being a part of romantic and fun adventures, even in a supporting role. I know I do.

Rate this adventure with a plus if you would like to find yourself in a similar situation, and with a minus if you wouldn't. Give extra pluses or minuses if you have strong feelings either way.

HER ANSWER	HIS ANSWER

Do you have any reservations about asking your friends or family to help you carry out an adventure? If so, think about some times you've helped your friends. Was it fun? Would you do it again?

HER ANSWER	HIS ANSWER

Message in a Bottle
Fred and Darlene's Romantic Adventure

Fred took his beloved Darlene to a Colorado resort for a romantic weekend. They had been dating for a couple of years, and he decided it was about time to pop the question. He had a diamond ring hidden in his suitcase and was just waiting for the right time.

After checking into their hotel, they walked around town and visited some of the shops. Fred noticed a concession stand on small lake that rented paddle-boats and thought that an early evening outing on the lake would be very romantic indeed. In a bookstore, he saw Nicholas Sparks' book, *Message in a Bottle,* and with a spark of romantic inspiration, he knew exactly what to do.

Fred had previously arranged for Darlene to get a massage in the afternoon. As his plan started to come together, he realized he would be very busy during that time. He needed to think of some reason to be gone a little longer than her massage might last, so he told Darlene he was going to the golf course to see if he could play nine holes or hit some balls at the driving range.

When she left for her massage, he made a beeline for the lake. He talked to the attendant and asked for his help. As luck would have it, Josh had just gotten to work and would be there through closing. Fred explained his plan and Josh was eager to help.

Fred's next stop was the restaurant they had considered for dinner. He made a reservation and asked the hostess if they had an empty wine bottle with a cork. Amy told him the trash in the dumpster had been hauled away earlier in the day. When Fred explained to Amy what he was going to do with the wine bottle, she offered to let him look through the kitchen trash. Soon Amy and Fred were digging through the trash together, trying to find a cork to go with the bottle of merlot that still had about a half inch of wine in it. The manager passed by the trashcan just as they found the matching cork; his surprised look suggested that it was inappropriate for Amy to be assisting this hopeless wino. Fred rinsed the bottle in hot water, which raised him in the eyes of the manager from hopeless wino to merely hopeless.

A gift shop just a few doors down had some costume jewelry. Fred caught the attention of the sales clerk as he was trying to find a ring small enough to fit through the opening of the wine bottle. Feeling slightly embarrassed, Fred felt compelled to explain his situation to the clerk. She helped him to find an adjustable ring that would fit. Fred bought a sheet of handmade paper, and she offered to write his message in calligraphy.

Fred went back to the bookstore where he saw *Message in a Bottle*. He had the book gift-wrapped.

> *The business of life is to enjoy oneself; everything else is but a mockery.*
> NORMAN DOUGLAS

His last stop was to go back to the lake. After testing the seaworthiness of the bottle, he left it with Josh. He gave Josh a $20 tip, a tidy sum for a college student, and reserved a boat.

When Fred got back to the room, Darlene was freshening her make up. He told her the golf course was very busy so he did some shopping instead. He gave her the book. She was thrilled since another Nicholas Sparks book, *The Notebook*, was one of her favorites. She was a true romantic at heart.

While they dressed for dinner, Fred told her he made a dinner reservation. On the way out the door, Fred slipped the ring box in his right pocket, being careful to keep Darlene on his left. Fred suggested a stroll by the lake before they ate. Much to his delight, when they got to the lake, Darlene wanted to go for a boat ride. This was too good to be true, he thought. Nonchalantly Josh took Fred's money for the boat.

They paddled to the south to check out some fish jumping in the water and admired wild flowers on the shore. Fred watched as Josh took off in a paddleboat for the center of the lake. As smooth as a pickpocket, Josh dropped the bottle in the lake and headed back to shore. There were only a few other boaters on the lake at the same time, but Fred didn't want to take a chance that someone else would steal his thunder, so he began to head indirectly for the drop point.

When the bottle was about thirty yards to the left of the boat, Darlene spotted it. She's a stickler for litter, which is one thing Fred was counting on. Darlene asked Fred to go by the bottle so she could pick it up. When they got a few feet away, Darlene said it looked like there was something in it. Fred's heart was beating wildly in anticipation.

Darlene picked up the bottle and said it looked like a message. She struggled to get the cork out, which Fred had pushed in perhaps a tad too far in his quest to make the bottle waterproof. Fred offered the corkscrew on his Swiss Army knife.

Amy removed the cork, and then pulled on the message. At first the faux diamond ring wrapped around the message stuck, but she was finally able to get the whole thing out intact.

She unwrapped the message and read aloud:

> *Dearest Darlene,*
> *You'll make me the happiest man alive if you'll be my bride. Will you marry me?*
>
> > *All my love,*
> > *Fred*

She recognized his handwriting even before she read the words.

"Yes, yes, I will!" she answered, and she started to unbend the ring to fit her finger.

"That was a test. I figured if you'd marry me with that ring it was true love. Since you passed, I have another ring for you." Fred pulled the ring box from his pocket, and spoke the words, "Will you marry me?"

Darlene's eyes filled with tears as she slipped the diamond solitaire on her finger. "Yes, I'll marry you since you passed my test, too."

"What test was that?" Fred asked.

"You were smart enough not to put a real diamond in a wine bottle in the middle of the lake."

Fred and Darlene talked for a while, deciding whom to tell first and tossing around some dates, and then headed back to the dock. On the way Fred noticed Josh and a small crowd watching their arrival. When Fred gave Josh a thumb's up, the crowd responded with whistles and applause.

They arrived at the restaurant a few minutes early. Amy greeted them, looked for the ring on Darlene's finger, and then offered her congratulations. She escorted them to a window-side seat overlooking the lake.

The manager stopped by to offer his best wishes and a complementary bottle of merlot. When the hostess explained the situation to him after Fred's earlier departure, the manager's opinion of Fred changed from hopeless, to hopeless romantic.

It's not only friends who are willing to help with romantic adventures. People practically came out of the woodwork to assist Fred. He managed to pull everything together in just over an hour with the help of total strangers. Everyone who helped Fred was not only willing but *eager* to help.

Rate this adventure with a plus if you would like to find yourself in a similar situation, and with a minus if you wouldn't. Give extra pluses or minuses if you have strong feelings either way.

HER ANSWER	HIS ANSWER

How would you feel if you had the opportunity to assist some strangers in their romantic adventure?

HER ANSWER	HIS ANSWER

Does Anyone Know French?
Our Romantic Adventure

Since Jim and I are not gamblers, we had no reason to return to Las Vegas after the one day we spent there on our two-week honeymoon twenty-two years earlier. My friends, Louise and Judy, had convinced me there was a lot more to Las Vegas than gambling. I wanted to see *Cirque du Soleil* after missing it in Denver. Finding out that *Cirque du Soleil's Mystere* was playing in Las Vegas was reason enough to return for Jim's upcoming birthday.

I invited Louise and Judy to join us and surprise their husbands with a trip to Las Vegas for Jim's birthday. One of Louise's favorite restaurants in Las Vegas was a French restaurant.

A theme was starting to emerge. We planned a Las Vegas vacation with a French flair.

On the day we were to leave, I asked Jim to take the afternoon off and go to a restaurant near his office at 2:00. Louise and Judy told Kurt and Michael to go to the restaurant and have a drink with Jim for his birthday. Our daughter-in-law, Karen, was a bartender at this restaurant. When Jim arrived, she brought him a martini. After Kurt and Michael arrived and settled in, she delivered their drinks along with a letter. A videographer, who had been setting up her equipment as if she were there to shoot a commercial, revealed her true mission as she zoomed in on the action.

The introduction in the letter read as follows:

> Dearest Jim,
>
> "Je t'aime" is "I love you" in French. To find out what fabulous French delights await you for your birthday, translate this message as quickly as possible. You must be ready to leave by 3:00.
>
> Je t'aime,
> Mary

The foreign message that followed had been written with the assistance of a French-speaking friend. The beauty of this plan was that Jim, Kurt and Michael couldn't speak more than a handful of French words. Karen had taken some French in college so she could throw in a few words here and there. Jim, Kurt and Michael had to enlist the help of other diners to translate the letter. After asking several people for help, they finally found a woman who spoke French. A cheer from the curious spectators went up when they got the message to throw their wives a kiss on video.

> You are forgiven for your happiness and your successes only if you generously consent to share them.
> ALBERT CAMUS

An hour later a limousine arrived to take the trio and the videographer to the airport. In the meantime, Louise, Judy and I had packed for our husbands and arrived at the airport in time to check their luggage. We were waiting curbside when the long white stretch limo arrived. The men piled out of the car, laughing, talking in horrid French accents, and telling us they knew exactly where they were going.

We demanded proof that the letter had been translated. After passing through airport security, we sat down at a nearby gate announcing a Phoenix departure and asked for a translation. The woman in the bar had accurately translated the message:

> *Three fun-loving women have a weekend of mystery planned for you and your buddies. For the next half hour, please enjoy your drinks. We will watch you later on video, so be sure to throw us a kiss. Prepare to be pampered in a grand French style. You will be warmed by the sun, enjoy fine dining, and delight in sensual pleasures. Where do you think you are going? Are you ready to have some fun? We promise you will.*

With the hint about the sun, they guessed we were going some place warm like Mexico, Arizona or Nevada. Michael was convinced it was Las Vegas. Jim and Kurt, noticing the Phoenix flight, were less sure. I kept an eye on the crowd boarding the Las Vegas flight a few gates down the concourse, and at the last minute asked the group to come with me.

Michael and Kurt were delighted with the destination. I could tell Jim had some doubts but was too much of a gentleman to let it show. Jim's image of Las Vegas was smoke-filled casinos inside and 100-degree temperatures outside. I was certain that with what we had planned, he would enjoy his Las Vegas birthday.

We had second row center seats to *Cirque du Soleil* on Friday night and dinner reservations at a French restaurant on Saturday. We watched the pirate ships battle at Treasure Island and visited Zigfried and Roy's tigers. While Louise, Kurt, Judy and Michael gambled, Jim and I read by the pool or escaped to our room. A good sport willing to try anything once, Jim spent $20 and a short 15 minutes at the blackjack tables with Kurt.

Friends and strangers helped us with this adventure. Our friends were eager to join us for the trip. Later, upon viewing the videotape, I saw how much everyone enjoyed being part of translating the mysterious love letter.

Rate this adventure with a plus if you would like to find yourself in a similar situation, and with a minus if you wouldn't. Give extra pluses or minuses if you have strong feelings either way.

HER ANSWER	HIS ANSWER

Romance in the Rainforest
Manuel and Elevinia's Romantic Adventure

Jim and I had the good fortune to run a bed and breakfast for some friends in Costa Rica for two months in 2001. The five employees at the Villa Decary spoke only Spanish, and most of their guests were English speaking, which is why the owners needed us. When we decided to embark on this adventure, we signed up for our first Spanish class, and five months later we went to Costa Rica. Our Spanish was marginal, but with the help of an ever-ready dictionary and sign language we got along famously with the staff.

One afternoon around quitting time, 20-year-old Manuel gestured for me to follow him into the office. He handed me a handwritten note and indicated that he wanted me to type it on the *"computadora"* and make it look pretty. It was addressed to *"El amor de mi vida."* I knew enough Spanish to know that the letter was to "the love of my life," but not enough to violate his privacy (at least not without a dictionary). I was absolutely delighted to help out with what I initially thought was a marriage proposal. I went to work right away, stopping only when necessary to look up some of the juicier words like *"dueño de mi corazón"* (owner of my heart) and *"novio"* (fiancée). Without a doubt, the letter contained a pledge of eternal love. I searched high and low to find a question with the word for "marry," but to no avail. It wasn't until I typed the last line that I realized the letter wasn't from Manuel, it was TO him. The letter didn't have the marriage proposal I thought it might, but I was touched by the love expressed in this letter and the sentimental value of having it typed as a keepsake.

When Manuel got to work the next morning, I showed him the words that didn't make it through the spellchecker on the Villa Decary computer (their computer was bilingual, mine wasn't), and then copied the file to my computer for a wider selection of fonts. I printed the letter in four different fonts trying to determine his favorite, but he said he wanted all of them. Not more than an hour later, he was back with another letter. This one was to *"Mi único y gran amor"* (My only and great love) and it was FROM Manuel. The perplexing thing was that both letters were in the same handwriting. The only explanation I could guess was that her handwriting was less legible than his, especially to someone who didn't know the language, so he transcribed it for me.

Jim, Dwayne (a friend who was a guest at the inn), and I made two trips to the small town of Arenal to find some nice stationery, but came home empty handed both times. Manuel and Elevinia have four copies of each of their love letters, on plain paper, to share with their grandchildren.

Manuel wanted this keepsake so much that nothing held him back from asking. Since Manuel kept the hotel grounds beautifully landscaped while my responsibilities kept me inside most of the time, I had not had a lot of interaction with him. His English was even worse than my Spanish so we seldom said much more to each other than *"¿Cómo está usted?"* He certainly didn't know I'm a pushover for anything romantic. All he knew was that I knew how to use a computer. I was thrilled to help him, especially since we were there during the slow season.

Rate this adventure with a plus if you would like to help someone in a similar situation, and with a minus if you wouldn't. Give extra pluses or minuses if you have strong feelings either way.

HER ANSWER	HIS ANSWER

This is Your Captain Speaking
Jason and Gina's Romantic Adventure

When Gina and Jason met, he was training in judo at the Olympic Training Center. He had competed all over the world. Jason loved to fly, and during his frequent travels, he started thinking about how much fun it would be to become engaged on a plane. After dating Gina for three years, he found the opportunity to make his fantasy a reality.

In December 1998, Gina and Jason were flying to Philadelphia to spend Christmas with Jason's family. He told her that he would be gone a few minutes to use the restroom. She went back to reading her paperback novel.

When he had been gone just a short while, she heard the captain's voice on the speaker. "Ladies and gentlemen, this is your captain speaking. Please stay tuned for a special announcement." Just a plain old announcement is something that even infrequent fliers will tune out, but when Gina heard the words "special announcement" she half-heartedly diverted her attention from the mystery unfolding in her book.

The captain said, "I'd like to draw your attention to Gina in seat 18A." In those first few moments when one is thrust unexpectedly from anonymity into the spotlight, things don't always make sense. Gina knew she heard her name, but there was no logical reason. What was the rest of the message? Jason was gone – had something happened to him?

When Gina heard Jason's familiar voice, the energy surging through her body transformed from panic to relief to astonishment in an instant. Jason said, "Ladies and gentlemen, I have known Gina for three years, and those three years have been the best years of my life. She is, without a doubt, the most beautiful, kind, and wonderful woman I have ever had the privilege to know. I am in love with her and want to spend the rest of my life with her. Gina, will you marry me?"

Gina is truly beautiful, kind, and wonderful, but she is not the type to run down the aisle yelling her answer. Jason knew that, too. Gina heard the captain say, "Gina, we all want to know your answer. If it's yes, push the flight attendant call button." All eyes were upon her when she shyly peeked her head above the seats. When she touched the call button to say "Yes," the passengers on the plane cheered and whistled their approval.

Gina stood in the aisle as Jason came back to their seats. Amidst the tears and smiles and best wishes, the happy couple confirmed their commitment with a kiss. He pulled a diamond ring from his pocket and slipped it on her finger. The flight crew sent back a bottle of champagne. Thanks to Jason and Gina, everyone on their plane got a memorable dose of romance for Christmas.

Rate this adventure with a plus if you would like to find yourself in a similar situation, and with a minus if you wouldn't. Give extra pluses or minuses if you have strong feelings either way.

HER ANSWER	HIS ANSWER

A Trail of Roses

Martin and Tina's Romantic Adventure

Martin and Tina had been dating for years and it was understood that they would eventually marry. She was frustrated by his unwillingness to commit. He simply wanted to do things his own way and in his own time. Unbeknownst to Tina, Martin was making plans.

Tina had been under a lot of stress at work and was dreading an upcoming business trip. She would be manning a booth at a software trade show. To make matters worse, after working long hours on Thursday and Friday, she would have to pack up the booth on Saturday and stay in San Francisco by herself on Saturday night. She needed a Saturday night stay to get the best airfare. While she loved San Francisco, she hated being there alone on a Saturday night. She hated it even more because that Saturday night was Valentine's Day. She dreaded being in the one of the world's most romantic cities alone on a day celebrated by lovers. What a reminder that her own relationship had stalled! She felt depressed as she packed for the trip.

Martin called to say goodbye on Wednesday afternoon. He wished her a good trip and said he'd see her on Sunday. He had a busy veterinary practice and worked Saturdays. Tina had asked him to join her in San Francisco and was disappointed by his predictable response – "I'd love to, but Saturdays are my busiest days."

Tina arrived at the airport just in time to check the bags and rush through the security checkpoint. She got to the gate after the last boarding call. The plane was full. Most of the seats were already taken, and a dozen people stood in the aisle adjusting their belongings.

As Tina approached her aisle seat, she felt slightly irritated when she noticed a single long-stem rose lying in her seat. Surely it belonged to the woman seated next to her. She was just about to ask the woman to hold her own flower when she saw the card with her name written on the outside. Still not believing the card and the flower was for her, she asked her seatmate, "Is this for me?"

"It is if your name is Tina," the woman replied with a smile.

Tina opened the card with trembling hands. Joy rushed through her body as she read the words, "Just because I love you, Martin." Her feelings of being rushed and irritated instantly gave way to the feeling of being loved.

After Tina settled into her seat, Martha said, "That is one romantic guy you have."

Tina confessed that Martin was not usually this romantic. "Do you know how this got here?"

Martha said, "A flight attendant dropped it off a few minutes ago."

Tina was absolutely in awe that Martin took the time to have a rose and card delivered to her flight. He never took time away from his practice during office hours. She was excited to call him as soon as she got to her hotel.

> *When you have once seen the glow of happiness on the face of a beloved person, you know that a man can have no other vocation than to awaken that light on the faces surrounding him.*
>
> ALBERT CAMUS

After Tina's plane landed in San Francisco, she collected her bags and started to leave the baggage claim area. She was startled when a man in a tuxedo stepped in front of her and called her by name. He was holding a single red rose and an envelope with her name on it – in Martin's handwriting. The card read, "Please accept this limo ride – just because I love you, Martin."

Tina was sure she had entered a parallel universe occupied by some other Tina and some other Martin. Until this cosmic glitch got straightened out, she figured she would enjoy the ride.

The trade show was held at the convention center, and Tina stayed at a large hotel nearby. When she checked in at the front desk, the clerk said, "Oh yes, we've been expecting you. Your boss felt bad about sending you here on Valentine's Day, so he upgraded you to a suite." Tina smiled in spite of herself. In those days of corporate belt tightening, staying in a suite was unheard of in her company. Even though the events of the last couple of hours had definitely lightened her mood, she still wondered how much fun a suite could be alone, without Martin.

She finished the paperwork and picked up her purse to leave. The clerk said, "Oh, there's one other thing. It seems that you have an admirer." He handed her a red rose and a card. Again the card read, "Just because I love you, Martin."

Tina followed the bellman up to her suite. After he opened the door, the first thing she noticed was a beautiful vase with a single red rose. There was no card this time; instead rose petals spelled out the message on the table, "I love you, Martin." She added her other three roses to the vase.

As soon as she was alone, Tina dialed Martin's number at work. His receptionist told her he was doing an emergency surgery on a ferret. Tina left her number and asked to have Martin call her when he was free. Tina eagerly awaited the call, but it never came.

During the next thirty-six hours, she received four more roses. She found rose number five in a Gatorade bottle sitting in the middle of the disarray of boxes when she arrived to set up her booth.

In the afternoon, a lone woman approached and presented her with a rose and card. She was tight lipped and soon disappeared.

Back at the hotel, Tina ordered room service. When the bellman brought dinner, he wheeled in a cart with her meal, a glass of chardonnay, a red rose and a card.

As Tina left her room on Friday morning, she nearly stepped on her next rose. It was lying on top of the USA Today that had been delivered to her door.

In the afternoon, Tina noticed the elegant yet efficient concierge from the hotel heading her way. She was carrying a red rose and a card. The concierge greeted her warmly, and then offered the card and the rose. The card read, "I know you'll be tired after the show. I've arranged for you to have a massage tomorrow morning at 11:00. Just because I love you, Martin."

"When did Martin call you?" Tina asked, wondering why Martin had time to call everyone but her.

"My lips are sealed," replied the concierge, "but I know you'll love the massage."

"I can't believe this is Martin. He's never been this romantic," Tina said.

"He must really love you," the concierge observed.

"I know he loves me, and I love him, too. He's just never expressed it in such a grand way before. I can't wait to see him again."

Tina's boss came for the end of the show, and they planned to have dinner together on Friday night. By this time, Tina fully expected anyone she met to be carrying a red rose. When Mike showed up empty handed, she was almost disappointed, especially since Martin and Mike were friends. Mike seemed genuinely surprised when Tina told him about the trail of roses that had been following her since she left home.

Tina returned to her room to find a rose on the pillow along with the customary chocolate the hotel provided with their evening turn down service. Tina dialed Martin's number, and once again was disappointed to hear Martin's voice on the answering machine.

The convention center was noisy with the sounds of the booths being disassembled, boxed and moved when Tina arrived on Saturday morning. Her booth was relatively simple to break down. She had everything packed and turned over to the shippers in less than an hour. She worked a little faster than usual knowing a fabulous massage awaited her.

The massage was just what Tina needed. Her back was sore from lifting boxes, so she went directly to the spa so she could sit in the hot tub and steam room before her massage. The massage therapist gave a wonderful deep tissue massage. When the session ended, the therapist left the room so Tina could dress. When Tina sat up, she saw a red rose – the eleventh one – lying on top of her clothes. "Happy Valentine's Day," the card read, "I love you, Martin."

Feeling more loved than ever, Tina returned to her room. Before she opened her door, she heard music playing inside her room. She knew she hadn't left the music on. She suspected that the bellman had been there, left another rose, and turned on the music.

The first thing she noticed when she opened the door was a trail of rose petals leading to the table with the roses. The curtains were closed. The only light came from some candles on the table. When she walked toward the table, she caught a movement out of the corner of her eye. She could not have been more surprised when she saw Martin, holding a white rose. The many questions racing through her mind seemed to paralyze her vocal cords.

Martin walked toward her, knelt down on one knee, and said, "I gave you the red roses because I love you. This one is different. It's white. Red and white roses together symbolize unity. With this white rose, I'm asking you to be my wife."

"Yes," she whispered, her voice choked with emotion. "I thought you'd never ask."

Martin took a ring box from the dresser and gave it to Tina. The box contained a breathtaking ring. Eleven little rubies surrounded a large diamond. Martin wanted her to wear a reminder of the dozen roses for the rest of her days.

The Valentine's Day that Tina had been dreading for months had become the best day of her life.

Here's Martin's version of the story

I had been planning to propose to Tina on Valentine's Day since July. When Tina told me in December that she would have to go to on a business trip then, I was bummed at first. When I got the idea of surprising her in San Francisco, I really got into it. I found another veterinarian to cover for my practice for a few days.

The day she left I went to the airport. I got there as soon as the plane landed so I could give the rose to the flight attendant and be long gone by the time she arrived.

Tina's boss, Mike, has been a buddy of mine for many years. He helped me a lot with the planning. He told me which hotel she would be staying in, provided her schedule to me, and he contacted the conference coordinator to get someone to deliver the rose during the set up time. As an engagement present, he upgraded her room. Mike and I even flew out to San Francisco together. I stayed in his room on Friday night. We had a great time talking about Tina's response after they had dinner together.

The hotel concierge was very helpful. She recommended a limo company, arranged all the rose deliveries at the hotel, and bless her heart, even found a customer at the tradeshow to deliver the rose to Tina on Thursday afternoon. I mailed all of the cards (except for the first one) to her and she got them to the right people.

The hotel has a strict policy about letting anyone into someone else's hotel room. The concierge even helped me here, although she wanted to be sure I wasn't some wacko stalker. That's the reason she personally delivered the rose to Tina at the show. Tina's enthusiastic response and probing questions convinced her I was on the up and up.

At first I was reluctant to use so many strangers in this scheme, thinking they wouldn't want to get involved. I couldn't have been more wrong. Every person I talked to was eager to help, and that was even before they knew that I would be a generous tipper.

The hardest part for me was not taking Tina's calls from San Francisco. I knew if I talked to her I would reveal more than I intended. My office was pretty excited about the scheme, too. They had a good time covering for me. From the message she left on Friday night, I could tell she was flattered and excited, but she was starting to get annoyed that I hadn't returned her calls.

Our engagement was really fun for both of us, and definitely worth the effort it took to put it together. Tina said she felt very loved, and that was the whole point.

With the heightened security at airports and other public venues, this adventure might not be as easy to set up today. Since only ticketed passengers are permitted beyond security checkpoints, getting an unattended rose and card on the plane these days might prove to be challenging, if not impossible. It could be tough to convince hotel management to let anyone into someone else's room. If this adventure sparked ideas for an adventure of your own, don't despair. Find new solutions that work in today's world.

Rate this adventure with a plus if you would like to find yourself in a similar situation, and with a minus if you wouldn't. Give extra pluses or minuses if you have strong feelings either way.

HER ANSWER	HIS ANSWER

Fears and Concerns
An Exercise

Do you have any fears or concerns about expressing your love or planning romantic adventures? Some common ones are:

♡ Fear of rejection

♡ Fear of failure

♡ Takes too much time

♡ Costs too much money

♡ Effort won't be appreciated

♡ What to do with the children

♡ It won't make a difference

♡ I'll plan something and he/she will cancel it at the last minute

Think about your own fears or concerns. Write them down on a piece of paper. Now destroy them. Rip them into little pieces or burn them. Throw them in the fireplace or campfire. As you tear them up or watch them burn, say, "I release this fear" or "I overcome this obstacle."

This symbolic act doesn't magically make fears and concerns disappear. Don't expect the world's most dependable babysitter to call you offering her services just because you burned a piece of paper that said, "There's no one to watch the children." However, identifying your fears or concerns in the first step in overcoming them.

Sometimes destroying the paper is enough to relieve some of the anxiety around the issue. You may realize your fear of failure isn't enough reason to not try. If you still have some concerns after doing this exercise, do some problem solving with your beloved. Perhaps your efforts in the past have been unappreciated because you were speaking two different love languages. If money is a concern, set a reasonable budget for a date or adventure. If you think you don't have the time to plan an adventure, invite people to help.

Sparks that Ignite the Romantic Flame

♡ Consider the creative ideas of the people you invite to help you, but remember it's your adventure.

♡ Welcome the enthusiasm of friends and strangers alike that can bring excitement to your adventure.

♡ Have fun asking strangers for help when you're on an adventure, whether you're the planner or the honoree.

♡ Use body language or refer to a foreign language dictionary to communicate your request if language is a barrier. The desire for romance is universal.

♡ Don't take it personally if someone you ask to help can't. Before you ask, consider heightened security restrictions in some public venues that may preclude any involvement.

♡ Tell your beloved about all the people who helped pull off an adventure. He or she will feel honored and be amazed.

Make an Adventure of Presenting Your Gift

Gifts are heartfelt symbols of love and affection. Even the simplest gift lets the receiver know that someone cared enough to search for a gift. If you want your beloved to think about you not only when the gift is given, but to smile at the memory of the gift for years to come, make an adventure of the presentation.

Just giving or receiving a gift is special in itself, but the gift can be made even more memorable if it is presented with pizzazz. A brightly wrapped package is always a welcome surprise. An activity planned around the gift is a way to crank up the enjoyment meter.

This habit is more about the presentation of the gift than the gift itself. The gift doesn't need to be expensive to be worthy of an adventurous presentation. You'll see how one man planned an adventure around the gift of a book.

> *The manner of giving is worth more than the gift.*
> PIERRE CORNEILLE

You'll also see how a special presentation is even more valuable when the gift is not a surprise. Stories about a golf club, mountain bike, and leather coat illustrate ways to celebrate an anticipated gift. If you have a hard time selecting a gift, ask your beloved to select his or her gift with you. Once the selection has been made, the adventure of the presentation can begin.

Finding Excitement in the Expected
Our Romantic Adventure

For me, part of the joy of Christmas was surprising Jim with a perfect yet unexpected gift. One year we both knew what we were getting from each other. Jim needed a new pair of backcountry skis to replace his 20-year-old cross-country skis. I wanted a small TV for the kitchen to keep me company when I cook. Only our "stocking-stuffer" gifts would be a surprise. I wanted to do something different to keep the magic of surprise in our gift giving. Jim must have been thinking the same thing.

On Christmas Eve Jim told me that he was going to get up thirty minutes before me and I was not allowed to leave the bedroom until he came to get me. Since Jim is naturally an early riser and I'm not, I didn't expect this to be a challenge for me. Curiosity, however, disturbed my sleep and I lay in bed wondering what Jim was up to. After what seemed like a long thirty minutes, Jim came to get me, closing the bedroom door behind him.

A piece of red yarn under the door extended in to the room about eight feet. After dressing in my lacy red Christmas best, I quickly began to wind the yarn into a ball. When I opened the bedroom door, I could see red yarn crisscrossing all over the house. Ducking under yarn and winding furiously, I followed the path to find a glass ornament, a paperback novel, and a pair of earrings. I quickly found myself at the end of the trail of red yarn. The yarn disappeared into a cabinet in the kitchen, where Jim had installed the TV and prohibited me from opening before Christmas.

Before Jim opened his gifts, we enjoyed eggs Benedict and champagne for breakfast. We adjourned to the living room for Jim's turn to open presents. I gave him several gifts, including a shirt, a CD, and a book. The last thing I gave him was a card. The card started him on a treasure hunt for his skis. He was told to look in the lovely gift he gave me the previous year.

Perplexed, he said, "I gave you several gifts last year." The truth was he could not remember what he had given me the previous year.

I asked, "Which gift was especially lovely?"

After a few moments, he walked over to a blue glass vase and looked inside. He found a note that told him to look behind a sentimental memento of our twentieth wedding anniversary. We talked about what we did on our twentieth anniversary – we had gone on a hot air balloon ride, privately renewed our vows on a mountaintop, and had a party two days later.

"What did we say to each other during our vow renewal?" I asked.

"Well, we reminisced about the past, shared our hopes for the future, read that poem…" Jim jumped up and went to search around the framed poem penned in calligraphy we used for our vows.

Attached to the back of the frame was a note telling Jim to find one of the sensual treasures we used on our 25th wedding anniversary. He needed no prompting this time. He went to our bedroom and opened the drawer holding massage oils and dusting powder. A fourth note told him to find the pictures of the event the last two celebrations com-memorated.

> *The habit of giving only enhances the desire to give.*
> WALT WHITMAN

"Our wedding?" he asked. After an affirmative nod from me, he set out to find our wedding pictures. As luck would have it, he could not remember which of the thirty-some photo albums housed our wedding pictures. As he randomly opened albums, we relived old vacations, remarked about how young we both looked, and laughed at the old bellbottoms.

In the wedding album, he found a note telling him to look under "the site of our earliest conjugal visits." He smiled and looked under the bed in our guest bedroom that I bought before we were married. There he found his skis with a big red bow on the tips.

I was delighted that Jim and I had independently decided to give our gifts to each other in such unique yet similar ways. We both wanted to add some excitement in our gift exchange since we both knew what we were getting.

Rate this adventure with a plus if you would like to find yourself in a similar situation, and with a minus if you wouldn't. Give extra pluses or minuses if you have strong feelings either way.

HER ANSWER	HIS ANSWER

Would you enjoy a treasure hunt to find a gift from your beloved?

HER ANSWER	HIS ANSWER

An Unexpected Driver
Lisa and Jim's Romantic Adventure

Lisa wanted to plan a memorable anniversary celebration for her husband Jim. He had asked for and even picked out a new golf club, but she wanted to do more to commemorate ten years together. She decided to surprise him with a limousine-driven treasure hunt. Lisa sent a limo to pick up him at work. His employees knew what was going on and led him outside to the limo. Jim was suspicious that someone was playing a practical joke on him and was reluctant to get in the limo. Only after the limo driver showed him his wife's signature on the order, he agreed to go along.

Lisa had arranged for the limo to stop at several locations. First, Jim went to a music store and used a gift certificate Lisa provided to pick out a CD. Next, he went to a wine store to select a bottle of wine. The driver then took Jim to a driving range. He was relieved to see Lisa, who was holding a bucket of balls and a new driver with a bow on the grip. Jim was thrilled with his new golf club, but the adventure was just beginning.

When he finished hitting balls, Lisa and Jim got into the limo together. To kill some time, Lisa told the driver to go through the drive-up window at Wendy's to order a soft drink. They felt like celebrities behind the darkened glass, especially when the clerks at the drive-up window tried to get a glimpse of them.

> *You give but little when you give of your possessions. It is when you give of yourself that you truly give.*
> KAHLIL GIBRAN

They took a leisurely drive through the Garden of the Gods, a park nestled in the foothills of Colorado Springs. They admired the towering sandstone rock formations. Passing by the romantic formation called "Kissing Camels" inspired some kissing and cuddling of their own. Their hearts soared while they looked at majestic Pikes Peak against the brilliant blue sky, feeling thankful to be together in such a magnificent place.

When Lisa and Jim arrived at their house, Jim's suspicious nature was aroused once again. The door was unlocked, and a couple of strangers had made themselves at home. Savory aromas and piano music filled the air. Lisa explained that she had hired Soraia to prepare a four-course meal and Geoff to entertain them on the piano with Eagles and Fleetwood Mac tunes. Jim was pleased to find the wine he'd picked up earlier was a perfect complement to their dinner.

Since Jim had picked out his own anniversary gift, he didn't expect much more than that. He assumed they would have a nice dinner and call it a night. Once he got over his initial uneasiness about the limo and saw Lisa at the driving range, he was thrilled with his adventure. He felt so thankful to have such a beautiful, loving and creative wife. Years later, he still thinks of these feelings when ever he pulls his driver out of this golf bag.

Rate this adventure with a plus if you would like to find yourself in a similar situation, and with a minus if you wouldn't. Give extra pluses or minuses if you have strong feelings either way.

HER ANSWER	HIS ANSWER

If your beloved planned a limousine-driven treasure hunt for you, would you need any reassurance at the beginning of the adventure? Would you be suspicious of a limousine trying to whisk you away? Would you trust that this was an act of love and not a practical joke? Discuss any reassurances you would need with your partner.

HER ANSWER	HIS ANSWER

A Painting Worth a Thousand Feelings
Dutch and Joan's Romantic Adventure

Joan and Dutch spent a weekend in Taos enjoying the fine cuisine and visiting the many art galleries in this charming New Mexican town. They wandered into a gallery that displayed works of art in several different rooms. Joan and Dutch admired the art at their own pace, and soon they became separated. Joan spotted a painting of an eagle she particularly liked. She was leaving the room when Dutch entered. She said, "My favorite painting in this whole town is in this room. You'll know it when you see it."

Dutch looked around and immediately spotted the eagle painting. When they met up again in another room, he said, "It's the painting of the eagle, right?" They agreed it was a beautiful painting, but did not discuss actually purchasing it.

Being a romantic at heart, Dutch's mind went to work. He arranged to buy the painting and surprise Joan with it on their next anniversary, which was still nine months away. He wanted the presentation to be as memorable as the gift itself.

Dutch began searching for a bed & breakfast where he and Joan could spend their anniversary. Décor was important; it needed to match the painting. He found a room that fit the bill, and the proprietor was very accommodating. Before Dutch took Joan to the room, the manager helped Dutch replace a painting on the wall with the eagle painting.

When Joan and Dutch checked in the B&B, Dutch tried to keep his eyes away from the painting. Joan looked around and admired the room. Her eyes stopped on the painting.

"Dutch, that looks like the painting from Taos." Since it had been many months since she had originally seen the painting, she had to study it for a while to be sure. "I can't believe these folks bought this painting for this bed and breakfast. Isn't it amazing that we loved the same painting? What a coincidence!"

Dutch nodded his agreement, but the look in his eyes told Joan there was more to the story. Dumbfounded, Joan asked, "Did you get this for me?"

Dutch confessed, and Joan fought back tears.

The painting now holds a place of honor in their home. When first-time visitors come to their house, Joan loves to tell them the story of the painting. Dutch smiles with modest embarrassment, as this story never fails to bring out enthusiastic admiration from the women and occasional sneers from the men.

Rate this adventure with a plus if you would like to find yourself in a similar situation, and with a minus if you wouldn't. Give extra pluses or minuses if you have strong feelings either way.

HER ANSWER	HIS ANSWER

Do you and your beloved have similar tastes? Take note when your beloved admires a piece of art. You don't necessarily have to buy it, but you'll find out more about his or her taste. When you do see something special that moves you to purchase it, think about a special way to present it.

HER ANSWER	HIS ANSWER

or record your answers in your private notebook.

Wind In His Sails

Our Romantic Adventure

In the late eighties my husband Jim became interested in windsurfing. At the time I was a full-time graduate student and money was tight. I saved for six months to buy Jim a used windsurfer. I wanted to make the giving of the gift as special as the gift itself, but the beginning of May in Colorado is way too cold to be playing in the water. Since I was giving Jim a new toy, I decided to have a birthday party for him and have his friends bring him toys suitable for a youngster.

> *When you love you wish to sacrifice and you wish to serve.*
> ERNEST HEMINGWAY

His party would have delighted any eight-year-old boy. His birthday cake had Spiderman on it. We played pin-the-tail-on-the-donkey. He opened his presents: a few toy trucks, softball, and some action figures. His last package contained the sail to the windsurfer.

It doesn't happen often, but for just a few seconds Jim was speechless. He recognized the sail from the board he had rented in the past. Everyone else in the room seemed to fade into the background as we looked into each other's eyes.

He asked, "Is this what I think it is?" I told him it was. I knew his next question, even though it was unspoken. "I saved my extra spending money to buy it for you." We knew then – and we still know now – that there is something precious about saving and making sacrifices in order to give a special gift.

Rate this adventure with a plus if you would like to find yourself in a similar situation, and with a minus if you wouldn't. Give extra pluses or minuses if you have strong feelings either way.

HER ANSWER	HIS ANSWER

Is there something your beloved would like to have that you both consider too expensive? How can you raise the money (besides credit card debt) to buy a gift that is just a bit over your budget? Consider buying a used item, or, depending on what the item is, making it yourself.

HER ANSWER	HIS ANSWER

or record your answers in your private notebook.

Mountain Bike Rally
Kelly and Vince's Playful Adventure

For Vince's fortieth birthday, he wanted a new mountain bike. For months he'd been looking at and test-riding bikes. He finally found "the one," and Kelly bought it for him. They agreed that Vince would not be allowed to ride the bike again or even see it until his birthday. The bike shop would store the bike until the big day. Vince was excited about his new bike, and even though he knew what he was getting, Kelly wanted to make the presentation special.

Kelly hired me to arrange a mountain bike rally for Vince's birthday. If you've never heard of a mountain bike rally, let me explain. One day as I was riding my bike in the National Forest near my home, I was appreciating the varying degrees of difficulty of the trails, which seemed to offer something for everyone. That thought sparked the idea of a mountain bike rally, and for the next five years I organized mountain bike rallies for my friends.

At these rallies there were three trail teams: hard, medium, and easy. I would plan the routes and plant clues along the way to lead all three teams to the picnic location. I spent hours finding funny cards and Trivial Pursuit questions to use as clues. Here's an example of a Trivial Pursuit clue: "What film has Cary Grant being attacked from a biplane crop duster? *(North by Northwest.)* Take the trail in the direction indicated by your answer."

On Vince's birthday, his biking friends were instructed to be at the trailhead at the appointed time. Vince didn't know what was happening, but he knew something was up. Kelly told him he was supposed to follow directions and not ask questions. She handed him a card and left the house.

The card directed Vince to dress in biking clothes and go to various stores to pick up a few unnecessary items like Gatorade and film. This diversion allowed Kelly time to pick up the bike and gave me time to organize things at the trailhead. After his last stop, Vince called Kelly on her cell phone to get further directions. She told him to come to the trailhead.

When Vince arrived at the parking lot, he found his high-performance bike garishly decorated with a big red ribbon on the handlebars, Happy Birthday crepe paper laced though the wheels, and an American flag waved from the seat post.

At this rally we didn't have three teams; we were all on Team Vince. Vince was our captain and called all the shots. He read all the clues and took the first crack at solving the riddles. At one spot, some non-biking female friends hid in waiting. When Vince got off his bike, they covered his face, arms and legs with bright red lipstick kisses.

At a second location a relay race had been set up. We organized ourselves into three teams. A member from each team tied panty hose around his or her waist. An orange had been placed in one toe of each pair of panty hose. The goal was to run (actually it was more like a waddle for most of us) from the starting line to the bottle, a distance of about thirty feet, and knock over the bottle with the orange. The tricky part was swinging the orange without using our hands. Elvis Presley could have learned some new moves from our swiveling hips. After someone knocked over a bottle, he tied the panty hose around the next team member's waist and the relay continued.

After the rally, Vince was blindfolded and taken to a friend's house nearby for a party with his biking and non-biking friends. No one that had not been at the rally believed Vince's story of how he got so many lipstick kisses on his body.

Rate this adventure with a plus if you would like to find yourself in a similar situation, and with a minus if you wouldn't. Give extra pluses or minuses if you have strong feelings either way.

HER ANSWER	HIS ANSWER

Do you have a hobby or sport that you enjoy doing with friends? Does your beloved? Brainstorm some ideas for celebrating this interest.

HER ANSWER	HIS ANSWER

or record your answers in your private notebook.

Do you have access to a special place you could share with others?

HER ANSWER	HIS ANSWER

or record your answers in your private notebook.

Bringing Italy Home
Tony and Maria's Romantic Adventure

Maria had three passions: Italy, reading, and cooking. For her birthday, Tony gave her *Under the Tuscan Sun: At Home in Italy* by Frances Mayes. Tony's manner of presenting the book impressed her as much as the gift itself.

Tony promised Maria a whole day of reading in her bedroom. He would cook all her meals and do the dishes. *I could get used to this*, Maria thought as he brought a tray of toast, strawberries and coffee to her bed.

While Maria read, Tony transformed their house into an Italian villa. Posters of the Tuscan countryside covered their walls. Italian music filled the air. A bouquet of calla lilies and lavender sat on the dining room table. A dozen candles in Chianti bottles were placed around the living room and dining room.

Tony went to work in the kitchen, using recipes from *Under the Tuscan Sun*. For lunch he made crostini, little rounds of bread topped with olives, peppers and mushrooms. Tony joined her for a picnic lunch on the bedroom floor. They enjoyed a romantic interlude, feeding each other and fantasizing about a trip to Italy.

Early in the evening when the aromas coming from the kitchen were making Maria's mouth water, Tony came to the bedroom and asked her to dress for dinner.

Tony had invited three other couples for an Italian dinner party. He printed individual menus and placed one at each place setting.

Maria's Birthday Menu

ANTIPASTI
Bruschette with Grilled Eggplant

SECONDI
Honey-Glazed Pork Tenderloin with Fennel

CONTORNI
Garlic Flan
Warm Portobello Salad with
Roasted Red and Yellow Peppers

DOLCI
Lemon Cake

Maria's friends had been advised of the Italian theme. They gave her gifts having to do with Italy: *Cinema Paradiso* on DVD, a Venetian feather mask, and a pair of Italian drinking glasses. Without a doubt, her favorite gift was the book and the time to read it in her makeshift Italian villa.

> *Every gift which is given, even though it may be small, is in reality great, if it is given with affection.*
>
> PINDAR

Tony gave Maria a full day to indulge in two of her three passions. As much as she liked to cook, she was just as happy to enjoy the fruits of his labors rather than indulge the third.

Rate this adventure with a plus if you would like to find yourself in a similar situation, and with a minus if you wouldn't. Give extra pluses or minuses if you have strong feelings either way.

HER ANSWER	HIS ANSWER

Does your beloved like to read? Can you think of a day you could plan for him or her around a book?

HER ANSWER	HIS ANSWER

or record your answers in your private notebook.

Deep Pockets
Sam and Eva's Romantic Adventure

Eva and Sam were strolling through some shops in an upscale shopping district. It was summer and neither of them intended to look at leather coats. There was a sale tag on a beautiful full-length leather coat with a fox fur collar. The textures of the soft buttery leather and the furry collar invited their touch. The sales woman encouraged Eva to try on the coat, but she hesitated since she wasn't even sure she liked the idea of wearing fur, even on the collar. Eva had never faced this ethical dilemma since not only were fur coats out of her price range, they didn't fit with her lifestyle, either. In spite of that, she was seduced by the luxury and comfort of the coat, and thirty minutes later they walked out of the store with Eva's Christmas present. She was actually looking forward to cold weather and fancy dress occasions.

Even though the coat was on sale, it still cost more than their typical Christmas budget for each other. Eva and Sam agreed that this would be her only present. Sam gift-wrapped the coat so that she would have a Christmas present to open.

On Christmas morning, they watched the kids open their gifts. Sam opened his, and then it was Eva's turn. She was looking forward to having the coat, but the anticipation was different since she knew what was in the box. The kids oohed and aahed as she tried it on. When she slipped her hand deep into the pockets, she felt an envelope. Sam had purchased *Phantom of the Opera* tickets so that Eva would have some place special to wear her new coat on Valentine's Day.

Rate this adventure with a plus if you would like to find yourself in a similar situation, and with a minus if you wouldn't. Give extra pluses or minuses if you have strong feelings either way.

HER ANSWER	HIS ANSWER

Are there items you would not want to receive as a gift due to personal beliefs? Make sure your beloved understands these beliefs.

HER ANSWER	HIS ANSWER

Think of a nice gift you gave your beloved in the last couple of years. How could you have presented the gift differently to have more of an adventure? This isn't to diminish any past gift giving. Use this as an opportunity to brainstorm with your beloved and to talk about likes and dislikes.

HER ANSWER	HIS ANSWER

or record your answers in your private notebook.

The Stress of Giving and Receiving

As wonderful and loving as gift giving is, it can also be stressful, for both the giver and the receiver. British author Pamela Glenconner said, "Giving presents is a talent; to know what a person wants, to know when and how to get it, to give it lovingly and well. Unless a character possesses this talent there is no moment more annihilating to ease than that in which a present is received and given."

Gift giving is not one of Carol's natural talents. She is a testament to "ease annihilated" by gift giving. As a child, she received few gifts. Gifts that she gave were criticized or ignored. She never learned how to accept a gift graciously. She dreaded selecting gifts for her husband.

Carol's main reason for enrolling in *The Art of Romance and Fun* was to deal with her phobia of giving and receiving gifts. I told her about one of the exercises we would do as part of the workshop, when she would practice giving and receiving an inexpensive gift in a low-risk environment. I could see the anxiety in her eyes when I explained this exercise to her, but she was willing to give it a try. The "Gift Giving Exercise" is covered in detail on page 181.

> *A gift consists not in what is done or given, but in the intention of the giver or doer.*
> SENECA

This exercise is always one of the class favorites, even among people who don't like to shop or aren't comfortable giving or receiving gifts. After the workshop Carol said, "The gift buying was fun with the helpful 'list.' Having the other person open the gift was the hard part."

In *The Five Love Languages,* Gary Chapman lists receiving gifts as one of the five ways people express love. He says, "If receiving gifts is his/her primary love language, almost anything you give will be received as an expression of love. (If she has been critical of your gifts in the past and almost nothing you have given has been acceptable, then receiving gifts is almost certainly not her primary love language.)"

Receiving gifts is not now and will never be Carol's primary love language, but she wanted to at least learn some of the basics of this expression of love so foreign to her. She wanted to approach Christmas and birthdays without dread. She wanted to raise her children without a stigma attached to gift giving and receiving. She wanted to receive and appreciate the love offered by her husband's gifts.

If you are not a natural gift giver, this isn't necessarily a character flaw and is only a problem if your beloved values gifts as an expression of love. For the vast majority of couples I have worked with, gift giving is usually important, even if it's not

> *Giving is the highest expression of potency. In the very act of giving, I experience my strength, my wealth, my power...I experience myself as overflowing, spending, alive, hence as joyous.*
>
> ERICH FROMM

necessarily the primary love language. This means that unless you both have expressed a sincere dislike for gift giving and receiving, it's probably a good idea to express your love with a gift occasionally.

No matter how you feel about gift giving, I recommend this exercise. If you love gift giving, this is a way to make it even more fun. This exercise was inspired by a couple who enjoyed gift giving, but didn't have time to do so before the start of their adventure. I promised them a shopping experience as part of their adventure. This activity turned out to be one of their favorite things during their four-day adventure. If you hate gift giving, this exercise helps you take a few baby steps in easing the discomfort associated with giving and receiving.

Moe Dullard Goes Shopping

I can see how Moe might have some anxiety about buying a gift for Bea if she returns every one. On the other hand, Moe doesn't seem like the type to put much effort into selecting the right gift.

A Moment with the Dullards

"It doesn't matter what size or color it is. She'll return it anyhow."

If your gifts are as uninspired as Moe's or your tastes are as finicky as Bea's, let's hope your primary love language isn't receiving gifts. That would surely raise the stress level of gift giving.

There's a lesson to be learned from Bea and Moe, and the lesson is doing whatever it takes not to be like them. If you have some Bea-like tendencies, next time you get a gift that you wouldn't have selected yourself, unless it doesn't fit or it's defective, don't return it. Imagine what the giver saw in the gift that spoke of you. I've received a few gifts I would have passed over in a store. I try to see myself reflected in that object. Even if I only wear it, display it, or use it a few times, I think of the giver whenever I see it. If you exchange it for something else, chances are it won't remind you of the giver.

If your gift-giving style is dangerously close to Moe's, remember that a gift is a heartfelt symbol of love and affection. It doesn't have to be expensive, but it does need to be thoughtful. The gift should reflect the receiver's interests, personality, and style.

Gift Giving
An Exercise

Fill out the following checklist of shopping hints about the gift you want to receive. There are two lists, one for you and one for your beloved.

The checklist has three columns for hints about physical characteristics, emotional characteristics, and store type, respectively. The first column describes what physical characteristics the gift should have, such as soft, a favorite color, or high tech. The middle column specifies emotions the gift may evoke: humorous, practical, or sentimental. The last column indicates where to shop. Specifying a jewelry store, bookstore, or golf pro shop could be the most helpful hint of all.

Next you must agree on how much to spend. In my workshops this is easy because I set the limits: the spending limit is $10 and the shopping time limit is 30 to 40 minutes.

Putting those kinds of constraints in place takes off some of the pressure of finding the "perfect" gift. These constraints don't give you the luxury of finding a "perfect" gift, just one that is suitable. Your expectations of the gift you will receive or give will be tempered by the constraints.

Decide how much money to spend. If this is your primary gift for an anniversary or Christmas, you might want to use your normal gift budget. I can assure you, however, this exercise can be just as much fun on a limited budget. It encourages you to be more creative.

Another decision to make is whether you shop at the same time in different stores as part of an adventure, or in preparation for an upcoming adventure. It could be fun to make the gift giving exercise part of a romantic getaway weekend. Go to a shopping district, set off in different directions to find a gift, then reconvene at a specified time.

If you would prefer to use these lists as preparation for an upcoming adventure, how long you shop is less important than when you'll exchange gifts. Perhaps you have an anniversary coming up in two weeks. Fill out the checklists, exchange them with your beloved, and shop at your leisure. If you don't like shopping, you could ask a friend to come along with you.

Each gift must be wrapped and given with a card containing a hand-written note. It's easy for some people to write personal notes to their beloved, but for others it's a stretch to come up with more than a few words in addition to their names. Include a minimum of four or five sentences. You can write whatever you want – your feelings for your beloved or what it was like to do this exercise. If you need some suggestions for your note, here are some ideas other couples have used:

💗 **My initial reaction when I first saw your word choices:**

"I was surprised that you picked mechanical" or "I was uncertain when you said 'my favorite color' as to whether I should look for blue or green."

💗 **What I was looking for:**

"The word that I thought was most unusual for you was mystical so I wanted to honor that request" or "I love the adventurous part of you so I started looking for a travel guide for Costa Rica."

💗 **What I found and how I knew it was the right gift:**

"I saw a book in a used book store by your favorite author, so I decided to go with 'contains text' instead."

💗 **How I imagined you using this gift:**

"I hope these earrings look good with your black dress."

💗 **Anything else that strikes your fancy:**

"At first, forty minutes didn't seem like enough time to find a gift for you. I found this candle in about ten minutes and I knew you would love it. After that, the time seemed to drag. I was looking forward to seeing you, holding you, kissing you. I had time to think about what you mean to me and how much I love you. I admire your kindness and your sense of humor. Life with you is so much fun."

The final step in the Gift Giving Exercise is to exchange gifts. You can give them right away or wait a few hours to build a little anticipation. When you do give your gift, consider reading your card to your beloved aloud. I find that sometimes in my excitement of getting a gift, I rush through the words on the cards without intending to and without letting the message sink in.

A few years ago Jim and I started reading aloud our cards to each other. When I hear Jim say the words he has written to me, the message is received in a whole different way. His words enter through my ears, bypass my mind, and go directly to my heart.

Gift Giving Exercise for Her

NAME _____   SPENDING LIMIT _____

START TIME _____   STOP TIME _____

WHEN TO EXCHANGE GIFTS _____

S H O P P I N G   H I N T S

Physical characteristics	Emotional characteristics	Store type (optional)
☐ Beautiful	☐ Admiration	☐ Antique shop
☐ Contains text	☐ Adventurous	☐ Art store
☐ Delicious	☐ Athletic	☐ Book store
☐ Flat	☐ Bewildered	☐ Clothing store
☐ Fuzzy	☐ Challenged	☐ Computer store
☐ Hard	☐ Frivolous	☐ Department store
☐ High tech	☐ Happy	☐ Florist
☐ Irregular shape	☐ Humorous	☐ Gift shop
☐ Mechanical	☐ Joyful	☐ Grocery store
☐ My favorite color	☐ Love	☐ Hardware store
☐ Mystical	☐ Mischievous	☐ Jewelry store
☐ Natural	☐ Playful	☐ Kitchen store
☐ Old	☐ Practical	☐ Liquor store
☐ Rough	☐ Relaxed	☐ Music store
☐ Round	☐ Satisfied	☐ Novelty store
☐ Sensuous	☐ Sentimental	☐ Office supply store
☐ Shiny	☐ Spiritual	☐ Restaurant
☐ Soft	☐ Shocked	☐ Shoe store
☐ Solid	☐ Thankful	☐ Specialty store
☐ Symbolic	☐ Unexpected	☐ Sporting goods store
☐ Unique	☐ Useful	☐ Toy store
☐ Other (specify)	☐ Other (specify)	☐ Other (specify)

Gift Giving Exercise for Him

NAME _____   SPENDING LIMIT _____

START TIME _____   STOP TIME _____

WHEN TO EXCHANGE GIFTS _____

S H O P P I N G   H I N T S

Physical characteristics	Emotional characteristics	Store type (optional)
☐ Beautiful	☐ Admiration	☐ Antique shop
☐ Contains text	☐ Adventurous	☐ Art store
☐ Delicious	☐ Athletic	☐ Book store
☐ Flat	☐ Bewildered	☐ Clothing store
☐ Fuzzy	☐ Challenged	☐ Computer store
☐ Hard	☐ Frivolous	☐ Department store
☐ High tech	☐ Happy	☐ Florist
☐ Irregular shape	☐ Humorous	☐ Gift shop
☐ Mechanical	☐ Joyful	☐ Grocery store
☐ My favorite color	☐ Love	☐ Hardware store
☐ Mystical	☐ Mischievous	☐ Jewelry store
☐ Natural	☐ Playful	☐ Kitchen store
☐ Old	☐ Practical	☐ Liquor store
☐ Rough	☐ Relaxed	☐ Music store
☐ Round	☐ Satisfied	☐ Novelty store
☐ Sensuous	☐ Sentimental	☐ Office supply store
☐ Shiny	☐ Spiritual	☐ Restaurant
☐ Soft	☐ Shocked	☐ Shoe store
☐ Solid	☐ Thankful	☐ Specialty store
☐ Symbolic	☐ Unexpected	☐ Sporting goods store
☐ Unique	☐ Useful	☐ Toy store
☐ Other (specify)	☐ Other (specify)	☐ Other (specify)

Sparks that Ignite the Romantic Flame

♡ Give gifts that are heartfelt symbols of love and affection.

♡ Make an adventure of the presentation. The memories may last longer than the gift itself.

♡ Make the occasion memorable for everyone involved, not just the recipient, with the activities surrounding the gift's presentation. This works especially well for sporting goods.

♡ Save and sacrifice if necessary to give a special gift. This makes the gift even more precious.

♡ Don't think the gift needs to be expensive to be worthy of an adventurous presentation.

♡ Let a unique presentation be the surprise when giving a gift that's expected.

♡ Write a personal note about the gift you're giving. Read it aloud to your beloved.

HABIT EIGHT

Prolong Special Occasions

Really special events deserve more than just a daylong celebration. After all, how many times do you get married, turn fifty, or retire? You can even turn an ordinary birthday or anniversary into an extended adventure, as long as the planning doesn't wear you out or set up unrealistic expectations for the big events yet to come.

If you do plan a multi-day celebration, be sure that you don't promise more than you can deliver, and what you do promise gets delivered on a timely basis.

I once helped a woman plan a special birthday for her ten-year-old son. She promised him ten special gifts or activities during the month of his tenth birthday. She gave him eight great gifts, and then ran out of steam. When I saw him six months later I asked him how his birthday was. He said it was fun, but his mom still owed him two gifts. Most children and some adults will remember broken promises more than the gifts received.

Tying a long celebration together with a theme can be a fun way to generate some creative ideas. This chapter offers several suggestions for themes that will make special occasions more memorable.

Top Ten Reasons

Randy and Loretta's Romantic Adventure

To set the tone for this story, think David Letterman's Top Ten Lists, written with romance in mind.

When my dear friend Randy married his true love, I offered to help make their honeymoon extra special. I asked Randy to list the things he loved most about Loretta. Randy is a romantic at heart and had no trouble coming up with a long list. His challenge was to narrow it down to his top ten. Next, he thought of a token gift or activity that symbolized that quality he loved about her. My role was to create ten greeting cards to accompany the ten gifts Randy would give to Loretta starting on the eve of the wedding and ending on the last day of their honeymoon.

The chart on the next page should give you an idea of how the cards worked. The text on the front was the same for every card, "Randy's Top Ten Reasons for Marrying Loretta," but the graphics on the card front and the message inside varied to give hints about what was to come. Since the cards weren't numbered in a countdown fashion, he had flexibility in deciding when to give which card.

For example, Randy was sure Loretta would want to shop at some time during their trip. On the day they decided to browse in some art galleries, he gave her a card with an art museum on the front and a message on the inside that said "She has good taste in art." He suggested they choose a painting as a honeymoon souvenir. Each day he gave her a card, always at a different time to keep her guessing. He enjoyed surprising her as much as she looked forward to finding out what clever things he had planned.

The gifts or activities do not need to be expensive; in this case it truly was the thought that counted. Randy's reasons and gifts are listed on the next page.

Randy's Top Ten Reasons For Marrying Loretta

MESSAGE INSIDE CARD	WHEN GIVEN	PRESENTATION/GIFT
She is his partner to share adventures	Day before the wedding	Travel book about honeymoon destination
Her warm and ready smile and melodic laugh fill him with joy	Wedding day	CD of Spanish music to honor her Hispanic heritage
She believes in magic	Any time they feel like playing a game	*An Enchanted Evening*, a romantic board game
She is open to the possibilities of life	On a warm starry night	Lie on a blanket and look at the stars
She loves her family and friends	Any day	Photo albums & note cards
She deserves to be spoiled with breakfast in bed	Any morning	Serve breakfast on tray with flowers in bud vase
She cries in romantic movies	When they feel like watching a movie	*Top Gun* video or DVD, her favorite movie
She has good taste in art	When she wants to shop	Choose a painting together as a memento of honeymoon
She enjoys romantic dinners for two	Any day; give cookbook mid day and cook dinner together that evening	The gift is *InterCourses: An Aphrodisiac Cookbook*. Choose menu, shop as necessary and cook together. Set table with candles and flowers.
Randy loves Loretta	On the way home	His love

I liked this idea so much I suggested it to other clients as well. When Shelley and Dave celebrated their tenth anniversary, she came up with her own top ten list of clever reasons and corresponding gifts. Because Dave was a good dad, she gave him a family portrait of the kids; because he is nurturing, she gave him a massage; because he always has time for her, she gave him a watch.

> *The very essence of the creative is its novelty, and hence we have no standard by which to judge it.*
> CARL ROGERS

Rate this adventure with a plus if you would like to find yourself in a similar situation, and with a minus if you wouldn't. Give extra pluses or minuses if you have strong feelings either way.

HER ANSWER	HIS ANSWER

Top Ten Reasons
An Exercise

Make a list of the ten things you love about your sweetheart. Think of an inexpensive gift or activity to celebrate each of those qualities. Separate his and hers lists are provided; however, if you don't want to share your list with your beloved at this time, record your list in a separate notebook.

Her Top Ten Reasons for Loving Him

What You Love	How to Celebrate
1.	
2.	
3.	
4.	
5.	
6.	
7.	
8.	
9.	
10.	

or record your answers in your private notebook.

His Top Ten Reasons for Loving Her

What You Love	How to Celebrate
1.	
2.	
3.	
4.	
5.	
6.	
7.	
8.	
9.	
10.	

or record your answers in your private notebook.

An Adventure in Leather
Lydia and Bill's Romantic Adventure

This list of traditional and modern anniversary gifts has inspired many anniversary celebrations. For Bill and Lydia it inspired an adventure.

Bill and Lydia had celebrated their first two anniversaries with gifts inspired by the traditional anniversary suggestions. On their first, or paper, anniversary, Bill gave Lydia a framed watercolor painting and she gave him a book. For the second, or cotton, anniversary, they gave each other clothes.

Bill liked the idea of staying within the traditional guidelines, but he wanted to be more creative on their third anniversary, which was leather. He used a brainstorming technique to visually arrange his ideas. His mind map of possible leather gifts looked like this:

Year	Traditional	Modern
1	Paper	Plastics, clocks
2	Cotton	Cotton, china
3	Leather	Crystal, glass
4	Flowers	Linen, silk, nylon, appliances
5	Wood	Silverware
6	Candy, iron	Wood
7	Copper, wool	Brass, desk sets
8	Bronze	Linen, appliances
9	Pottery	Leather
10	Tin	Diamond
11	Steel	Jewelry
12	Silk, linen	Pearl
13	Lace	Textiles, fur
14	Ivory	Gold
15	Crystal	Glass, watches
20	China	Platinum
25	Silver	Silver
30	Pearl	Pearl
35	Coral	Jade
40	Ruby	Garnet
45	Sapphire	Sapphire
50	Gold	Gold
55	Emerald	Turquoise
60	Diamond	Gold

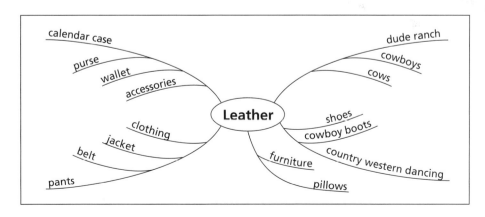

Since it was their third anniversary, he wanted to give her three gifts. Rather than just handing her three packages, he wanted to plan some fun around each gift. For her first gift, he decided to book a room for the weekend at a dude ranch in the mountains. On their first afternoon, they went on a horseback ride that ended with a chuck wagon dinner.

Lydia's second gift was a pair of leather cowboy boots. The next evening they went to a barn dance. Dancing was something they both enjoyed, but dancing in new cowboy boots for more than a couple of hours proved to be a challenge. This was not a bad thing; leaving the dance early simply left more time for romance back in their room.

The third gift was a new leather binder for Lydia's Day Timer. Bill had taken the liberty of penciling in a few dates in her calendar.

Since they had agreed to the theme, Lydia also bought Bill leather gifts. Using two different colors of scrap leather from a local leather shop, she glued squares to a board to make a new chessboard. She also gave him an African drum and signed him up for drumming lessons, something in which he had expressed an interest.

What impressed Bill was that Lydia came up with leather gifts he never even considered, even with his brainstorming session. They are now both working on clever floral gifts for their fourth anniversary.

Rate this adventure with a plus if you would like to find yourself in a similar situation, and with a minus if you wouldn't. Give extra pluses or minuses if you have strong feelings either way.

HER ANSWER	HIS ANSWER

Traditional or Modern Anniversary Gifts
An Exercise

Here's your chance to brainstorm some ideas about incorporating traditional or modern anniversary gifts into your own celebrations. A good way to develop this brainstorming technique is to use a past anniversary. This doesn't suggest there was anything wrong with past celebrations; use this only as a way to be creative in the future.

If you and your beloved are doing these exercises together and either of you has a low tolerance for surprises (Type 1), use this exercise to plan your next anniversary together.

In any case, determine which anniversary you will use for this exercise and record it here. Make a note of the traditional and modern gifts for that year.

Anniversary	Traditional Gift	Modern Gift

Now write down everything you know about the gift suggestion for that anniversary. Brainstorm gift ideas. One way to get really creative is to laughingly go to extremes, and then find reasonable possibilities in the absurd answers. In the early years it could be fun to give one gift for each year of marriage like Lydia and Bill did, but as the years progress that may not be practical, reasonable or necessary. Pick out a few of your favorite ideas and tie them all together in an adventure.

HER ANSWER	HIS ANSWER

or record your answers in your private notebook.

Twelve Days of Fifty
Our Romantic Adventure

On my husband Jim's fiftieth birthday, I went all out. I planned a twelve-day celebration for him based on the *Twelve Days of Christmas*.

I made twelve cards. The front of each card said, "On the (nth) Day of Fifty My True Love Gave to Me." The verses on the inside of the cards and what went with them are listed below.

> *Creativity requires the freedom to consider "unthinkable" alternatives, to doubt the worth of cherished practices.*
> JOHN W. GARDNER

About half way through the twelve days, Jim said, "I feel so loved. I don't think anyone has ever had a birthday like this."

On the (nth) Day of Fifty
My True Love Gave to Me

WORDS TO THE SONG	WORDS INSIDE CARD	GIFT OR ACTIVITY
A partridge in a pear tree	A taste of luxury	The mayor (who worked in the same building as Jim) escorted him to a limousine, which took him to a five-star hotel for a spa treatment. I met him there for dinner.
Two turtle doves	Two bare breasts	Details not necessary. You get the picture.
Three French hens	Three French kisses	I gave him three kisses, mostly as a diversion. The real event that day was a surprise party with his family and friends.
Four calling birds	Four calling birds	Jim is a bird watcher. I gave him four CDs with birdcalls and music.

On the (nth) Day of Fifty My True Love Gave to Me (continued)

WORDS TO THE SONG	WORDS INSIDE CARD	GIFT OR ACTIVITY
Five golden rings	Five golden things	Jim was out of town on business. Room service delivered five micro brew beers to his room in a Styrofoam cooler so that he could enjoy them later at his leisure.
Six geese a laying	Six geezers playing	Four friends joined Jim and me for a night of board games and cards.
Seven swans a swimming	Seven Swanson dinners	I bought seven Swanson TV dinners, took out the food and added small gifts, like a chocolate bar, biking gloves, and silk boxer shorts.
Eight maids a milking	Eight maids a milking	Seven friends and I dressed up like French maids, drank milk to get the mustaches, and posed for silly pictures. I gave the pictures to Jim in an album, wrapped up in one of the frilly aprons.
Nine ladies dancing	Nine ladies dancing	Tickets to performance of *Beauty and the Beast.*
Ten lords a leaping	Ten lords a leaping	Videotape of Michael Flatly's *Lord of the Dance.*
Eleven pipers piping	Eleven lattes piping	A card entitling Jim to eleven lattes at a local coffee shop. This was one of his favorites since it lasted so long.
Twelve drummers drumming	Twelve drummers drumming	Mickey Hart's CD *Planet Drum.* Jim got a bonus here since there were thirteen songs on that CD.

Rate this adventure with a plus if you would like to find yourself in a similar situation, and with a minus if you wouldn't. Give extra pluses or minuses if you have strong feelings either way.

HER ANSWER	HIS ANSWER

Twelve Days of Anything
An Exercise

Come up with your own play on words to the *Twelve Days of Christmas*. You could celebrate the twelve days of fifty, the twelve days of marriage, or the twelve days of vacation. Be creative. Pick any twelve-day period, then have fun figuring out how to celebrate it.

Love is that condition in which the happiness of another person is essential to your own.
ROBERT A. HEINLEIN

What activities would you suggest to celebrate each day? What gifts would you give? It's not necessary to give a dozen extravagant gifts or plan as many lengthy activities. Find twelve thoughtful tokens or playful pastimes that fit the theme.

Separate his and hers lists are provided; however, if you don't want to share your list with your beloved at this time, record your list on a separate piece of paper.

CELEBRATING HIM:
On the (nth) Day of Anything My True Love Gave to Me

WORDS TO THE SONG	YOUR OWN WORDS	GIFT OR ACTIVITY
A partridge in a pear tree		
Two turtle doves		
Three French hens		
Four calling birds		
Five golden rings		
Six geese a laying		
Seven swans a swimming		
Eight maids a milking		
Nine ladies dancing		
Ten lords a leaping		
Eleven pipers piping		
Twelve drummers drumming		

or record your answers in your private notebook.

CELEBRATING HER:
On the (nth) Day of Anything My True Love Gave to Me

WORDS TO THE SONG	YOUR OWN WORDS	GIFT OR ACTIVITY
A partridge in a pear tree		
Two turtle doves		
Three French hens		
Four calling birds		
Five golden rings		
Six geese a laying		
Seven swans a swimming		
Eight maids a milking		
Nine ladies dancing		
Ten lords a leaping		
Eleven pipers piping		
Twelve drummers drumming		

or record your answers in your private notebook.

A Foreign Affair

Donna and Rich's Romantic Adventure

Donna went to Greece on business, leaving her husband Rich at home to care for their young children. In her free time, she managed to take in some of the cultural sites. She found herself missing Rich terribly, especially when confronted with erotic Greek images in gift shops and museums. She bought some playing cards of Ancient Greek Lovers and a set of coasters with more sexy drawings. These gifts sparked the idea for an evening she began to plan for Rich. On her last day she found a decorative box and a bottle of ouzo for him, and a Greek cookbook and music CD for herself, all part of the master plan.

On her way home, Donna reflected on her life with Rich. They loved to travel, but with kids, jobs and a limited budget, they didn't get to travel as much as they liked. She decided to plan mini-vacations for Rich at home.

A short time later, she began to turn her fantasy into reality. In the decorative box, she put the names of three countries — Greece, Mexico, and Russia — on small pieces of paper. She prepared three separate packets to go with each country. In the Greek package, she put the playing cards, the coasters, and some postcards she had picked up of her favorite Greek attractions. For Russia, she gathered a bottle of vodka, some scrub oak branches and pictures out of a National Geographic of the Russian countryside. The box for Mexico had a seashell and two DVDs, *Like Water for Chocolate* and *Y Tu Mama Tambien*.

That night Donna told Rich she wanted to spend some time with him after they got the kids in bed. This got Rich's attention since he didn't know whether he was in trouble or in for a good time. After the kids were settled, Donna poured each of them a small glass of ouzo. Rich thought this was probably a good sign, but he still couldn't be sure. Donna handed him a gift-wrapped box. Rich tore off the paper to find the decorative Greek box, with the names of three countries inside.

Donna said, "I know I've already told you how much I appreciated your support while I was in Greece. I'd love to go back with you sometime, but I know that won't happen for a while. We can still have some exciting foreign adventures, right here at home. I've prepared some mini-adventures where we can experience foreign cultures for a night. All you need to do is draw a country. I'll take care of everything else, including getting a babysitter for the evening. Our first trip is scheduled for Saturday night. Where are we going?"

Rich was intrigued when he randomly picked "Russia" out of the box. Donna went to the closet where the other packets were hidden and returned with the one marked "Russia." She let Rich open the box and enjoyed the perplexed look on his face when he saw the scrub oak branches.

"Are you going to tell me what these are for?" he asked.

"Nope, you get to wonder."

On Saturday she told him to pack for an overnight trip. They dropped the kids at her sister's house, and she drove him to a Russian banya. Rich had no idea what to expect, but he was ready for anything.

The literal translation for banya is a bathhouse, but a banya session includes so much more. At this spa, the session started with a soak in their private hot tub, followed by massages. The next stop was the sauna, where water was poured on the rocks to raise the heat and humidity. This was where the scrub oak leaves came in. The banya assistant soaked bundles of dried scrub oak leaves in water, and then used them to beat the backs of the trusting folks under his care. This really isn't a violent act. It actually feels good, and it's said to rid the body of toxins. Next, honey was spread on their bodies, which they expected to be very sticky. They were sweating so much at this point it slid right off. Just when the heat became almost unbearable, the banya assistant brought in a bucket of cool water and poured it over them. In Russia, a banya session ends with a plunge into icy cold waters. At this banya, the cold-water plunge had been replaced with a lukewarm shower.

> *A man travels the world over in search of what he needs, and returns home to find it.*
> GEORGE MOORE

"When I saw those oak leaves you put in the box, I never imagined that I would be beaten with them," Rich said.

"I never imagined I would enjoy being beaten as much as I did," Donna laughed.

Donna took Rich out to a Russian dinner, and they enjoyed a night in a downtown hotel.

Over the next three months, Rich drew each of the other countries. For Mexican adventure, Donna made a feast of fajitas and margaritas. They stayed home (without the kids) and watched two very sexy Mexican movies.

For the Greek tour, Donna used her Greek cookbook to make a delicious dinner. When she served the ouzo on the coasters with the sexy drawings, Rich knew he was in for a special evening. After dinner, Donna gave him the playing cards. They started a game of strip poker, but soon lost interest in declaring a winner or loser. They were both winners that evening.

Rate this adventure with a plus if you would like to find yourself in a similar situation, and with a minus if you wouldn't. Give extra pluses or minuses if you have strong feelings either way.

HER ANSWER	HIS ANSWER

What countries would you like to visit? How can you celebrate those countries and cultures on your home turf?

HER ANSWER	HIS ANSWER

or record your answers in your private notebook.

Long Distance Love

When you can't be with the one you love, love him or her anyhow. Being separated from your beloved due to business travel or military deployment is not

Only in the agony of parting do we look into the depths of love.
GEORGE ELIOT

uncommon. It's possible to maintain emotional closeness in spite of the physical distance.

If you're the one who's going, leave behind tokens of your love. Make some easy to find; make others more difficult by requiring

direct hints via a telephone call or email. You might even consider a treasure hunt with clues planted all over the house. If you'll be gone a long time, hide notes or small gifts in places that your beloved will be sure to look at a certain time of the day, month or year. Here are ideas for hiding places and surprises to put in them:

- In a cereal box, include an "I love you" card to get the day off to a great start.

- In the entertainment center, include a CD of love songs or a romantic comedy on DVD reminiscent of a time you shared.

- In the place you keep monthly bills to be paid, include a crisp $20 bill for a frivolous treat for your beloved.

- In the box of Christmas decorations, hide a new ornament that represents something special from the past year.

- In the pocket of a winter coat, place a new pair of gloves with a note promising to provide a better hand warmer when you're together.

- Under the snow shovel, store a beautifully gift-wrapped heating pad.

- Next to an alarm clock hidden in a drawer or closet set to go off when your beloved will be around, hide some warm socks.

- With the gardening tools, stow some seed packages with a message about tending to your love and watching it grow.

One time Jim left for work while I was packing to leave for a business trip. At the last minute, I decided to leave him a reminder of me. After carefully making the bed, I turned back the sheets on my side. I made a head on my pillow out of a hat, sunglasses and gaudy earrings. To represent my torso, I placed a teddy inside of an unbuttoned, long-sleeved blouse. A pair of lace panty hose flowing from the bottom of the teddy, crossed at the knees, completed the image. One of the arms was stretched out to the nightstand, next to an empty wine glass and a bottle of wine. At the end of the other arm was a book of women's erotica and poetry. I'll let you guess what my homecoming was like.

If you're the one staying home, let your beloved find a few unexpected surprises during the journey. Consider these possibilities:

♡ Have a single red rose delivered to the hotel room (easier in an American hotel than a war zone).

♡ Hide some notes or small gifts in the suitcase.

♡ Give your beloved's traveling companion some surprises to present to your beloved somewhere along the way.

♡ Take pictures of things that happen while your beloved is gone, even the small things. Send them via email or in cards.

♡ Send along a "survival pack," a large envelope filled with love notes, promises of treats to be given upon his or her return, and blank postcards with appropriate postage. Instructions on the outside of the pack would say, "Select one at random whenever you need a boost."

♡ If your traveler's gone too long to save the entire newspaper, clip interesting news items, amusing comics, stories about favorite sports teams, and crossword puzzles. If it's an extended trip, mail them once a week. Otherwise, present them upon his or her return, along with a nice block of free time to enjoy them.

I was raised in a military family that endured two yearlong isolated tours. My mom still talks about the time my dad returned home from Turkey. My seven-year-old sister Connie was captivated by the love and affection between our parents. She left notes around the house that said, "Kiss again," "Kiss on the lips," or "Kiss in my room." They were happy to oblige.

Fifty-eight Days Without Him
Our Romantic Adventure

My husband Jim was able to take an early retirement. Before he retired, he used to dream about the things he would do when he could walk away from the stress of corporate life forever. He would plan with his friend and co-worker, Bruce, about the days and weeks they could spend on the beaches and golf courses of Mexico. Jim and Bruce retired the same year. Since I was working, I could only wish them luck as they prepared for their two-month adventure.

Some of my friends kidded me about Jim's vacation. "Don't let my husband know about this. I wouldn't want him to get any ideas," one of them said. Another joked, "I'd tell my husband he could go, but not to bother coming home."

While I felt Jim truly deserved this time to decompress in the Mexican sun after thirty-three years with his company, I couldn't imagine being without him for two months. We'd never been apart for more than a couple of weeks at a time, usually due to business travel, rarely for separate vacations. The dread of being alone was equal to the fear that he wouldn't miss me as much as I would miss him.

> *Absence lessens the minor passions and increases great ones, as the wind douses a candle and kindles a fire.*
> FRANÇOIS DUC DE LA ROCHEFOUCAULD

I was determined that Jim would be reminded every day how much I love him. I recruited Bruce as my messenger. The day before Jim and Bruce were due to leave, I delivered a box to Bruce filled with cards and presents.

They were due to be gone fifty-eight days. I bought fifty-eight cards and a dozen or so little gifts to be given at various times. I numbered each card, and wrapped and labeled each present. The labels on the presents indicated when they should be given: golf balls for the first game of golf, instant hand sanitizers for when they get to Mexico, a bag of pistachios to go with some cold Mexican beers, and sunscreen for the sunny days.

Jim called home most days. Once he told me the name of the beach town where he was staying. As soon as we ended our call, I went to the atlas to find the town. When I opened the atlas to the map of Mexico, I was surprised to find a card with my name on it. Jim had written, "Look behind your favorite Saturday morning lovemaking music." In back of the John Klemmer CDs in the music case I found a small package containing a pair of earrings. I was delighted that he had found his own way of reminding me of his love while he was gone.

Jim and Bruce enjoyed their trip. Jim endured a large share of Bruce's good-natured teasing, but Bruce benefited from the treasures almost as much as Jim did. Jim let Bruce read the funny cards, and shared most of the gifts with him. Most importantly, Jim came home knowing that he was loved.

If you found yourself facing a similar situation, how would you rate this solution? Give it a plus if you liked it, and a minus if you didn't. Give extra pluses or minuses if you have strong feelings either way.

HER ANSWER	HIS ANSWER

or record your answers in your private notebook.

How can you let your beloved know how much you love him or her when you're not there?

As you were reading this story, you may have thought of things you could do in a similar situation. Jot down your ideas.

HER ANSWER	HIS ANSWER

or record your answers in your private notebook.

Sparks that Ignite the Romantic Flame

♡ Promise only what you can deliver, and deliver on a timely basis.

♡ Give big events the attention they deserve with a multi-day or multi-faceted celebration.

♡ Consider borrowing from popular culture to find a theme for your adventure. Some suggestions are Top Ten Lists, The Twelve Days of Christmas, and the list of traditional anniversary gifts.

♡ Celebrate with a mixture of inexpensive gifts and activities.

♡ Choose a foreign or regional theme, then celebrate with that area's food, activities, dances, spas, movies or books while staying close to home.

♡ Find ways to express your love even when you are apart.

Practice Your Own Romantic Traditions

I'm always asking people to tell me about their romantic adventures. I've been particularly impressed with encounters that were so much fun they were worth repeating. They became traditions.

That made me think about why we have traditions.

They provide a link to our heritage. They give us a sense of belonging. They connect us to our past, and help us look forward to our future. We mark and celebrate changing seasons as well as the milestones in our lives.

It stands to reason that just as traditions evolve in different nations, regions and families, couples can and should create practices of their own. Isn't it time to create traditions that belong to just you and your beloved?

Think about the good times you've shared, especially the parts that are worth doing again. Repeat what you love, throw out what you don't, and add whatever you want to make your own personal mark. If you follow what's in your heart, your celebrations will evolve as your love grows and flourishes.

Just because it's your tradition, that doesn't mean it has to be conventional. Just because your grandmother served the Christmas turkey before you opened presents, that doesn't mean you can't wear your sexiest lingerie and open your gifts in bed. Make traditions your own.

Holidays, birthdays, and anniversaries are perfect for developing your own romantic practices. When the special day approaches, anticipation builds. Memories come to mind that can set the stage for romance and love.

Thanksgiving Thanks
John and Shannon's Romantic Tradition

My family has a tradition of giving thanks before we serve the Thanksgiving meal. Each person gets a chance to express appreciation and recount his or her blessings. One year my sister, Connie, and her husband, Ross, hosted nearly thirty people at her house. Ross's brother John planned to use this occasion to propose to Shannon. As we gathered in a circle to say a prayer and give thanks, the anticipation was almost palpable since everyone except Shannon knew John's secret.

As the host, Ross started the thanks tradition by expressing his gratitude for his family, their health, and his teenage son's relatively safe driving record. Heart-felt and humorous thanks continued in a clockwise direction. John stood to Ross's right so he would be the last person to give thanks. Shannon held on to John's hand as she talked about their loving and deepening relationship.

When it was John's turn, he said he was thankful for his family and Shannon. He said he loved her and wanted to spend the rest of his life with her. He talked about her kindness, her sense of humor, and her beauty, about how he felt when he was with her. At that point, he got down on one knee, pulled a ring box out of his pocket, and said with a quivering voice, "Shannon, there's only one thing that would make me even more thankful than I am right now. Will you marry me?"

The first sound out of Shannon was a gasp, followed quickly by "Yes!" A round of applause went up along with shouts of congratulations and whistles.

Sharing gratitude is a wonderful Thanksgiving tradition for anyone, but for John and Shannon it will always be a beautiful part of their love story.

Rate this tradition with a plus if you would like to create a similar practice and with a minus if you wouldn't. Give extra pluses or minuses if you have strong feelings either way.

HER ANSWER	HIS ANSWER

Whether you are married or not, how would you feel about proposing or being proposed to in front of a gathering of family and friends?

HER ANSWER	HIS ANSWER

The Rose Bowl
Andrea and Sean's Romantic Tradition

When Andrea and Sean met, they had two weeks to fall in love. They did. Then he left her alone for four months, which has been their pattern ever since.

Sean is in the U.S. Army's 7th Special Forces Group. In the nine years

> *The way to love anything is to realize that it might be lost.*
> G. K. CHESTERTON

they've been together, he's spent seven to eight months a year in places like Panama, Columbia, and Iraq.

While many couples would regard this as a hardship, Andrea chooses to focus on the benefits. She misses her husband when he's gone, which makes the time they're together even sweeter. The breaks in their togetherness help them appreciate each other more, although she admits her life has become more challenging with a four-year-old and an infant.

They consider themselves fortunate since, no matter where in the world Sean has been, he's always had access to the Internet and telephones. When he's deployed, they keep in touch with daily emails and weekly phone calls.

Most of their phone calls start with the same playful banter. "What are you wearing?" he asks in his most suggestive voice.

"I'm naked," she whispers.

"What are you doing?"

"I'm vacuuming – naked," she teases.

The Internet has also enabled their most cherished romantic tradition. Not once in nine years have they celebrated Valentine's Day together. Not once in nine years have they even been in the same state on Valentine's Day, usually not even the same country. Yet, not once in nine years has Sean failed to send roses on Valentine's Day. He says he can always get to a computer to order roses for his beloved.

Andrea has dried every rose he's ever sent. She keeps the buds in three large glass bowls. When I interviewed Andrea, I watched her eyes stop on one of these glass bowls. "Every time I see those roses, I know how much he loves me," she said.

That's a tradition to cherish.

You might expect her primary love language to be receiving gifts. It isn't. It's acts of service. When Sean's at home, Andrea feels most loved when he's making her breakfast in bed, cleaning the kitchen, or freshening the kitty litter. His primary love language is physical touch. She rubs his head every night before he goes to sleep.

> *Love knows not its depth*
> *till the hour of separation.*
> KAHIL GIBRAN

When they're apart, it's impossible to communicate in their primary love languages, so they do the next best thing. He sends roses; she sends cards. They exchange words of affirmation in email and phone calls. They create an environment of love such that each reunion has the heightened emotions of an adventure.

Sean's schedule should keep him home this year, and they are anticipating their first Valentine's Day together. I'm betting this will be one to remember.

Rate this tradition with a plus if you would like to create a similar practice and with a minus if you wouldn't. Give extra pluses or minuses if you have strong feelings either way.

HER ANSWER	HIS ANSWER

It's not always possible or practical to communicate in your primary love language on a frequent basis. Is this true in your situation? If so, what can you do to adapt?

HER ANSWER	HIS ANSWER

A Twenty-Five Year Celebration of Romance
Charlotte and Tom's Romantic Tradition

Several years ago we were invited to a twenty-fifth anniversary party. When the time came to toast the happy couple, Tom and Charlotte used a pair of silver champagne flutes that had been given to them as a wedding present. Tom said that every year on their anniversary, no matter where they were, they toasted each other with these glasses. In the early years of their marriage when they didn't have a lot of money, they took them camping. Through the years these flutes become very well traveled, having been to China, Japan, and several states. The fact that these flutes looked well used made them even more precious.

Not only do Tom and Charlotte celebrate the anniversary of their marriage, they celebrate the anniversary of their engagement and the day they met. Each year on New Year's Day they get up early to celebrate their engagement anniversary with a champagne and omelet breakfast, then they go back to bed. Even when the children were young and would bound out of bed at 6 a.m., Tom and Charlotte would set the alarm and get up very early to honor this tradition.

Tom and Charlotte met on a cold winter's day in Chicago's O'Hare Airport. Their returning flights were delayed due to a snowstorm in Denver. They started talking while holding up the wall in the hallway. After getting off to a rough start – Charlotte claims she is never at her best when she is hungry and tired – the attraction between them rapidly grew. To this day Tom sends Charlotte flowers every December first as a reminder of the day she brought springtime into that winter day.

Jim and I have known Tom and Charlotte for over thirty years, and I have always been impressed with the level of romance they maintained in their relationship, especially while raising two children. When they attended the *Couples' Romance Weekend,* I asked them how they managed to do this. Charlotte said that every year they always took at least a one-week vacation with just the two of them – no children. Tom added that they focused on the relationship with each other even above the relationship with the children, since their relationship needed to survive and flourish after the children left home. It worked. They raised two well-adjusted, successful children who saw how good marriages were nurtured by watching their parents. Tom and Charlotte's relationship is stronger than ever after nearly thirty years together.

Rate this tradition with a plus if you would like to create a similar practice and with a minus if you wouldn't. Give extra pluses or minuses if you have strong feelings either way.

HER ANSWER	HIS ANSWER

Can you imagine the healthy relationships we would have if all of our parents had modeled this kind of love, commitment, romance and passion for us? Can you imagine giving this gift to your own children? If you have children at home or plan to have them, talk about what you can do to keep the romance alive while raising them.

HER ANSWER	HIS ANSWER

My Private Christmas
Our Romantic Tradition

Holidays are vivid with established traditions, and our families of origin or our children often influence many of our practices. For those who celebrate gift-giving holidays, opening presents is an established part of each family's celebration. Early in our marriage, I never considered breaking those long-held customs. It took years for us to develop some of our own romantic traditions.

Opening presents on Christmas morning was a long-standing and cherished tradition in my parent's home. Younger siblings, and later a niece and nephew, added to the joy and mayhem at my parents' house on Christmas morning. With the energy and determination of a pack of wolves tracking down dinner, youngsters would beeline to their cache of gifts, having spent the preceding weeks arranging and rearranging their gifts under the tree, thereby marking their own personal gift turf. Santa in his infinite wisdom always left his gifts in the appropriate territory.

Adults would forage through the remaining loot, finding gaily-wrapped packages tagged with their names. Sounds of ripping paper and shouts of surprise and gratitude filled the air. A mere ten minutes after the frenzy began, the wolf pack – oops, I mean my family – would sit back, surveying the bounty with glazed eyes.

Jim's family's traditions were more polite, or perhaps more civilized. People opened gifts one at a time, allowing each gift time to be savored and appreciated. Even the children did this, offering their gifts and encouraging each other to go first. Given my background, you can imagine my surprise when I saw three siblings under the age of seven voluntarily acting like this.

For the first fifteen years of our marriage, Jim and I alternated spending Christmas in Albuquerque with my family and staying in Colorado with his. The idea of spending Christmas morning with just my husband seemed as unlikely as a skinny Santa sporting a kilt.

After years of subtle and not-so-subtle suggestions, Jim finally convinced me to try a private Christmas morning with him. My resistance to this was in part due to my underlying belief that children made Christmas more fun. Perhaps I feared that not having children around would show the folly in our decision to remain childless. To my surprise, I found Christmas morning with no children in the mix could be a relaxing and sensual adventure. Jim and I would get out of bed at our leisure. We dressed in our Christmas morning best, sensual silks and fabrics that felt good against our own skin and invited touch.

Jim would put on a pot of coffee and I would serve a plate of fresh fruit and date nut bread. Music from Mannheim Steamrollers' Christmas CD filled the air. We opened our gifts to each other, taking time to savor each gift. We might try on new clothes, read a few paragraphs aloud from a book, or listen to a new CD. Sometimes we would take a break to get in the hot tub to enjoy the early morning view of the mountains. We would talk, and then make love. In this way we could stretch out the joy of gift giving over four or five hours.

After doing this for several years, I realized we had claimed this as our own Christmas tradition. I made a transition from feeling a need to be surrounded by

> *I have found that among its other benefits, giving liberates the soul of the giver.*
> MAYA ANGELOU

family and friends on Christmas morning to protecting that special time Jim and I have together. It's not that we've decided to ignore our families at this time. After several hours, we rejoin the hustle and bustle of holiday travelers to be with our loved ones. On rare occasions when we weren't able to be alone on Christmas morning, we scheduled our rendezvous for another time.

Rate this tradition with a plus if you would like to create a similar practice and with a minus if you wouldn't. Give extra pluses or minuses if you have strong feelings either way.

HER ANSWER	HIS ANSWER

What are your most romantic memories of past holidays?

HER ANSWER	HIS ANSWER

What can you do during the next holiday season to add some romance?

HER ANSWER	HIS ANSWER

Does the idea of a romantic interlude during the holidays appeal to you but not enough to replace current family traditions? If so, schedule some other time during the week for some one-on-one time with your beloved.

HER ANSWER	HIS ANSWER

Romance on a Dollar a Year
Mabel and Frank's Romantic Tradition

It's important to note that gift-giving traditions need not be expensive. When I was researching this habit, Marylin told me a story about a friend of hers who had recently died in her eighties.

Mabel had a companion for the last eighteen years of her life. Neither she nor Frank needed or wanted more material possessions. Early in their relationship they agreed to limit their spending for each other's gift to $1 for each year they'd been together, and then make a contribution to the other's favorite charity.

On their sixteenth Christmas, Mabel was thrilled that she could spend $16. She found a collectable book at a thrift store. Inside the book she tucked a package of nails because she'd just made a contribution in his name to Habitat for Humanity.

They found a creative yet socially responsible way to celebrate Christmas.

> *Love is, above all, the gift of oneself.*
> JEAN ANOUILH

Rate this tradition with a plus if you would like to create a similar practice and with a minus if you wouldn't. Give extra pluses or minuses if you have strong feelings either way.

HER ANSWER	HIS ANSWER

How The Reindeer Saved Christmas
Ann and Michael's Romantic Tradition

Ann had started to dread trimming the Christmas tree. Her children were grown and her partner, Michael, wasn't interested in decorating for the holidays. It was up to Ann to get the tree, trim it, and take it down after Christmas. What was once a festive occasion was now a lonely burden.

Feeling alone against the world, Ann went out to get the Christmas tree and some outdoor lights. A pair of reindeer antlers in the Christmas aisle at Wal-Mart sparked an idea. She tried the antlers on for size, and then found a few other items to complete her outfit.

When Michael got home, he found a fire glowing in the fireplace and Christmas music playing. An unadorned tree stood next to boxes of ornaments and lights. Michael's eyes widened as Ann entered the room wearing only reindeer antlers, a new red teddy, and spiked heels.

Michael moved toward her, but she stopped him. "You're not allowed to unwrap this present until after we've trimmed the tree."

That promise was all that was needed to turn Michael into a playful, enthusiastic helper. In fact, this worked so well that Ann ups the ante every year. He looks forward to seeing what new outfit she will be wearing. One of their recent favorites was a red outfit inspired by Barbara Eden on *I Dream of Jeannie*. The only thing Michael has come to count on is that his beloved's outfit will be red, and very, very sexy. Trimming the tree is once again a festive occasion in their house.

Rate this tradition with a plus if you would like to create a similar practice and with a minus if you wouldn't. Give extra pluses or minuses if you have strong feelings either way.

HER ANSWER	HIS ANSWER

Sweet Tuesday
Linda and Gene's Romantic Tradition

Gene and Linda met on a Tuesday. The attraction was instant and mutual. The following Tuesday he gave her a card, just a silly little card, but it meant a lot to Linda. Gene did more than just sign his name; he wrote about how much he enjoyed their first date and subsequent phone calls.

As they continued to see each other, Gene continued to give Linda cards on Tuesday. Some cards were funny, some romantic. He bought most of them, but occasionally he made one. He always wrote something about what they had done that week or how he was feeling. He apologized for upsetting her; he thanked her for cooking dinner for him.

Linda saved these cards in a box. On the first anniversary of the day they met, she presented him with a scrapbook containing every card he had given her. Together they looked over the cards, and reminisced about their first year together.

Tuesdays have always been special for Linda and Gene. He proposed to her on a Tuesday. Getting married on a Tuesday posed logistical problems for family and friends coming from out of town, but the happy couple did get their marriage license on a Tuesday.

I met them just once several years ago. At the time, they had been married for seventeen years, and they had known each other for almost nineteen. Gene has never missed giving Linda a card on Tuesday, even during some rough times. She was working on their nineteenth scrapbook.

They still celebrate the day they met. Linda was planning a vacation to Hawaii for their thousandth Tuesday.

Not only is this a wonderful romantic tradition, it's a great way to document their love story.

Rate this tradition with a plus if you would like to create a similar practice and with a minus if you wouldn't. Give extra pluses or minuses if you have strong feelings either way.

HER ANSWER	HIS ANSWER

Keeping the Flame Alive and the Bathroom Clean
Paul and Barbara's Romantic Tradition

Paul and Barbara both had demanding jobs, and she was a part-time student. Keeping their apartment clean on top of every thing else was more than they could handle. Clutter was something that bothered Barbara more than it did Paul. He didn't even notice when a room was messy, whereas having dirty dishes in the sink made her very cranky.

When Barbara's birthday approached, Paul started thinking about how to make her day special despite a low budget. He took the day off without telling her. He kissed her goodbye and left for work at the usual time, but as soon as she was gone, he hurried back home.

The first thing he did was to start a load of laundry, which was stacked up a good two feet above the laundry basket. Then he changed the sheets on the bed, scrubbed the toilet bowl and shower, and waxed the kitchen floor.

In the early afternoon, he drove to Barbara's office. He wanted to wash her car and change the oil. When he found her car, he backed it out of its parking place, leaving his to hold the space. At a self-service car wash, he changed the oil and filter, vacuumed the inside, ran it through the car wash, and washed the windows. He returned her car to its original parking place. On the driver's seat he left a single long stem rose and a birthday card.

Paul still needed to buy groceries for dinner. He was starting to worry that he might not have enough time to get all this done. He dashed though the aisles in the store, grabbing a couple of steaks, salad fixings, a cake mix and a few other items.

He was relieved when he checked messages and found Barbara had called to say her friends from work wanted to take her out for a birthday drink. Paul called her to say he was running late and would be home about 7:00. He said he would take her out to dinner for her birthday then.

Back at the apartment, he continued his attack on the laundry, baked a cake, and marinated the steaks. He broke a sweat while running the vacuum and was surprised that high-intensity housekeeping could have the same effect as a workout at the gym. He was grateful that their apartment was small.

When Barbara walked to her car after work, she stopped dead in her tracks. Her car, which had been wearing the aftermath of a month's worth of rain and mud puddles, was replaced with a sparkling look-alike. The license plate confirmed it was hers. She slowly walked around it, approaching it like a farmer would approach crop circles in his field. The rose and card addressed to her in Paul's handwriting provided the answer she was looking for. She was thrilled. Barbara called Paul at work to say thanks, and was disappointed to get his voice mail. She wondered if he had to work late to make up the time he took off to wash her car.

At home, after Paul set the table, he had just enough time to jump in the shower. He dressed, put on some music, and started cooking. He checked his voice mail, and heard Barbara's delight at finding her car washed. She assured him she'd be home by 7:00.

Barbara was so excited to see Paul that she made excuses to her friends to bow out a little early. She felt so loved by him; she was

Tradition does not mean to look after the ash, but to keep the flame alive.
JEAN JAURES

looking forward to seeing him. When Barbara walked though the door, she smelled a chocolate cake and heard the music. Seeing the clean apartment glowing in candlelight and Paul cooking in the kitchen overwhelmed her.

"How did you get all this done?" she asked.

"I took the day off," Paul confessed. "Happy birthday."

This was the best birthday she ever had.

Barbara and Paul have been together for six years. Paul takes the day off on her birthday every year to cook and clean for her. It's no longer a surprise, but something she looks forward to. Knowing how much this meant to her, he made a conscious effort to be more helpful throughout the year.

Habit Nine reminds you to create your own romantic traditions. Remember, it is not the money behind the tradition that counts most, but the feelings that will make it a memorable event of love.

Rate this tradition with a plus if you would like to create a similar practice and with a minus if you wouldn't. Give extra pluses or minuses if you have strong feelings either way.

HER ANSWER	HIS ANSWER

What acts of service could you do for your beloved that would make him or her feel loved?

HER ANSWER	HIS ANSWER

What would you like to have done for you?

HER ANSWER	HIS ANSWER

Our Own Tradition

An Exercise

Do you have some traditions? If so, what are they?

HER ANSWER	HIS ANSWER

If you already do some things that work for you, keep doing them, but also consider adding some new ones.

The first step in creating a new tradition is doing something once that is so much fun you'll want to do it again and again. The charts on the following pages have some suggestions for adventures, dates or loving gestures that could be repeated and turned into traditions if they are a hit with you. It doesn't matter if it's a grand adventure or a simple loving gesture. It will strengthen your relationship no matter where it falls on the Romance Pyramid.

These charts have suggestions for every combination of love languages a couple can have. Read them all, marking the ones you like with a plus (+), and the ones you don't with a minus (-). If it doesn't move you either way, leave it blank.

Remember, your primary love language is how you like to receive love, not give it. If you want most to hear "I love you" or "I appreciate you," your primary love language may be words of affirmation. If, more than anything else, you want your beloved's undivided attention at some point during the day, your priority might be quality time. If some tangible token of your sweetheart's affection speaks louder than words, it might be receiving gifts. If actions speak louder than words, specifically actions like when your beloved cooks dinner or takes out the trash, you probably fall in the acts-of-service camp. If you feel most loved when your beloved reaches out to hug you, count yourself among the physical touch aficionados.

When you get to your own primary love languages, notice if the suggestion fits for you. This list is simply a place to start generating ideas for a new romantic tradition. Perhaps these pages will trigger fresh ideas of your own. It doesn't matter if your favorite traditions are totally unrelated to your primary love languages. The important thing is to find something that appeals to you enough to make a habit of it.

Finding Our Own Traditions

BASED ON PRIMARY LOVE LANGUAGES

No.	Hers	His	Occasion	Tradition	Hers	His
	Primary Love Languages		**Suggestions**		**Ratings**	
1	Words of Affirmation	Words of Affirmation	Thanksgiving	They include a "Gratitude Circle" at their Thanksgiving dinners. Everyone has the opportunity to talk about what they are thankful for. They praise each other in the presence of their guests.		
2	Words of Affirmation	Quality Time	Anniversary	They set aside time for a conversation about good memories of the past year, qualities they love in each other, and their hopes and dreams for the future.		
3	Words of Affirmation	Receiving Gifts	Christmas	When they exchange gifts, they write cards to each other about why each gift was chosen, why their beloved deserves this gift. They read these cards aloud to each other.		
4	Words of Affirmation	Acts of Service	His birthday	She washes his car, irons his shirts, and fixes dinner. He writes words of thanks and devotion and hires a calligrapher to pen them.		
5	Words of Affirmation	Physical Touch	Every night	He tells her what he loves about her or one thing she did that he appreciates. She lightly rubs his back as he falls asleep.		

Finding Our Own Traditions
BASED ON PRIMARY LOVE LANGUAGES

	Primary Love Languages		Suggestions		Ratings	
No.	Hers	His	Occasion	Tradition	Hers	His
6	Quality Time	Words of Affirmation	Anniversary	Over an intimate dinner, they toast each other using their silver wedding goblets.		
7	Quality Time	Quality Time	Valentine's Day	They take turns planning a romantic getaway. They focus on each other, blocking out the rest of the world for a few hours or a few days.		
8	Quality Time	Receiving Gifts	His birthday	She buys him gifts they can enjoy together. Maybe it's a board game they can play, a book they can both read and discuss, or tickets to a sporting event.		
9	Quality Time	Acts of Service	Halloween	They both enjoy decorating for Halloween. She picks up pumpkins and gathers the carving tools. They set aside an evening to express their creativity by carving jack-o-lanterns.		
10	Quality Time	Physical Touch	Christmas	He helps her put up the Christmas tree. She wears sexy lingerie for the private tree-trimming party. They both enjoy the "after" party.		

Finding Our Own Traditions
BASED ON PRIMARY LOVE LANGUAGES

	Primary Love Languages		Suggestions		Ratings	
No.	Hers	His	Occasion	Tradition	Hers	His
11	Receiving Gifts	Words of Affirmation	Christmas	He gives her a charm bracelet. Every year, he adds a charm representing a special event. She never misses an opportunity to brag about his thoughtful gift.		
12	Receiving Gifts	Quality Time	First of the month (any regular time period will do)	He gives her a card every month. He writes about what's going on in their lives. She collects the cards in an album. Once a year, they enjoy reminiscing.		
13	Receiving Gifts	Receiving Gifts	Anniversary	They do Habit Seven's Gift Giving exercise. After the shopping spree, they reserve time to exchange gifts.		
14	Receiving Gifts	Acts of Service	Any time	He knows what chores she'll be doing. He hides wrapped gifts in various locations. He might slip a box with earrings into the dishwasher before she empties it, or a book in the linen closet.		
15	Receiving Gifts	Physical Touch	Valentine's Day	He never fails to give her thirteen roses. Why thirteen? So that she'll still have a dozen left after she pulls one to sprinkle the petals in their bubble bath.		

Finding Our Own Traditions

BASED ON PRIMARY LOVE LANGUAGES

	Primary Love Languages		Suggestions		Ratings	
No.	Hers	His	Occasion	Tradition	Hers	His
16	Acts of Service	Words of Affirmation	Her birthday	He cleans the house, washes her car, cooks dinner, and does the dishes. He's her slave for a day. She sincerely appreciates him. She tells him so in a love letter.		
17	Acts of Service	Quality Time	Spring planting, if she's a gardener	He helps her select and plant the garden. She gives him as much focus as the garden.		
18	Acts of Service	Receiving Gifts	Reading Day	They both love to read and often give books as gifts. They each get to select one reading day per year. The reader gets to read all day long while the other does any necessary chores such as cooking, cleaning, or childcare.		
19	Acts of Service	Acts of Service	Their birthdays	On her birthday, he does her chores while she hikes with friends. That evening, they dine on the meal he prepared. When it's his turn, he plays golf while she cooks for him.		
20	Acts of Service	Physical Touch	Lawn mowing day	He looks forward to mowing the lawn, and the reward his efforts bring. After he drinks his ice-cold lemonade, he lies in the hammock while she massages his hands and feet.		

Finding Our Own Traditions
B A S E D O N P R I M A R Y L O V E L A N G U A G E S

	Primary Love Languages		Suggestions		Ratings	
No.	Hers	His	Occasion	Tradition	Hers	His
21	Physical Touch	Words of Affirmation	Valentine's Day	She puts a love note to him in the classified section of the newspapers. He gives her a sensual massage in front of the fireplace.		
22	Physical Touch	Quality Time	Every Thursday	He heats up the massage oils and rubs her feet. She tunes out everything except her beloved. This is a time to talk and share about their day.		
23	Physical Touch	Receiving Gifts	His birthday	She buys him a CD by his favorite artist. They dance cheek-to-cheek to the slow songs in the living room.		
24	Physical Touch	Acts of Service	Most days	As she cooks his favorite meals or does his laundry, he slips up behind her to kiss her neck, pat her bottom, or give her a hug.		
25	Physical Touch	Physical Touch	Sensual day (once or twice a year)	They set aside a full day to be together. They bathe together, exchange massages, and make love. While this is a day devoted to touch, engaging all of the senses will enhance it.		

What is your primary love language?

HER ANSWER	HIS ANSWER

Of the suggestions you marked with a plus (+), which ones are your three favorites?

HER ANSWER	HIS ANSWER

What did you like best about your three favorites?

HER ANSWER	HIS ANSWER

What new activity would you like to try that might become a tradition? Work on this together to agree upon one complete idea. After you've enjoyed the experience, decide if it was something worth repeating. If it stands the test of time, you may have found a new tradition.

OCCASION	TRADITION

Sparks that Ignite the Romantic Flame

♡ Have fun celebrating your love. If you do something that's worth repeating, consider making it a tradition.

♡ Follow traditions of your own, just as traditions are practiced in nations, regions, and families.

♡ Make a tradition uniquely yours. It doesn't have to be conventional.

♡ Repeat what you love, throw out what you don't, and add whatever you want to make your own personal mark.

♡ Consider incorporating both of your primary love languages into your romantic traditions.

♡ Enjoy adventures as one-time events if you don't have the desire or opportunity to repeat them. There's nothing wrong with that, it's just not a tradition.

♡ Practice traditions whether they are grand adventures or simple loving gestures. They will strengthen your relationship no matter where they fall on the Romance Pyramid.

Enjoy the Bumps on the Road to Adventure

American football coach Chuck Knox once said, "Always have a plan and believe in it. Nothing happens by accident." To which I'll add my own philosophy: It's a good idea to begin with a plan, but sometimes things do happen by accident. With the right attitude, even mishaps can lead to great fun.

This element may appear to contradict itself, but actually it's just romantic common sense: Plan the journey, but embrace the side steps of the adventure. Or as my friend Yella Werder says, "It's always nice to have a plan to abandon."

In spite of the best planning, something might go wrong. Have contingency plans whenever possible for key elements, the critical items that will be disastrous if

> *The friends who fail you are always replaced by new ones who appear at the critical moment and from the most unexpected quarters.*
> HENRY MILLER

they go astray. For instance, if you are depending on others to deliver instructions as to what your beloved should do next during a treasure hunt, provide your cell phone number in case they miss making the connection.

Some deviations from the plan will require major readjustments, especially if your safety is compromised. For example, if your adventure includes a snugly warm weekend in a secluded snowy setting, the "critical item" would definitely be a cabin. If unforeseen circumstances prevent you from getting to that remote location, do whatever's necessary to secure lodging, and then continue with the modified adventure.

Beyond the critical items, however, if something doesn't work out as intended, bless it and let it go. Figure out how to make the best of the situation. Focus on your goal.

My niece Caley shared one of her favorite childhood memories. Her family had loaded up the station wagon for a picnic in the mountains. By the time they got to their location, it was pouring rain. They spread out the blanket in the back of the wagon and laid out the food. The five of them crawled over seats and squeezed themselves into the cozy space. Caley loved being warm and dry while watching the dramatic afternoon thunderstorm from the safety of the car. A family picnic was their goal, and a turn in the weather didn't prevent it from happening.

> *Those who say only sunshine brings happiness have never danced in the rain.*
> UNKNOWN

Whether you're on the giving or receiving end, don't complain about minor inconveniences or mishaps. Keeping a positive attitude in spite of a few challenges makes the adventure more fun for everyone. Unless you can actually change the situation by registering a tactful complaint, get over it.

Once Jim planned a birthday celebration for me that involved a series of events throughout the day with different friends. As my day unfolded I enjoyed a catered breakfast in the Garden of the Gods, a mountain bike ride, and a watsu, a unique style of massage done in warm water. Jim had arranged that I would do each new activity with a different friend. When I dressed after the watsu, I kept my disappointment to myself when I realized Jim didn't think to bring my makeup or hair essentials. Gone were the makeup and hairstyle I'd carefully attended to only a few hours earlier. It wasn't worth worrying about; I figured anyone else on my agenda surely accepted me with or without makeup.

Sometimes a little misadventure sprinkled in an adventure serves to make the time all the more memorable. Emotions are heightened when you are overcoming adversity. It's possible to feel even more receptive to love and happiness after overcoming obstacles.

Confessions of a Wayward Daughter
Our Romantic Adventure

Only once in my life have I ever disregarded my mother's advice never to accept a ride with a stranger. Well, Mom, I thank you for all your good advice, and I hope you're sitting down as you read about the one time I didn't follow it.

On a very cold, wintry day in February 1986, Jim was returning home from a business trip. I had planned to give him a very *warm* welcome. The plan was set in motion when I left work early and stopped at a gas station a couple of miles from the airport to put gas in my car.

In 1986, full service gas stations were still plentiful and I always took advantage of them. I hated pumping my own gas. As I pulled up to a vacant pump, I noticed a helpful attendant heading my way. He was dressed in an oily, chocolate brown uniform with a patch on his right chest identifying him as "Al." He came up to my window, smelling like a combination of Wrigley's Juicy Fruit gum and Pennzoil.

> *An adventure is only an inconvenience rightly considered. An inconvenience is an adventure wrongly considered.*
>
> G.K. CHESTERTON

Watching Al work over his fresh stick of Juicy Fruit with gusto, I could only hope Jim would greet me with a similar enthusiasm, although I did hope Jim would express his enthusiasm differently. In between loud smacks Al asked, "Can I help you?"

"Fill it up with premium, please," I responded.

I grabbed my bag from the back seat and went to the bathroom, a greasy little one seater. I caught my reflection in the dingy and splattered mirror. As I braced myself for the impending metamorphosis, I said good-bye to the woman in the mirror wearing a conservative Pendleton suit and sensible pumps.

I locked the door – tight. I took off all my clothes and felt a shock of cold air blowing in under the door. I proceeded to take some goodies out of my bag. First I took out some black lace panty hose, put them on, and straightened the seams in the back. Then I took out a red and black satin teddy and slipped into that little number. Next I went to work on my hair and makeup. I took the big hair craze of the day to new heights. I teased it and sprayed it until it stood out inches from my head. I put on lots of eye shadow and false eyelashes and fire engine red lipstick. I slid my feet into a pair of wicked 4-inch spiked heels and took a few wobbly practice steps. Last but certainly not least, I put on the ankle-length black cape I borrowed from a friend.

Who was that woman in the mirror? Not someone I knew. Perhaps not someone my husband would recognize at first glance. Certainly not the sensible, modest daughter my dear Catholic mother raised.

The reflection in the mirror looked a bit like Elvira, except for the teased blonde hair. The false eyelashes were a bit too Tammy Fay-ish, so I trashed them and settled for heavy mascara. When I was satisfied that my appearance would have the desired effect on Jim, I glanced over my shoulder, attempted a dramatic twirl with the cape flowing, and dubbed my alter ego Vanes-s-s-s-s-s-a!

Vanessa was ready for her debut. Al would be her first test. I left the bathroom and walked toward the car. Al watched me cross the parking lot, the Juicy Fruit doing double time, but it wasn't until I handed him my credit card that he recognized me. The wad of Juicy Fruit dangled precariously from his upper molars, bounced off the name patch and landed on his shoe. Vanessa had passed her first test.

I wanted everything to be perfect for greeting Jim. I knew my appearance would get his attention, but I found I was a bit squeamish about letting other people see me this way. Rather than arrive at the airport early and suffer the curious looks of strangers, I decided to use the fifteen minutes I had to spare to run the car through the car wash just around the corner.

In my desire for perfection, I overlooked one important thing. The same water that gets a car clean also freezes in winter. The car wash exited onto a sloped ramp, which was a solid sheet of ice. As I drove from the level safety of the steamy car wash, my tires hit the slippery slope and — BAM! — crashed into the curb.

Have you ever been able to change a bad dream by wishing it wasn't happening? I tried that, but it didn't work. There I was, stuck on a sheet of ice, and as soon as I opened the door I could hear the hiss of air draining from my front tire. Even though I was dressed like a Barbie doll, I was smart enough to know that my high heels and sexy attire might be exciting for Jim, but they'd be less than attractive sprawled on an icy pavement.

I got back into the car and slowly returned to the station. As soon as Al saw me drive in, he noticed my rapidly deflating tire.

As I tell you what happened next, I shudder to think what my mother would have said if she would have seen me in such daring attire demanding a ride from a total stranger.

> *Obstacles are those frightful things you see when you take your eyes off your goal.*
> HENRY FORD

I prefer to say that I was absolutely, positively focused on my goal of meeting Jim's plane.

Al said, "Looks like you got a problem."

"It's worse than you think. I need to be at the airport in ten minutes to meet my husband's plane. I need to borrow your car," I insisted.

"You can't borrow my car."

"Then you have to take me and we have to leave right now," I said, leaving Al little room to deny me.

"Okay," he agreed.

I'm glad Al's mother didn't warn him about giving rides to strange women.

So I climbed into a large, rusty pickup truck with my good buddy Al and we headed to the airport. While Al worked over a fresh stick of Juicy Fruit, he kept one eye on the road and the other on his wayward passenger.

When we got to the airport, Al said he would wait at the curb. I rushed inside, saying a prayer that I would not see anyone I knew other than Jim, and that his plane would be on time. I checked the arrival time on the monitor for flight 409 and ran, with black stilettos wobbling and cape fluttering, to the gate. I was aware of the stares and long looks from passersby but did my best to ignore them.

Maybe I didn't make myself clear in the specifics of my prayer – or maybe God was just having a little fun. There was no plane on the other end of the jet way. There was no plane taxiing toward me on the runway. There was no plane approaching in the nearby skies.

> *The gods too are fond of a joke.*
> ARISTOTLE

To my horror, I ran into an acquaintance from graduate school and her mother. Not only that, my former classmate recognized me. Where was Vanessa when I needed her?

Katie – who was wearing a Pendleton suit and sensible pumps – brought her mother along to meet her husband's plane.

I wore lady-of-the-night heels and brought Al.

After hearing my frantic story, Katie and Mom offered to take Jim and me to the gas station when the plane arrived. The plane was a few minutes late so I had time to run back out to Al's truck and tell him I found a ride and I would meet him back at the gas station. I begged him to fix my tire as soon as possible.

I dashed back to the gate, feeling the wind resistance on my big hair, and arrived just as the passengers were getting off the plane. The look on Jim's face was priceless. He hugged me and kissed me and whispered in my ear. I could feel that he was ready for the afternoon. I whispered back in my sexiest voice that the fun really started thirty minutes ago when I wrecked the car.

I really should be better at whispering sweet nothings.

Jim and I walked with Katie and family to their car. Knowing I didn't blend into this conservatively dressed group, I felt like a streetwalker at a Mother's Day brunch. Jim and I squeezed into the back seat with Katie's mom, who did a fine job of eliminating any dead air space with small talk and nervous laughter. I could only imagine that Katie's mom wanted reassurance from her daughter that she would never dress like me, while her husband was thinking it could be fun.

> *Blessed are we who can laugh at ourselves for we shall never cease to be amused.*
> UNKNOWN

Al greeted us and said the car should be ready in an hour or so. Jim and I walked to the restaurant next door to wait. The hostess graciously gave us a cozy, very warm seat by the fireplace. Of course I dared not undo even one button on that heavy wool cape. Jim was only left to wonder what went with those 4-inch heels and lacy ankles. I did let him read the letter I had written to him describing the afternoon that I had planned for him.

Al eventually fixed my tire. Jim and I went on our way. We had a very exciting afternoon – both before and after we got home. Events that could have derailed the whole adventure only served to intensify our experience and make our reunion even more memorable. Jim and I were very much in love that afternoon as we enjoyed the bumps — and crashes— on the road to adventure.

Rate this adventure with a plus if you would like to find yourself in a similar situation, and with a minus if you wouldn't. Give extra pluses or minuses if you have strong feelings either way.

HER ANSWER	HIS ANSWER

Men, how would you feel if your beloved "dressed" to greet you? Women, what "dress up" fantasy are you willing to do for your beloved?

HER ANSWER	HIS ANSWER

We're Getting Married. Can We Use Your Laundry Room?

Debbie and Deane's Romantic Adventure

On a Wednesday night in a bygone April, I got a call from my dear friend Debbie who was on vacation in Arizona. She and her sweetheart, Deane, had some big news to share. Their relationship had been progressing nicely so I had been expecting to hear an engagement announcement.

"Guess what!" Debbie said.

"You're getting married," I ventured.

"Yes, but there's more. I'm pregnant." She was bubbling with excitement.

"Congratulations! When are you due and when are you getting married?"

"The baby is due in December. We're getting married this Saturday in Sedona. Can you make it?"

My happiness for Debbie and Deane left no room for any answer other than "Yes, of course I'll be there."

All I had to do was buy a plane ticket. Debbie and Deane had a wedding to plan in two days. Debbie enlisted her friend Susan who lived in Phoenix to help with the wedding logistics. Susan made a hotel reservation for Debbie and Deane and the five guests who would attend the wedding.

Debbie and Deane got the marriage license and hired a judge to perform the ceremony. They found a beautiful spot in Oak Creek Canyon north of Sedona where they would hold the wedding. The apple trees next to the creek were in full bloom. Debbie bought a white cotton skirt but ran out of time before she could complete the wedding ensemble. Debbie asked Susan to find a white cotton blouse and a pair of shoes.

On Saturday morning the wedding guests gathered at Susan's house, and then drove to Sedona in a flashy red convertible. We met Debbie and Deane for a pre-wedding lunch. In our excitement, we were oblivious to the possibility that anything could go wrong, especially with such simple wedding plans.

Our bubble burst when Susan tried to check us into the hotel in Oak Creek Canyon. Our reservations were for MAY 27, not April 27. Oops! In spite of Susan's demands and tears, there was simply no room at the inn. The hotel's management was not accommodating when we begged for any space at all where we could change our clothes, but they did help us book rooms in Sedona. The problem was we didn't have time to drive back to Sedona, change clothes and be back to Oak Creek Canyon in time for the wedding.

There was a place across the street that offered quaint cabins. They didn't have any rooms available, but after hearing our tale of woe, they graciously offered us the use of their laundry room and tool shed. That was good enough for us. The two men went to the tool shed, and the five women went to the laundry room.

Any hopes of taking a shower or washing our wind-blown hair were gone in a flash. A few of us felt a brief moment of regret about that carefree convertible ride. Susan, one of the most meticulously groomed women I know, was desperate for a bath. She ran about six inches of water in the laundry sink and folded her 5'10" frame into it. The picture of Susan with her legs hanging over the edge of the sink and a shelf of laundry detergent and cleaning supplies over her head captured the spirit of the day.

The brook would lose its song if you removed the rocks.
AMERICAN PROVERB

Our focus was on making Debbie look beautiful for her wedding. We rolled her hair and did her make up. She was radiant, as all brides are. There wasn't enough time for the rest of us to do anything but change clothes and put smiles on our faces.

The judge arrived at the wedding site just as we did. The ceremony itself went off without a hitch. When the judge pronounced Debbie and Deane husband and wife, Debbie let out a spine-tingling holler. In our heightened emotional state, there wasn't a dry eye among us.

♡　♡　♡　♡　♡

I've been to lots of wonderful weddings, and even had the privilege of helping to dress the bride on several occasions, but I've never heard of a wedding where the getting there and dressing the bride were as much of an adventure as the wedding itself.

Rate this adventure with a plus if you would like to find yourself in a similar situation, and with a minus if you wouldn't. Give extra pluses or minuses if you have strong feelings either way.

HER ANSWER	HIS ANSWER

Have you ever planned an important event only to find a key element went awry? How did you handle it? Is there anything you could have done differently?

HER ANSWER	HIS ANSWER

Lights Are Out and They're at Home
Louise and Kurt's Romantic Adventure

Early in their relationship, Louise invited Kurt to dinner at her house. She spent the day cooking and cleaning. She made a salad and planned to pop the salmon in the oven when Kurt arrived. Soft jazz was loaded in the CD player. Everything was ready, and she wanted this evening to go perfectly for this new man.

A Moment with the Darlings

"Now that I know how much sweeter cake tastes from your fingers, maybe I'll drop all our cakes on the floor.

Kurt arrived with a bottle of wine in one hand and flowers in the other. Just after Louise put the flowers in a vase, the electricity went out. They looked out the window to find the whole neighborhood was dark. Louise lit the candles in the living room and dining room, and pulled a dozen more candles out of their hiding places to provide some additional lighting. Kurt helped her build a fire in the fireplace to ward off the frigid January temperatures. Except for the lack of music, the power outage made the environment even more romantic.

The problem, of course, was how to cook dinner. A call to the power company brought the unwelcome news that the outage could take a couple of hours to repair. Louise got to see Kurt's creative side at work in the kitchen. Using the garden salad Louise had already prepared as a base, Kurt added a can of tuna, feta cheese, a few olives and some spices. They spread a blanket out to eat picnic style in front of the fireplace.

It wasn't the dinner Louise had planned, but it was still a rousing success. When the electricity came back on, it seemed like an intrusion. They turned off the lights and silenced the music. Seeing how graciously each of them handled the minor inconvenience increased the attraction between them.

Rate this adventure with a plus if you would like to find yourself in a similar situation, and with a minus if you wouldn't. Give extra pluses or minuses if you have strong feelings either way.

HER ANSWER	HIS ANSWER

A Loving Farewell
Kelly's Loving Gesture for Jim

Shortly after Kelly and her sweetheart, Jim, took *The Art of Romance and Fun* workshop, he had to go out of town on business. She had a previous appointment and was unable to take him to the airport to give him a proper sendoff.

When Kelly's appointment finished early, she decided to surprise Jim by showing up at the airport to say goodbye. She thought it would be a great loving gesture. His plane was due to depart in fifty minutes. Since the airport was a thirty-minute drive, she had no time to waste.

> *If I create from the heart, nearly everything works; if from the head, almost nothing.*
> MARC CHAGALL

She arrived at the airport and parked the car with fifteen minutes to spare. She searched the monitors to find Jim's departure gate. As she hurriedly made her way through the security gate and rushed to gate A-25, her heart sank when she saw the last of the passengers enter the jet way. The plane, so close, yet off limits to the unticketed, was due to depart in five minutes.

On an impulse, Kelly ran into the gift shop next to the gate. Her eyes went immediately to a card and a Valentine Beanie Baby. She grabbed both of them and waited her turn for the cashier. While waiting she scribbled an "I love you" on the card and Jim's name on the envelope.

> *When one door of happiness closes, another opens; but often we look so long at the closed door that we do not see the one which has opened for us.*
> HELEN KELLER

The ticket agent was closing the doors when Kelly got back to the gate. She gave him the card and bag and asked him to deliver them to Jim. The ticket agent gave the goods to a flight attendant. After the flight was airborne, Jim heard an announcement asking him to push the flight attendant call button.

Puzzled and slightly concerned, he pushed the button. The approaching flight attendant had a broad smile, which put his mind at ease. She explained that a lovely lady had delivered this package just after the passengers had loaded the plane.

He was pleasantly surprised, especially when he read the card. He had just picked up the same card for her in the airport gift shop. At no time in his adult life had anyone given him a stuffed animal. He felt truly loved.

Giving Jim a loving goodbye was Kelly's intention. Not being able to do that face-to-face did not change her intention.

Rate this adventure with a plus if you would like to find yourself in a similar situation, and with a minus if you wouldn't. Give extra pluses or minuses if you have strong feelings either way.

HER ANSWER	HIS ANSWER

Where There's Fire, There's Romance
Nick and Joan's Romantic Adventure

The summer of 2002 was dry and dangerous in the western United States. Wild fires raged out of control in Colorado, Arizona, California and several other states. Many communities were evacuated as the fires encroached on residential neighborhoods.

The Hayman Fire in central Colorado burned 137,000 acres. Thousands of residents were evacuated from their homes or put on standby to evacuate. One-hundred-thirty-three families lost their homes.

Nick and Joan were among the evacuees. Their neighborhood consisted of mostly wooden homes surrounded by ponderosa pines and scrub oak on two-acre parcels. Rather than accept offers of lodging from friends who were far from the front lines of the fire, Nick, Joan and five other families in their neighborhood decided to camp out together just a few miles from the evacuation zone. Barbara and Bob, who lived on several acres near a small lake, opened their land and their hearts to this group of evacuees. They were far enough from the fire to be out of harm's way, but close enough to maintain an emotional connection to their endangered homes.

The first couple of days of exile were tense. Each news report brought emotional highs and lows. When the wind blew out of the north pushing the border of the fire toward their community, each person suffered with his or her own tortured images of personal property and natural beauty destroyed by fire. The air was heavy with smoke, and at times the ashes falling from the sky was like a winter snow. When the wind blew from the east clearing the smoke from the cloudless blue sky, they could breath easier and almost forget the imminent danger for a moment or two.

The third day was a good one. A slight breeze blew from the east and afternoon rain clouds held a promise of help for firefighters. Nick and a few of the neighbors were playing a spirited game of horseshoes. Some kids were exploring on the parched banks of the lake recently exposed by the drought; some others were making a fort out of an abandoned boathouse. Joan and Barbara were making a grocery list for an evening picnic. Since all open outdoor fires were strictly prohibited, Barbara's kitchen was always filled with people preparing meals. To an outside observer, the group looked more like a happy family reunion than a group under duress.

> *Many waters cannot quench love, neither can floods drown it.*
> SONG OF SOLOMON 8:7

In all the chaos, Nick had almost forgotten that Joan's birthday was two days away. Under normal circumstances, he would buy her a nice present and take her to dinner, but things were hardly normal. Going out for a nice dinner was out of the question; they left with clothes for camping, not fine dining. Buying material possessions at a time when their home could go up in smoke with a shift in the wind seemed inane to Nick. In all the years they had been together, Nick had never given Joan a birthday party. It seemed like the perfect time to change that.

Nick asked several of his friends to help him plan a party. Working on the party was like having a magic elixir; first it lifted the spirits of the conspirators and then the good cheer started to ripple out to people who had not yet become involved. Nick and his cohorts planned the menu, bought food, drinks and decorations, and worked on one very special surprise. The day before Joan's birthday, Nick explained to the nine kids in residence what was going on and enlisted them to help.

No one had said anything to Joan about her birthday, and she hadn't given it much thought either. She assumed it would be forgotten this year in light of more pressing business.

On the morning of Joan's birthday, she was awakened by a verbal "knock, knock" outside her tent. Barbara told Joan that as the birthday girl, she could have the first shower. Joan was surprised that Barbara even knew it was her birthday, but she wasn't going to turn down a shower. Since her internment began six days earlier, she'd only had one lukewarm sun shower and a couple of sponge baths. None of the campers wanted to take advantage of Barbara and Bob's generosity, so they had all limited their water usage. Starting the day with a warm shower and clean clothes sounded like a luxury indeed.

When Joan emerged from the bathroom feeling freshly scrubbed, she was surprised to see a dozen or so people in the kitchen. Nick stood in the center of the room holding a cheese and mushroom omelet with a candle in the middle of it. Everyone began to sing "Happy Birthday" to her. She was delighted. They remembered. Nick told her they had several activities planned in honor of her birthday.

The day was filled with fun and games. They played volleyball and horseshoes, had a scavenger hunt, reminisced about old times, ate good food and drank beer and soft drinks. In the late afternoon, a couple of people pulled out their guitars and began a sing along. It had been a wonderful day, when everyone was able to forget their troubles for a while and celebrate what they had.

The party seemed to be winding down, but no one was leaving. Joan whispered to Nick that she was ready to call it a night. She expected him to slip quietly away with her, but instead he stepped forward and announced to the group, "Ladies and gentlemen, Joan is ready for bed." Cheers went up and two young girls, Heather and Emily, grabbed her hands. "Close your eyes and come with us," they said. Nick put a blindfold on her for good measure. The girls turned her around a couple of times to disorient her, and then they started walking. Joan could tell the whole group was coming along with them.

Joan had no idea what was going on. She walked over the uneven surface of the ground, then felt the surface even out as if she were on a wooden deck. The girls led her a short distance before they let go of her hands. Nick took off the blindfold and told her to open her eyes.

Nick and the kids had transformed the abandoned boathouse into a romantic hideaway. Nick and Joan's sleeping bags were laid out in the center of the room. Floral sheets covered up some of the damaged walls. Matching pillowcases were draped over cardboard boxes to make nightstands.

Candles and vases of wild flowers sat on the makeshift nightstands. Several of the children had drawn pictures for the walls. Someone pushed the button on the boom box and soft music filled the air.

"I wanted to take you away for your birthday, but this is as far as our friends would let us go," Nick said. "But at least we have more privacy here than we did in tent city."

"Do you like my picture?" Emily asked. "It's your house so you would know what it looked like in case it burns."

"I love it. I love the picture, I love the boathouse, and I love all of you. I feel so honored," Joan said. "Thank you all for everything."

With that, Barbara and Bob led the procession out of the hideaway. Emily and Heather weren't ready to leave. They didn't understand that their starring roles could be over so quickly.

As soon as the door was closed and the dock was quiet, Nick and Joan took advantage of their newfound privacy. That was the best gift of all.

The good news was that several days later, they were allowed to return to their property. None of them lost their homes.

There wasn't a person among them who wasn't eager to return home, but even as they packed up, there was a bittersweet quality to leaving. It was like going home after a great vacation. There's no place like home, but the memory of their temporary home will always have a place in their hearts.

Rate this adventure with a plus if you would like to find yourself in a similar situation, and with a minus if you wouldn't. Give extra pluses or minuses if you have strong feelings either way.

HER ANSWER	HIS ANSWER

I Feel Really Loved When...
An Exercise

One definition of a dyad is an interaction between two people. This exercise is a dyad in which you will each complete one sentence, repeatedly, for three minutes while looking into each other's eyes. The sentence stem is "I feel really loved when…" When your beloved has the floor, you are only there to listen, not to respond in any way, not to laugh, not to agree or disagree.

Three minutes may not seem like much now, but it can feel like an eternity when you are doing the exercise. If you run out of things to say, repeat yourself. The purpose is to dig a little deeper, to mine some new nuggets, some previously unspoken or unknown truths. For example, your monologue might sound like this:

> "*I feel really loved when you tell me you love me.*
> *I feel really loved when you touch me.*
> *I feel really loved when you put lotion on my feet.*
> *I feel really loved when you talk to me.*
> *I feel really loved when I see your smile.*
> *I feel really loved when I hold our kids.*
> *I feel really loved when I'm with my parents.*
> *I feel really loved when you touch me.*
> *I feel really loved when you kiss my neck.*
> *I feel really loved when you cook for me.*
> *I feel really loved when you touch me.*
> *I feel really loved when you take time to be with me.*"

You'll notice that some items were repeated rather than to allow any silence. As you look for things to say, you may discover new things about yourself. When you keep on talking after you've run out of things you rehearsed in your mind before the exercise started, you begin to talk from the heart.

You will need a timer that you can set to alert you after three minutes. Watching a clock while doing the exercise can be distracting.

Determine who will go first. Sit facing your beloved, with nothing between you and nothing in your lap. Uncross your arms and legs. Put both feet on the floor. Look into your beloved's eyes. Set a timer for three minutes. The first person talks for three minutes. Reset the timer for the second person.

When you are both done, thank each other for sharing. Discuss what you learned about yourself and your beloved. Did the primary love languages of you and your beloved come through loud and clear? Any surprises? Did you learn any new ways to demonstrate your love or ask for love?

Write about this exercise in your notebook for ten minutes.

A Public Date
An Exercise

Each of you will plan a three-hour "date" or "mini-adventure." This will be a public adventure, anything you enjoy doing together. You may know exactly what you want to do, but here are a few ideas:

♡ Dine in a nice restaurant
♡ Hike in the forest
♡ Dance to your favorite music
♡ Shop together
♡ Make pottery at a you-paint-it pottery place
♡ Visit art galleries
♡ Attend a concert or play
♡ Play golf
♡ Ride bikes
♡ Have a picnic

Make your plans and set the date. When you go on your date, notice if any thing goes wrong. If it does, your attitude and intention to have a good time together will make all the difference.

Sparks that Ignite the Romantic Flame

♡ Plan the journey, but embrace the side steps of the adventure.

♡ Adapt quickly to unforeseen circumstances. In spite of the best planning and good intentions, something might go wrong.

♡ Show your best side by reacting with grace under pressure.

♡ Look on the bright side. Sometimes a little misadventure sprinkled in only serves to make the adventure all the more memorable.

♡ Make romance your intention, and don't let minor inconveniences or mishaps change that.

Cherish Intimacy

I know there is a fair amount of planning and structure that goes into these adventures I've described. However, I don't want you to think every minute is carefully choreographed. On the contrary, most of the time you are free just to be together. All the stuff leading up to the big event only serves to make the private time more special. Once the stage is set for romance and fun, let nature take its course. What happens after the plan is set in motion is what's most important.

There are two parts to cherishing intimacy. First, find a place conducive to romance. As much as possible, protect yourselves from unnecessary interruptions, whether it's in a quiet restaurant, your own home, or a romantic inn. Where can you retreat to a fortress for some one-on-one time with your beloved?

Once you're in the right environment for romance, the second part to cherishing intimacy is the interaction between the two of you. How do you focus on each other and make your conversations, your feelings, and your caresses more tender and intimate?

> *The best feelings are those that have no words to describe them.*
> MICHELLE HAMMERSLEY

Finding Romance in Great Aunt Gertrude's Guest Bedroom

If you're looking for a change of venue for your romantic rendezvous, here are some things to consider about lodging.

Many people think of a bed and breakfast as the ideal romantic get-away. Jim and I have certainly enjoyed several romantic evenings in B&Bs. However, some of our least intimate encounters have been in what I thought were promising B&Bs, while some truly memorable occasions happened within the confines of large, formal hotels.

The key to intimacy, to no one's surprise, is privacy. Some charming B&Bs are private homes converted to and licensed as public lodging. Private bathrooms may or may not be available. Location of the bedrooms could be adjacent to a gathering place. While privacy may be expected and likely to be promised in small B&Bs, the actual feeling could be like being a guest in your Great Aunt Gertrude's home.

Of course, this is not always a bad thing. When we were traveling in New Zealand, we occasionally would seek out small B&Bs so that we could get to know our hosts. Our goal here was not intimacy; we wanted to immerse ourselves in the culture and meet the people of New Zealand. Years later I fondly remember the people we met at three B&Bs as some of the highlights of our trip.

In our search for romance, however, Jim and I have stayed in some places that were not suited to that purpose, and it is not easy to tell from the brochure whether or not you will have privacy. For a special occasion we once stayed in a beautiful B&B in downtown Denver. Based on the brochure's description, we had reserved a specific room, which had a private bath, fire-place, sitting area and king-sized bed. The room was every bit as luxurious as the brochure promised. However, it was right next to the reception area and reservation desk on the first floor. Every time new guests checked in we could hear their entire conversation with very little effort. Not only that, when I sat on the edge of the bed to change shoes I was greeted by a loud squeak, which promised to announce all our intimate movements to the outside world. Needless to say, when we returned to our room after dinner, we spent a somewhat quiet and inhibited evening. We asked for a different room the next morning. On the busy holiday weekend, the only room available was a small one on the third floor. This room did not have the view or the amenities available in the other more expensive room, but it had some thing far more precious to us – privacy.

For an anniversary I once found a B&B in a small town in central Colorado. The woman who owned it had two rooms she could rent. I told her I was looking for a room with a private bathroom. The two rooms shared a bath so she promised not to rent the other one during our stay. Her home was lovely. Since this place was off the beaten path, she cooked dinner for us. She could not have been more gracious and accommodating, treating us like welcome guests in her home. Therein was the problem. We felt rude if we spent too much time in the bedroom. She ate dinner with us. While we were the only ones using the bathroom, we had to put on a robe and leave our bedroom to get to our "private" bathroom.

Neither of these experiences ruined our weekend. We made the best of the situation, but we weren't eager to return. I've learned not to recommend a specific B&B for a client unless I've at least done a site visit or preferably stayed there overnight.

In defense of B&Bs, we have also had some fantastically romantic stays. Beyond the typical amenities, here is what I look for in a romantic B&B:

♡ Private bathrooms, with private entry from the bedroom to the bathroom

♡ Entry to the bedroom away from common areas, like the reception desk or sitting room

♡ Thick common walls or separate cabins

♡ More than two guest rooms, unless you *want* to feel like a guest in someone's home

♡ The option for breakfast in bed, if desired

♡ CD player

Who Cares What the Bellman Thinks?

On the other hand, large hotels, considered impersonal by some, may provide an excellent environment for romance. A certain degree of privacy is a byproduct of anonymity. After you check in, no one knows how long you stay in your room. You will not be missed at the community breakfast table if you order breakfast in bed. If a few moans escape your lips, no one will give you that knowing look in the lobby.

> *A successful marriage requires falling in love many times, always with the same person.*
> MIGNON MCLAUGHLIN

Best of all, you can order any or all of your meals through room service. You can eat dinner in your sexiest lingerie and sip wine from your beloved's navel if you want to. Nobody can see you, nobody can hear you, nobody will care who made those wine stains on the sheets.

What is the most romantic place you've ever stayed? What made it so romantic?

HER ANSWER	HIS ANSWER

Have you ever been disappointed by what promised to be "romantic" lodging? If so, why?

HER ANSWER	HIS ANSWER

An Intimate Encounter
An Exercise

Here is a chance for you to plan a three-hour "date" or "mini-adventure" either at home or in a hotel or B&B. Make this an intimate encounter. Remember to set the stage and engage the senses. Make sure the space looks, smells, feels, tastes and sounds like romance.

Dress for the occasion. Wear something that makes you feel beautiful or handsome, sexy and sensuous. This is your chance to wear some of your favorite lingerie or something that is just a little too risqué for public viewing.

An intimate encounter does not necessarily mean lovemaking, although it certainly can. The main thing is to focus on each other for the entire time. Other activities to consider are:

♡ Massage each other

♡ Feed finger foods to each other, and get messy if you want to

♡ Play games that encourage conversation and/or touch, like *An Enchanted Evening*

♡ Just talk – really talk – and listen

♡ Read poetry or love stories to each other

♡ Sing or play a musical instrument

♡ Slow dance to a love song

♡ Soak in the hot tub

♡ Shadow dance to a sexy instrumental

What's a shadow dance? It's a slow dance anyone can do, even people who don't necessarily know how to dance, and it's a lot of fun. I know people who consider it a form of foreplay. Just follow these three simple rules:

1. Maintain eye contact.

2. Touch your fingertips.

3. Take turns leading and move in time to the music. When you are following, it is your job to mirror your partner's every move.

> *One should dance because the soul dances.*
> HOLBROOK JACKSON

After your shadow dance, here's an idea for making your hot tub soak more interesting. Get a bucket of marbles. Ask your lover to put his feet on the bottom, head on the edge of the hot tub, and straighten out on a diagonal through the water. Slowly drop marbles one at a time near his throat, letting them slowly roll over his body, gently massaging his body as they slide down. If his body is not on a straight diagonal, some of the marbles might get stuck in certain angular body parts. You may have to give them a nudge to get them rolling again. (Of course, that in itself could be fun.) Be sure you gather up all the marbles when you are done since it would hurt to step on them.

Something to Talk About

Free time is wonderful, but to make the most of it sometimes a little conversation prompting doesn't hurt. Here's an idea that grew from my desire to renew our wedding vows on our twentieth anniversary.

I wanted to have a big ceremony and invite our friends and family. Jim saw no reason to include anyone other than the two of us. We compromised. We had a private mountain top vow renewal on the morning of our anniversary, and several days later we had a party.

Since we would be conducting our own ceremony, I started thinking about what it should include. It would be primarily a conversation, but I wanted it to be a very special conversation about our love and our lives, about our past, present and future. In the weeks preceding our anniversary, we both took time to reflect on, and take notes about, memories of our past, qualities we love in each other, and our hopes and dreams for our future. Our preparation ensured that our ceremony was a tender, free-flowing interaction filled with fond memories, gratitude, and hope.

Snuggled together among the pine trees and boulders, we read my favorite poem by Steven Kowit. We felt a renewed commitment "till death do us part" as we read his eloquent words.

Our service ended when Jim slipped an Australian opal ring on my finger and said, "With this ring I re-wed." It may sound corny to you, but I can assure you at that moment it carried all of the emotion of *Jerry Maguire's* "You complete me" line.

This worked so well for us, I developed a line of greeting cards for couples. The "Romantic Couple" kit contains two sets of "past, present and future" cards.

Let the fire of my passion
glow in the eyes of my beloved.
Let it illuminate her path.
Let the liquid
of which my body is composed
be the river refreshing her
& the well
at which she quenches her thirst.
Let my spirit be the air
she breathes
& thru which she moves
till we are no longer ourselves
& I lie by her side in the earth.
Let our dusts be one.

STEVE KOWIT
after Govindadasa,
15th century Sanskrit poet

Each person fills out his or her own set of cards prior to an agreed upon date. Here are some examples of how these cards have been used in the past.

On Valentine's Day, one woman used the cards as part of a daylong adventure. She hired a limo to take her and her beloved to a matinee performance at the theater. On the way to the play, they talked about the good memories listed on their "past" cards. On the way home, they read their "present" cards with the qualities they love in each other. While listening to live piano music and being served a catered dinner in their own home, they referred to their "future" cards and talked about their hopes and dreams.

Other couples have used these cards to guide their dinner conversation on a picnic, in their own home, or at a restaurant. When and how they exchanged the cards were as varied as the couples themselves. Some randomly chose a card to read with each course. Some people simply read the cards; others read an item and talked about it before going on to the next.

> *Dream as if you'll live forever, live as if you'll die today.*
> JAMES DEAN

These cards have even been used before, during and after weddings. On the eve of their wedding, a couple used the cards to remind them of all of the good times they had shared. As part of their wedding vows, they read the list of qualities they love in each other. On their honeymoon, they shared their hopes and dreams for their future.

If this idea appeals to you, greeting card software and supplies are available in most office supply stores. Handmade cards with personal sentiments make wonderful keepsakes.

Past, Present and Future
An Exercise

Here's an opportunity to think about your lives together and make some notes. Use your answers to reminisce about your relationship, appreciate each other, and dream about your future at some later date.

If you'd like to create your own greeting cards, you can practice with the following prompts:

As I reflect on our life together, I remember the many good times we've shared. Some of my favorite memories are:

HER ANSWER	HIS ANSWER
or record your answers in your private notebook.	

How do I love thee? Let me count the ways.[1] Here are just a few of the qualities I love in you:

HER ANSWER	HIS ANSWER
or record your answers in your private notebook.	

[1] Elizabeth Barrett Browning (1806–1861), *Sonnets from the Portuguese XLIII*

Our lives together hold great promise. My hopes and dreams for our future, and my commitment to making them happen are:

HER ANSWER	HIS ANSWER

or record your answers in your private notebook.

Active Listening

There's so much more to having a conversation than talking. Have you noticed how satisfying it is when someone is truly *hearing* you?

Some people have a special talent for listening. My husband is one of them. Sometimes Jim senses what's going on with me before I do.

In the early 1960s, Carl Rogers explored active listening. In his book, *A Way of Being,* Rogers talked about the importance of listening with empathy or understanding. "It means temporarily living in the other's life, moving about in it delicately without making judgments; it means sensing meanings of which he or she is scarcely aware…"

Barry and Janae Weinhold are leaders in communication and conflict resolution and authors of twenty-six books. In working with hundreds of couples over the years, Barry has found that couples can benefit by listening more to what their partners are actually saying rather than what they think they should be saying. When I interviewed Barry, he said, "The best way to do that is through active listening. The rule is you cannot say what you are going to say in response to what your partner just said until you have repeated back to them what you heard them say and reach an agreement that both of you accurately heard what was said. This helps sur-face any fantasies or projections that might be present and keeps them from creating conflict and leads to true intimacy."

> Sometimes it is a great joy just to listen to some-one we love talking.
> VINCENT McNABB

Honor your beloved by being a good listener. Be attentive. Give your partner your full focus. Make eye contact. Listen without judgments, assumptions or interruptions. While it's easy for couples to finish each other's sentences, it can be annoying if it takes the con-versation in an unintended direction, or if the speaker feels discounted or cut off. Pay special attention to body language and what's not being said.

Sparks that Ignite the Romantic Flame

♡ Plan for adventure and set the stage for romance. Once the plan is in motion, let nature take its course.

♡ Remember that privacy is essential for intimacy.

♡ Find lodging that enhances intimacy.

♡ Order room service.

♡ Save some time for intimate conversations. Take a few notes ahead of time about favorite memories, qualities you love in your beloved, and your hopes and dreams for the future.

♡ Engage all five senses and express love with your primary love languages during your intimate encounters.

♡ Be a good listener.

Make Romance a Way of Life

Sometimes I wonder what my marriage would have been like if Jim and I hadn't stumbled onto a romantic lifestyle. We might still be married, but we could have developed our own interests and friends to the exclusion of the other. We could have become bored in our marriage. We might have been unwilling to forgive each other for mistakes we made. We might have become so irritated and intolerant that we'd be divorced.

Instead, we made our relationship a priority. That hasn't always been easy. We both went through periods of intense stress in our careers. Several years ago, Jim was working sixty

> *Love is an act of endless forgiveness, a tender look which becomes a habit.*
> PETER USTINOV

to eighty hours a week. Early in my career, I missed my sister's wedding to meet a deadline on a software delivery. When I realized how little difference that one day made to the project, I promised myself I would never again put work before family. Over twenty years later, neither the customer nor my boss at the time remembers that day, but my sister and I do. Whenever I've been tempted to put my job before my husband, I remember my priorities. Especially when Jim was overloaded at work, we knew how important it was to celebrate our love through loving gestures, dates, and adventures.

Because of the emphasis we put on our marriage, not only are we still married, we're also best friends and satisfied lovers. Not only do we share many common interests and friends, but we grow as individuals as we develop our unique interests and separate friendships. Because we have a love that continues to grow, the minor annoyances we experience dissipate quickly. We respect each other. Both of us know how to say "I'm sorry" and "I forgive you."

> *Love does not die easily. It is a living thing. It thrives in the face of all of life's hazards, save one – neglect.*
> JAMES D. BRYDEN

It's easy to say your relationship is a priority, but how much do you invest in it? When you invest money, you get interest, right? When you invest time and money in your relationship, the interest in it is compounded. It's a way to maintain the mystery – even after ten, twenty or fifty years. When you are falling in love, romance often comes naturally. New relationships are exciting, passionate and mysterious. Romance can be more of a challenge in long-term relationships, but it might be easier to recapture than you think.

Invest in Your Relationship

I've done my best to convince you your relationship is worth an investment. If you're still with me, you may ask, now what?

It depends on the status of your relationship. An adventure is an investment of time, money and creativity. If you're ready for that, jump in.

If you're still working your way up the Romance Pyramid and want

> *Grow old along with me! The best is yet to be.*
> ROBERT BROWNING

some more suggestions on loving gestures and dates, Gregory Godek's book *1001 Ways To Be Romantic* is the standard by which all other books of its type are measured.

Perhaps your relationship needs a boost beyond what a healthy dose of romantic adventure can provide. If you need help on specifics like conflict resolution or communication, or building a stronger relationship in general, there are many good counselors, therapists, and psychologists who specialize in these areas.

You don't have to look very far to find classes designed to help various aspects of your relationship. Many churches offer marriage encounters. Highly qualified experts offer romance and relationship seminars. Not only do all of the authors discussed in this section write valuable and interesting books, but they also offer seminars on their specialties. Some offer one-on-one counseling.

If you'd rather read a book and work independently, Harville Hendrix's *Getting the Love You Want* contains "a ten-week course in marital therapy you take in the privacy of your own home."

Sexuality can be a source of joy and disappointment in relationships. If you'd like to tip the scales to the joy side more often, Charles and Caroline Muir, authors of *Tantra: The Art of Conscious Loving,* offer weekend seminars across the U.S. and vacation seminars in Hawaii that teach physical, spiritual, and emotional methods of achieving ecstasy in lovemaking. Lana Holstein and David Taylor wrote *Your Long Erotic Weekend: Four Days of Passion for a Lifetime of Magnificent Sex.* If their "first-class sex retreat in a book" whets your appetite for more, you can experience the Partners, Pleasure and Passion workshop at the Miraval Life in Balance Resort and Spa.

Find a counselor, book or class that fits your beliefs and budget. Remember, investing in your love relationship pays big dividends in your life.

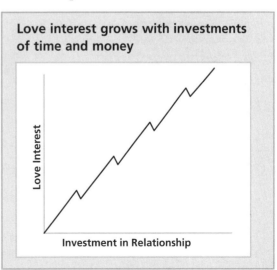

Love interest grows with investments of time and money

What's Important to You?
An Exercise

List fifteen aspects of your life that are important to you. What makes you happy? What makes you feel most fulfilled? What, at the end of your days, will make you feel like you've lived a full and worthwhile life?

My relationship with Jim, my health, and creative expression are just three of the things on my list. Other possibilities might include raising children, a successful career, a rich spiritual life, or making the world a better place by volunteering time for social causes or medical research.

HER ANSWER	HIS ANSWER
1	1
2	2
3	3
4	4
5	5
6	6
7	7
8	8
9	9
10	10
11	11
12	12
13	13
14	14
15	15

or record your answers in your private notebook.

Look back over your list on the previous page. Pick your top five, the five things that are more important than all the others. Estimate the number of hours you devote to each activity in the Top Five list. There are 168 hours in a week.

HER ANSWER		HIS ANSWER	
Top Five	Hours/week	Top Five	Hours/week
1		1	
2		2	
3		3	
4		4	
5		5	
or record your answers in your private notebook.			

Were you surprised at how little time you spend on some of your higher priorities? It's normal, considering how much of your week is devoted to things like commuting to your job, cleaning house, and grocery shopping. The purpose of this exercise isn't to suggest that you should be devoting most of your time to your Top Five. That isn't always practical, possible, or even desirable.

What I am suggesting is that you make the time you do spend on the Top Five count. Be sure there is something left for your beloved. When you give to your partner, you are also giving to yourself. Your partner will have more to return to you if he or she is really taken care of. Invest in your relationship, in yourself, and in your beloved.

Balancing Business and Pleasure

You know your beloved is more important to you than your business, but does your beloved know it? If you're like most people, you say you prioritize your relationship over your business. But take a look at how you spend a typical week. Does your calendar testify to your priorities? Probably not, but don't despair.

> *No matter what you've done for yourself or for humanity, if you can't look back on having given love and attention to your own family, what have you really accomplished?*
>
> LEE IACOCCA

You don't need me to tell you that American workers are busier than ever before. A recent issue of *American Demographics* reported that the average married couple works 717 hours more each year than a working couple in 1969. If I told you how to squeeze more pleasure into those dwindling leisure hours, would you do it?

Imagine that you have a scale that represents your life. Each arm of the scale has a large container hanging from it. The business container on the left represents your obligations, or your "must do's." The pleasure container on the right holds fun, romance, leisure activities, and other "want-to-do's."

Imagine that you fill these containers with little marble-sized nuggets whenever you take care of business or pleasure. The size of the nuggets is always the same, but the weight varies along a continuum from very light to very heavy. When you take care of a relatively small obligation, such as taking out the trash, the orb weighs about as much as a Styrofoam peanut. The nuggets for medium-sized obligations, like putting in a normal day at the office, are about as dense as a glass marble. Heavy lead marbles represent major obligations, like paying the kids' college tuition.

Your pleasure container gets filled up the same way. A quick kiss from your beloved puts a Styrofoam peanut in the container. A foot massage could be worth a glass marble. A romantic weekend rates a solid gold nugget.

As you go through your day, your business container gets pretty full and your pleasure container might get a few marbles. That's normal. While the majority of people have more business than pleasure nuggets, that doesn't necessarily mean it's impossible to balance the scales. It means that you need to make your pleasure nuggets count.

Work for some people is an obligation, and for others it is a joy. If you are one of the lucky ones whose business is a pleasure, remember that your partner may not derive the same satisfaction from your business as

> *Work consists of whatever a body is obliged to do... Play consists of whatever a body is not obliged to do.*
> MARK TWAIN

you do. Scales are balanced for both partners in successful relationships.

A successful adventure puts a heavy nugget in your pleasure bucket and makes obligations seem like less of a burden.

All it takes is some loving gestures, dates and adventures to tip the scales in the right direction.

Appreciate, Reciprocate, and Honor Commitments

For romantic adventures to become a way of life, the events must be appreciated and reciprocated. This is key to keeping romance alive. When I ran the Great Romantic Payback Contest, I noticed how many people told an inspiring romantic story, then followed it up with all the reasons why they haven't had the time or money for a repeat performance.

I like the idea of reciprocity when it comes to taking responsibility for romance. In many relationships, the responsibility for planning romantic outings often falls on one or the other, instead of being shared.

Once I helped a man plan an adventure for his wife's birthday – a weekend out of town in a charming inn, a visit to a museum, and a few extra touches. By all reports, they had a great time together. The following year I asked him if he had any special plans for Valentine's Day. He said his wife hadn't done anything for him since her birthday celebration so he didn't feel moved to go to great lengths for her. Whether he felt he was the only one working on romance or simply unappreciated, he had no motivation to pursue further romantic adventures.

Numerous times I've heard women say, "My husband really needs your class (or book)." If you're one of the women thinking your sweetheart needs lessons on romance, why not give him some? Take the initiative and plan a rock-his-world adventure for him. Don't think I am letting the men off the hook; I am simply proposing that romance is an equal opportunity event.

Let's suppose a "romantic" day is approaching – Valentine's Day, your beloved's birthday or your anniversary. The promise of romance is in the air. As a romantic guy, it's up to you to make reservations for a candlelight dinner, buy a sweet card, and order a dozen roses, right? As a woman in love, do you expect this, or resent your sweetheart if it doesn't happen?

> *Treat a man as he is, and he will remain as he is. Treat a man as he could be, and he will become what he should be.*
>
> RALPH WALDO EMERSON,
> ALSO ATTRIBUTED TO
> JOHANN WOLFGANG VON GOETHE

In this age of equality for women, some women have hung onto the traditional notion that men should do the romancing. Is it any wonder that some men may view romance as a burden?

It's not surprising so many of Cupid's arrows miss the romance mark and fester as disappointment for women and dread for men.

Beyond reciprocity, there's another important point here: give for the joy of giving, not for the expectation of getting something in return. I don't want to suggest that romance will only happen when all things are equal. The goal is for both of you to have such a good time that you don't keep score. I planned many romantic adventures for Jim before either one of us realized that it might be his "turn."

Showing appreciation is obvious – nobody wants to knock himself or herself out if the effort will not be appreciated – but there is more to showing appreciation than

Blessed are those who can give without remembering and take without forgetting.
ELIZABETH BIBESCO

merely saying thanks. You were taught to send thank you cards to your friends and family, but when was the last time you sent your beloved a thank you card?

Honoring commitments is another no brainer, but how often do we let life get in the way of romance? You planned on a date with your sweetheart, but something came up at the last minute. Make your beloved a priority. When you make a date, keep it. If you *must* break it, reschedule as soon as possible.

Commitment Letters
An Exercise

What changes are you willing to commit to as a result of reading this book? Find some nice stationery. Write a letter in your own words to your beloved, but cover the following points:

Point to cover	Sample
What is the purpose of the commitments you are making?	*Because our relationship is very important to me, I will show you beyond a shadow of a doubt that I absolutely love and adore you.*
What loving gestures are you willing to commit to on a daily basis?	*When we come together after being separated during the day, I will always give you a warm hug.*
What loving gestures that your beloved can do for you would make you feel really loved and adored?	*I feel really special when you call me just to tell me how much you love me. I also like it when you rub lotion on my feet.*
Within the next two months, what invitation for a date will you extend?	*Will you join me for a dinner at that new restaurant? Let's compare calendars and set the date.*
Are you willing to commit to an adventure? If so, when?	*I would like to surprise you with an adventure for our anniversary. I'll do all the planning.*

Pick a time to share your letters, maybe by candlelight over a glass of wine. Read them aloud to each other. Record the dates in your calendars.

It's Never Too Late
Cecil Pearl and Ace's Romantic Adventure

Carol's grandmother, Cecil Pearl, was burned by love several times, but she never gave up on romance. At fifteen, she married an abusive, alcoholic man, and had three kids before she divorced him. Later she married another abusive, alcoholic man who couldn't hold a job. That marriage, too, ended in divorce. Her third attempt was better. This man was kind and hard working, but he died at an early age.

Cecil Pearl remained single for many years. When she learned about the death of a friend, she sent the widower a note of condolence on the loss of his wife, citing fond memories of their friendship.

> *It's never too late to have a happy childhood.*
> TOM ROBBINS

They began to correspond, just friendly at first. When they started getting together socially, love bloomed. Ace sent her flowers at regular intervals. "No one's ever sent me flowers before," she gushed to her friends. Finally he proposed with a diamond engagement ring, the only one she'd ever had, and she accepted.

> *It's never too late to be what you might have been.*
> GEORGE ELIOT

When Cecil Pearl was seventy-eight, she was married in her first formal church wedding. Her daughter was her matron of honor, and her sons were the ushers. She wore an ivory and peach chiffon floor-length gown. Carol said it was the most romantic wedding she'd ever attended.

Cecil Pearl had never lived in a new house. Ace bought her a new house, where they lived happily for six years until

> *It's never too late to make romance a way of life.*
> MARY ZALMANEK

his death. She died two years later, knowing she'd been loved.

♡ ♡ ♡ ♡ ♡

Checklist for
Adventure Planning

Here's a checklist of items to consider when planning an adventure. Use this list as a starting place to customize your own checklist on the following page.

♡ Arrange for a babysitter.

♡ If you'll be gone overnight, arrange for pet care and someone to watch your house. Stop the mail and newspapers if necessary.

♡ Reserve the time on your calendars. If the adventure will be a surprise, arrange for time off work for your beloved.

♡ Determine appropriate activities if a theme will be used.

♡ Choose lodging and make reservations.

♡ Choose a restaurant and make reservations.

♡ Consider transportation alternatives. Buy tickets.

♡ Purchase tickets to entertainment or sporting event.

♡ Make massage appointments or pack massage oils.

♡ Buy cards for the occasion, and write personal messages in them.

♡ Purchase or make gifts and have them wrapped.

♡ Think about music for the adventure. Bring along a CD player for your favorite CDs, or hire a musician.

♡ Order or buy flowers and candles.

♡ Prepare instructions for anyone you will be depending on for this adventure, like a limo driver or babysitter. Include cell phone numbers.

♡ Pack clothing, shoes, cosmetics, vitamins, and prescription drugs.

♡ Bring along your camera and film. If you use a digital camera, be sure there's plenty of space on the memory card. Get fresh batteries.

♡ Consider backup options for essential items. What will you do if the babysitter gets sick or bad weather prevents a planned picnic in the park?

♡ Drop hints if you want to build anticipation.

Checklist for Your Adventure

You can use a checklist like this to help with your planning. Use the comments column to record prices, contact information, phone numbers, and addresses. If you've got someone helping out with certain items, you can track who's doing what in the "Assigned to" columns.

Task	Due Date	Status	Comments	Assigned to: You	Helper
1					
2					
3					
4					
5					
6					
7					
8					
9					
10					
11					
12					
13					
14					
15					

or record your answers in your private notebook.

Making Romance a Way of Life for Generations to Come

Linda and Richard's Romantic Adventure

My wish for you is that you take what you've learned from these twelve habits and create an adventure that is uniquely yours. That's what Linda and Richard did when they attended the *Couples' Romance Weekend.* They decided to plan a romantic adventure around an upcoming family vacation to Mexico. They had rented a seaside villa for their children and grandchildren.

They told their children about their intention for romance to be a part of the family's Christmas vacation. Part of their gift exchange was for each couple to bring something that could be used during a night of romance, like a romantic board game, candles, or massage oils. Each couple would have full use of the villa and all romantic gifts for one evening, while the rest of the clan went out to dinner and weren't allowed to return home until an agreed upon time.

When we began the exercise to plan an adventure in the workshop, my expectation was that their adventure would be for just the two of them. My students became my teachers. They showed me new possibilities.

Linda and Richard took what they learned and modeled romance for their children and grandchildren.

Relaxing some of the traditional expectations about romance can open your hearts to a new level of adventure. You might be surprised at how many more of the arrows in Cupid's quiver hit the bull's eye.

Sparks that Ignite the Romantic Flame

♡ Make your relationship a priority.

♡ Invest in your relationship with time and money.

♡ Use successful adventures to make the obligations in your busy life seem less burdensome.

♡ Appreciate and reciprocate the romance that comes your way so that it becomes a way of life.

♡ Give for the joy of giving. You'll have such a good time that you won't need to keep score.

♡ Remember to show your gratitude to your beloved. Send a thank you card.

♡ Keep the dates you make. If you must break one, reschedule as soon as possible.

♡ Start now to make romance a way of life. It's never too late.

♡ Remember romance is an equal opportunity occasion. Get rid of the notion that one person in the relationship should do all the romancing.

Appendix

Your Romance Profile

The Romance Profile gives you a place to summarize your answers for future reference. If you decide to seek help in planning adventures, this information will be useful to the person helping you. It will also serve as a reminder of what you learned about yourself and your beloved as you worked through this book.

There are two sample Romance Profiles for the Dullards and the Darlings and a blank Profile for you to fill out with your beloved. You'll notice the stark contrast between the two couples from the comics when you read their Profiles.

Bea and Moe Dullard

You can almost feel Bea blaming Moe for the state of their union and his defensiveness as you look over their Profile. For them to agree on two dates per year and three loving gestures per day is just short of a miracle.

Notice they couldn't even think of five shared interests or a single romantic tradition. The stories they picked as their favorites were selected to point out each other's shortcomings.

Gracie and Frank Darling

On the other hand, Gracie and Frank have a healthy Romance Pyramid. They enjoy showing their love for each other and naturally do daily loving gestures. They make time to go on ten dates a year. That's a solid foundation for romantic adventures. Their shared interests give them quality time together, yet they both have strong individual interests.

Use this Profile to focus on what's working in your relationship. Be realistic, but maintain a positive attitude.

Romance Profile for

COUPLE'S NAME
Bea and Moe Dullard

1. What are your combined totals on the Romance Pyramid?

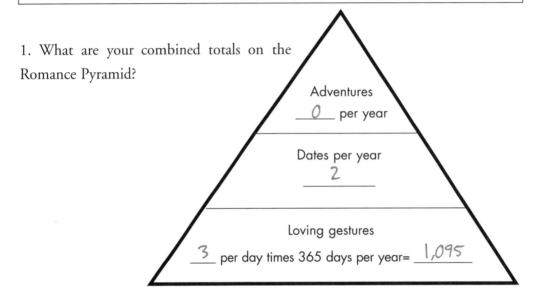

Adventures
___0___ per year

Dates per year
2

Loving gestures
__3__ per day times 365 days per year= _1,095_

2. What is your Primary Love Language?

HER ANSWER	HIS ANSWER
Receiving Gifts	Acts of Service

3. What is your Surprise Tolerance Type?

HER ANSWER	HIS ANSWER
Type 2	Type 1

4. What are your top five shared interests? List them in order of importance to you.

HER ANSWER	HIS ANSWER
Visiting family	Watching TV
Eating	Eating
Watching TV	Home Improvements
Home improvements	Visiting family

5. What are your top five individual interests?

HER ANSWER	HIS ANSWER
Working hard to get ahead in my career	Watching TV, sports
Shopping	Attending football games
Getting together with friends	Spending time alone
Volunteering on various boards	Fishing
Aerobics	Napping

6. What are your five favorite stories or ideas from the book, and why?

HER ANSWER	HIS ANSWER
A Painting is Worth a Thousand Words — a beautiful gift with a thoughtful presentation	An Elegant Evening at Taco Bell— it was cheap
Deep Pockets — I'm more likely to get a gift I like if I pick it out myself	Romance on a Dollar a Year — to show Bea how to have fun without breaking the bank
Top Ten Reasons — I'd love getting little gifts for 10 days no matter how small they are	Keeping the Flame Alive and the Bathroom Clean — I'd love it if Bea cooked for me and pampered me
I loved the shopping exercise — anything to get Moe to see how much fun it is to shop	I know Bea is too busy to iron my shirts, but she could at least pick them up at the cleaners. That would be a loving gesture
I'd like for Moe to realize that gifts are "heartfelt symbols of love and affection." He just thinks I'm too materialistic	I don't expect Bea to go fishing with me, but she could at least pack a picnic lunch for me when I go

7. What is your favorite romantic tradition you currently practice?

HER ANSWER	HIS ANSWER
We don't have one	Ditto

Romance Profile for

COUPLE'S NAME
Gracie and Frank Darling

1. What are your combined totals on the Romance Pyramid?

Adventures

___2___ per year

Dates per year

10

Loving gestures

___10___ per day times 365 days per year= ___3,650___

2. What is your Primary Love Language?

HER ANSWER	HIS ANSWER
Words of affirmation	Quality time

3. What is your Surprise Tolerance Type?

HER ANSWER	HIS ANSWER
Type 3	Type 2

4. What are your top five shared interests? List them in order of importance to you.

HER ANSWER	HIS ANSWER
Mountain biking	Golf
Skiing	Skiing
Entertaining family & friends	Mountain biking
Travel	Travel
Golf	Entertaining family & friends

5. What are your top five individual interests?

HER ANSWER	HIS ANSWER
Volunteering at Angela's School	Woodworking
Knitting	Crossword Puzzles
Singing	Volunteering for trail maintenance
Reading	Listen to music, especially jazz
Cooking	Reading

6. What are your five favorite stories or ideas from the book, and why?

HER ANSWER	HIS ANSWER
Drum Roll! – I can imagine how much our daughter Angela's class would have liked this	Love in a 1964 VW Bus – I'd love to have a place Gracie and I could retreat to
Limousine-Driven Treasure Hunt – 3 hours in a spa, that's why!	An Elegant Evening at Taco Bell – I can see doing this with friends.
This Guy Loves Surprises – Loved the mystery of not knowing what's next	Mixing Technology and Romance – What a great way to get Gracie to have fun with my "toys"
A Valentine Retreat – This couple knows how to make the best of rare alone time	A Valentine Retreat – It's realistic for couples with kids
A Foreign Affair – I want to try a Russian banya	Making Romance a Way of Life for Future Generations – I'd like to think Gracie and I show Angela the joys of romance

7. What is your favorite romantic tradition you currently practice?

HER ANSWER	HIS ANSWER
Taking turns planning a celebration for our anniversary	Making love on Saturday morning while Angela's at soccer practice

Romance Profile for

COUPLE'S NAME

1. What are your combined totals on the Romance Pyramid?

Adventures

_____ per year

Dates per year

_____

Loving gestures

_____ per day times 365 days per year= _____

2. What is your Primary Love Language?

HER ANSWER	HIS ANSWER

3. What is your Surprise Tolerance Type?

HER ANSWER	HIS ANSWER

4. What are your top five shared interests? List them in order of importance to you.

HER ANSWER	HIS ANSWER

5. What are your top five individual interests?

HER ANSWER	HIS ANSWER

6. What are your five favorite stories or ideas from the book, and why?

HER ANSWER	HIS ANSWER

7. What is your favorite romantic tradition you currently practice?

HER ANSWER	HIS ANSWER

Index

Bibliography
Recommended Reading and Cited Works

1001 Ways to be Romantic by Gregory J.P. Godek. Casablanca Press, Inc. Boston: 1991.

365 Ways to Date Your Love: A Daily Guide to Creative Romance by Tomima Edmark. The Summit Publishing Group, Fort Worth, Texas: 1995

50 Most Romantic Things Ever Done, The by Dini von Mueffling. Doubleday, New York: 1997

Alchemist, The: A Fable about Following your Dream by Paulo Coelho and Alan R. Clarke (translator). HarperCollins Publishers, New York: original 1988, English version 1993.

Born for Love: Reflections on Loving by Leo Buscaglia. SLACK Incorporated, Thorofare, New Jersey: 1992

Chicken Soup for the Couple's Soul by Jack Canfield, Mark Victor Hansen, Mark & Chrissy Donnely, and Barbara De Angelis, Ph. D. Health Communications, Inc., Deerfield Beach, Florida: 1999

Enchanted Love: The Mystical Power of Intimate Relationships by Marianne Williamson. Simon & Schuster, New York: 1999

Five Love Languages, The: How to Express Heartfelt Commitment to Your Mate by Gary Chapman. Northfield Publishing, Chicago: 1992. To order, call Customer Service at 1-800-678-8812 or visit the web site at mpcustomerservice@moody.edu.

Getting the Love You Want: A Guide for Couples by Harville Hendrix, Ph.D. Henry Holt, New York: 1988

Great Sex Weekend, The: A 48-Hour Guide to Rekindling Sparks for Bold, Busy or Bored Lovers by Pepper Schwartz, Ph.D. and Janet Lever, Ph.D. G.P.Putnam's Sons, New York: 1997

Gryphon, The by Nick Bantock. Chronicle Books, LLC, San Francisco: 2001

How to Write Love Letters by Michelle Lovric. Shooting Star Press, New York: 1995.

I Love You, Ronnie: The Letters of Ronald Reagan to Nancy Reagan by Nancy Reagan. Random House, New York: 2000.

Inter Courses: An Aphrodisiac Cookbook by Martha Hopkins and Randall Lockridge. Terrace Publishing, Memphis, Tennessee: 1997

Living, Loving & Learning by Leo Buscaglia, Ph.D. Charles B. Slack, Inc., Thorofare, New Jersey: 1992

Love: The Course They Forgot To Teach You In School by Gregory J. P. Godek. Sourcebooks, Inc., Naperville, IL: 1997

Man Who Ate the 747, The by Ben Sherwood. Bantam Dell, New York: 2000

Message in a Bottle, by Nicholas Sparks. Warner Books, Inc., New York: 1998

Notebook, The by Nicholas Sparks. Warner Books, Inc., New York: 1996

On Becoming a Person by Carl Rogers. Houghton Mifflin Company, Boston: 1961

Passionate Journey: Poems and Drawings in the Erotic Mood by Steve Kowit and Arthur Okamura. City Miner Books, Berkeley, California: 1984

Permission to Party: Taking Time to Celebrate and Enjoy Life by Jill Murphy Long. Sourcebooks, Inc., Naperville, Illinois: 2004

Prophet, The by Kahlil Gibran. Alfred A. Knopf, New York: 1923

Real Moments for Lovers by Barbara DeAngelis, Ph.D. Dell Publishing, New York: 1995.

S Factor, The: Strip Workouts for Every Woman by Sheila Kelley. Workman Publishing, New York: 2003

Tantra: The Art of Conscious Loving by Charles and Caroline Muir. Mercury House, Incorporated, San Francisco: 1989

Under the Tuscan Sun: At Home in Italy by Frances Mayes. Broadway Books, New York: 1996

Way of Being, A by Carl Rogers. Houghton Mifflin Company, Boston: 1980.

Yellow Silk: Erotic Arts and Letters edited by Lily Pond and Richard Russo. Harmony Books, New York: 1990.

Your Long Erotic Weekend by Lana Holstein, M.D. and David Taylor, M.D. Fair Winds Press, Gloucester, Massachusetts: 2004.

Quotation Books

Columbia Dictionary of Quotations, The edited by Robert Andrews. Columbia University Press, New York: 1993

Crown Treasury of Relevant Quotations, The edited by Edward F. Murphy. Crown Publishing Group, Norwalk, Connecticut: 1978

Familiar Quotations edited by John Bartlett. Little, Brown and Company, Boston: 2003

Home Book of Quotations edited by Burton Stevenson. Dodd, Mead and Company, New York: 1967

Illustrated Oxford Dictionary by Oxford University Press, Oxford: 1998

International Thesaurus of Quotations, The edited by Eugene Ehrlich and Marshall DeBruhl. Harper Collins Publishers, New York: 1995

Oxford Dictionary of 20th Century Quotations, The edited by Elizabeth Knowles. Oxford University Press, Oxford: 1988

Oxford Dictionary of Phrase, Saying & Quotation, The edited by Susan Ratcliffe. Oxford University Press, Oxford: 1997

Oxford Dictionary of Quotations, The edited by Elizabeth Knowles. Oxford University Press, Oxford: 2004

Simpson's Contemporary Quotations edited by James B. Simpson. Harper Collins Publishers, New York: 1988

What a Piece of Work Man Is! Camp's Unfamiliar Quotations from 2000 BC to the Present edited by Wesley D. Camp. Prentice Hall, Englewood Cliffs, New Jersey: 1990

Writers & Artists on Love: A Quotable Muse Journal edited by Eric Maisel. New World Library, Novato, California: 2003

Quotation Web Sites

www.1-love-quotes.com
www.affirmations-for-success.com
www.angelfire.com
www.bartleby.com
www.dailycelebrations.com
www.brainyquote.com
www.crystalclouds.co.uk

www.groups.msn.com
www.heartquotes.net
www.intangiblereverie.com
www.learningplaceonline.com
www.library.cornell.edu
www.paradise-engineering.com
www.quotableonline.com
www.quotations.about.com

www.quotationspage.com
www.quoteland.com
www.religioustolerance.org
www.romancestruck.com
www.sheetudeep.com
www.thinkexist.com
www.wisdomquotes.com